CW01371642

Margaret Thatcher: The Myths Exposed

The author would like to thank the following for their practical assistance and general encouragement when he was writing this book:

Ian Aylett, Ed Brandon, Alan Brooke, Mick Brooks, Jay Gearing, Ron Graves, Sean McCartney and Martin Upham.

© 2013 David Brandon. All rights reserved.
ISBN 978-1-300-94424-9

Contents

1. Introduction — 1-7
2. Economic Decline — 8-15
3. Post War Britain and the rise of Thatcher — 16-33
4. The Ideology of Thatcherism — 34-49
5. Thatcherite Economics - the theory — 50-58
6. The Tory Government 1979-83 — 59-69
7. The Falklands War — 70-75
8. Thatcher and the Miners — 76-101
9. Welfare and Privatisation — 102-115
10. Thatcher's Economics in Practice — 116-139
11. Thatcher and the Trade Unions — 140-151
12. Thatcher and Foreign Policy — 152-163
13. Public Order and Civil Rights — 164-171
14. Thatcher and Local Government — 172-177
15. Thatcher and the National Question — 178-182
16. The Thatcher Style — 183-204
17. Decline and Fall — 205-211
18. Conclusions — 212-222
Bibliography — 223-226

1. INTRODUCTION

If an interviewer was to go out on the streets and ask people, aged forty and over, which British politician of their lifetime has made the biggest impression on them, it is more than likely that the answer would be 'Margaret Thatcher'. Her reputation lives on. Even those born after she was forced out of office by her colleagues frequently have an opinion about her personality, her style and the policies carried out while she was Prime Minister. When she was no longer Prime Minister and party leader and even after she had left Parliament, she continued to exert a significant influence within the Conservative Party and in the wider world of politics. She never failed to attract attention while she played an active political role both in Britain and abroad and she has continued to do so ever since. In 2011 the film industry considered that she was still sufficiently controversial for it to be a worthwhile risk to make a film about her. This film, called 'The Iron Lady', was released early in 2012. Immediately Thatcher was once again at the centre of the news as controversy raged. Did the film put her in too favourable a light? Was it too critical? Should it have been made at all? Should it have been released only after she died? Did it dwell too much on personal rather than political issues? There were even anti-Thatcher demonstrations outside some cinemas, evidence of the strong emotions that this old and frail woman is still capable of provoking.

The argument here, in a critical assessment of Thatcher's attitudes, policies and activities, is that a huge amount of what has been and indeed is still being said about Thatcher's life and works is misleading. Frequently it is little better than myth. On occasion it is simply untrue. An image was created, packaged and presented that deliberately portrayed her as a resolute and radical leader of unusual strength and moral integrity who bravely sorted out any number of crucial issues that were facing Britain in the 1980s. According to this viewpoint, Thatcher effected what was virtually a revolution, reversing the damage she thought had been done by past generations of spineless politicians more concerned with compromise and consensus than with taking and implementing hard, possibly unpopular and yet necessary, economic and political decisions. She carved a swathe through and swept aside practices and institutions that she thought were holding back enterprise and entrepreneurialism and set Britain in a new direction restoring economic viability, international status and a sense of national purpose as she went. The result of all this, we were told, was a significant improvement in the country's economic position, an increase in her status in international circles and a significant turn for the better in the lives of her citizens.

Thatcher unquestionably thought of herself as a radical. No shrinking violet, she was intensely conscious of the role she wanted to be seen as having played in history. She saw herself following in the footsteps of Churchill in bringing back greatness to Britain. He was a man she greatly admired and was similarly the subject of much myth-making and controversy.

It is contended here that the policies carried out during her three terms as Prime Minister failed to restore the long-term health of the economy, did enormous damage to the country's economic and social fabric and bequeathed a highly toxic legacy to later generations. In the UK today we see social fragmentation, widespread deprivation and exclusion and senses both of helplessness and cynicism. We see the waste of human potential and the misery that inevitably accompanies the return of mass unemployment.

We have been made very aware of the eggshell fragility of the British economy. The nature of wealth creation has changed out of all recognition in the last 50 years and Britain has become largely a *rentier* and service economy, highly vulnerable to the predatory activities of strutting bankers, hedge-fund managers and other so-called financial wizards. It is also at the mercy of international economic movements and fluctuations which are largely beyond its control. Now nail bars, tanning parlours, health spas and retail parks proliferate where once factories stood while manufactured goods flood in from abroad and masses of people, especially the young, languish on the dole.

The harsh realities of life in Britain in the second decade of the twenty-first century are not simply the results of the general crisis currently afflicting much of world capitalism. Thatcher set out to tackle what she saw as the causes of the 'British Disease'. This was the unique set of reasons why the nation, once the proud 'Workshop of the World' and possessor of the largest empire that the world had ever seen, had subsequently tumbled down the league table of world economic and political powers. In 1982, during Thatcher's first government, Britain significantly became a net importer of manufactured goods. Although the decline was only a relative one, it rankled with Thatcher who came up with her own set of 'explanations' and 'solutions'. Both were equally flawed. In her own mind, however, she could do no wrong and she insisted that her governments were implementing policies which were restoring Britain to its rightful place in the international scheme of things. In reality these governments proved incapable of eradicating the underlying causes of malaise. The 'remedies' her governments and those which followed have implemented only succeeded in making the symptoms worse.

Margaret Thatcher, nee Roberts, was born at Grantham, Lincolnshire, on 13 October 1925. She won a scholarship to Kesteven and Grantham Girls' School, a selective secondary school where she became head girl in 1942-3. She went up to Oxford in 1943 to study chemistry and graduated in 1947. She became involved in politics at Oxford, joining the Oxford University Conservative Association and becoming President in 1946. While she was at Oxford she came across Friedrich von Hayek's book *The Road to Serfdom* which had a seminal influence on her and from which she obtained her belief that freedom and government intervention in the economy were incompatible.

She left Oxford to become a research chemist at Colchester where she became active in the local Conservative Association. Her rise in the Conservative Party was rapid and in 1951 she was adopted as prospective parliamentary candidate in the safe Labour seat of Dartford in Kent where she attracted media attention on account largely of her youth and, of course, of her sex. She worked extremely hard and succeeded in reducing the Labour majority. She married Denis Thatcher in December 1951. He was a divorced and extremely wealthy businessman who then paid for her to study Law. She qualified as a barrister in 1953, specialising in taxation.

In 1955 she was narrowly defeated in the Orpington by-election and then had the good fortune to be selected as candidate for the safe Tory seat of Finchley in 1958. She entered Parliament after the election of 1959. She rose quickly and in October 1961 Harold Macmillan promoted her to the front bench as Parliamentary Undersecretary at the Ministry of Pensions & National Insurance. When the Tories lost the 1964 election she became spokesperson on Housing and Land, enthusiastically advocating her party's policy on the selling of council houses. In 1966 she became a spokesperson at the Treasury and famously declared that the high tax policies of Labour governments tended not only towards Socialism but actually to Communism. Low taxes, she stated, were an incentive to hard work and economic regeneration.

She held other portfolios before being appointed Secretary of State for Education and Science in the Heath government elected to office in 1970. She hit the headlines when she was responsible for abolishing free school milk for school children aged seven to eleven. She gained notoriety being caricatured as 'Margaret Thatcher, the Milk Snatcher'. Later, in her autobiography, she wrote, 'I learnt a valuable lesson. I had incurred the maximum of political odium for the minimum of political benefit'.

The Heath government fell early in 1974 and with the Tories doing badly in both general elections of that year, there was widespread disillusionment within the party about the Heath leadership. A challenge to his leadership seemed likely but rather unexpectedly when it happened, Thatcher emerged as a frontrunner, having considerable support among the backbenchers. She defeated Heath on the first ballot and he promptly resigned whereupon she then defeated William Whitelaw who had generally been expected to be Heath's successor, in a second ballot. She became Leader of the Conservative Party on 11 February 1975.

There was an almost messianic fervour in Thatcher as she approached her first general election as party leader in 1979. The Tory manifesto for the election contained a foreword by Thatcher in which she stated: *For me the heart of politics is not political theory, it is people and how they want to live their lives. No one who has lived in this country during the past five years can fail to be aware of how the balance of our society has been increasingly tilted in favour of the state at the expense of individual freedom. This election may be the last chance we have to reverse that process and to restore the balance of power in favour of the people. It is therefore the most crucial election since the war. Together with the threat to freedom there has been a feeling of helplessness, that we are a once great nation that has somehow fallen behind and that it is too late now to turn things round. I don't accept that. We not only can but we must.*

Thatcher became Prime Minister on 4 May 1979, sweeping to victory in the general election. Hotly pursued by the press corps and the TV cameras, she made a speech in front of No.10, Downing Street which included the following words: *Where there is discord, may we bring harmony. Where there is error, may we bring truth. Where there is doubt, may we bring faith. And where there is despair, may we bring hope.*[1] We will argue that, as so often happened with Thatcher, her expressed intentions were totally at odds with their outcomes. In practice, her policies created discord, error, doubt and despair in equal measure.

Clearly here was a politician who saw herself on an urgent mission. It would be possible to juxtapose her talk of 'our society' in the manifesto with her later statement to the effect that there was no such thing as society, only individuals and families. It would also be possible to argue that her real mission was never to 'restore the balance of power in favour of the people'. Very much the opposite in fact because her real purpose was to reverse the decline of British capitalism and she believed that this could only be done by transferring wealth from the pockets of the working classes to the business sector to boost flagging rates of profit, encourage investment and enable companies to kick-start a recovery in their international competitiveness.

Since her spoken intentions were so often at variance with the outcomes of the policies she was carrying out, it might be suggested that Thatcher was insincere, given to saying one thing and actually meaning something completely different, like so many politicians. Yet she has been credited with being a 'conviction politician'. Indeed she projected herself as being a 'straight-talker' and hence a cut above so many other politicians. We shall see a fundamental conflict between Thatcher's expressed desire to encourage 'freedom' and 'market forces' and what the results of that were in practice. While she was fond of flaunting her 'principles', the needs of particular situations meant that in practice those principles frequently took a back seat to pragmatism. Thatcher was only a straight-talker when it suited her.

Essential to any understanding of Thatcher is the fact that she saw economics and morals as inextricably linked. As far as she was concerned, a free market untrammelled by obstructive state bureaucracy encouraged not only greater prosperity but positive moral virtues in the individuals that were part of it. Diligence, self-reliance, responsibility and judicious risk-taking were the very stuff that had made Victorian Britain great in her opinion and they could do so again through actively encouraging individual and corporate enterprise. This was a curiously anachronistic point of view given that capitalism in the late twentieth century was a very different creature from its nineteenth century manifestation. It had come to be dominated by massively powerful multi-national and even global corporations. They had little sense of social responsibility and scant concern for the integrity of nation-states. Their only real concern was maximisation of profits by whatever means were available and some had accrued so much power that they were able to dictate their wills to governments rather than vice versa. Her view of what capitalism should be was an idealised one, traceable to her upbringing, and it bore little resemblance to hard reality. The robust diligence and rugged self-reliance of the owner of a corner grocery store were soon snuffed out when a Tesco supermarket opened just down the road. The painstaking work put in to establish a small business could quickly be put to nought if the bank called in its overdraft.

The author believes that in assessing the role of political and other historical figures, factors of character and personality are less important than the objective role that the figure is playing, sometimes almost unconsciously, in expressing and attempting to further the interests of a particular social class or substratum within a class. Thatcher was a resolute supporter of British capitalism but capitalism is not a homogeneous entity and many of her policies were highly injurious, especially to its primary and manufacturing wings. Finance capital, on the other hand, underwent radical reform and enjoyed an explosion of growth. The nabobs of the City of London, both the long-established and the newly-enriched, had every cause to rejoice when the 'Big Bang' de-regulated their affairs and over twenty years later we are living with and paying for the dire results of allowing such people to act almost entirely as though the world had been created for their benefit. Elsewhere, the legacy of hate her policies generated lives on, decades later, especially in parts of Britain which were torn apart and devastated by policies carried out as part of her drive to make Britain great again. Try telling people to this day in some former pit villages in South Yorkshire, for example, that while it may have been painful it was all worth it because at least she put Britain back on a firm economic footing. The actions of her governments widened the gap between the richest and the poorest members of society. The 'freedom' to which she constantly referred and which we will examine later was of no more substance than a wraith for vast numbers of Britain's citizens.

It is exceptionally hard in the case of Thatcher to disentangle politics from the person since she put such a distinctive imprimatur on everything that she did in public life. Thatcher was convinced that her policies were both economically necessary and morally justifiable. She appeared incapable of considering that she might actually be mistaken and that there could be viable alternatives to her opinions and to the policies she wanted to implement. All too often she was praised for what were actually faults, not virtues. We were told, and indeed she never shrank from telling us, that she had resolution and strength of will in abundance. Such qualities are necessary in political leaders but only when tempered by the ability to listen to and seriously consider questions, criticisms and alternatives. She was immensely irritated by those who raised 'difficulties' and in doing so they were always likely to get short shrift. This intolerance and arrogance posing as 'firmness' and 'conviction' was a weakness, never a strength.

Deeply-rooted organic problems afflict economic, political and social reality in twenty-first century Britain. Many originate in processes extending back to the late nineteenth century and the changed role forced on Britain when she ceased to be the unchallenged 'Workshop of the World'. Generations of twentieth-century politicians struggled without much success to deal with the country's relative economic and political decline and reduced international status. Thatcher promised radical, innovative solutions with which to arrest and reverse this systemic decline but in practice these 'solutions' proved ineffective, particularly in the longer term. The largely derivative policies carried out by subsequent governments, both Conservative and so-called 'New Labour', have only emphasised and exacerbated Britain's continuing slow relative decline. Thatcher and her successors between them have contributed to the growth of a divided, cynical and disillusioned population and a mass of economic and social problems which appear to be entirely insoluble on the basis of the existing economic system.

Baroness Thatcher is now dead. Her death already prevoked a huge response in the media. Much of this will consist of fulsome, even cringingly, obsequious tributes. All the old myths and clichés about 'Maggie' will be taken off the shelf, dusted down and repeated as if they were self-evident truths. Incanting these orthodoxies uncritically and unquestioningly will be the expected and 'right' thing to do. The author believes that it is essential to question whether the orthodoxies actually bear any resemblance to historical reality. As Karl Marx and Friedrich Engels wrote in 1845: *The ideas of the ruling class are in every epoch the ruling ideas, i.e. the class which is the ruling material force of society is at the same time the ruling intellectual force.*[2] Thatcher's purpose was to promote the interests of the rich and powerful and to restore the long-term health of British capitalism. In pursing her mission she had heavyweight ideological support and it became almost heretical to call her views into question. While effectively achieving the first task, she failed very badly to achieve the second. One purpose of this book is to question, analyse and criticise what is still largely the orthodoxy concerning Thatcher. In doing so, it will become clear that the person and the politics are surrounded by misapprehensions, misunderstandings and myths.

The author lived through the 'Maggie years' and found that the praise systematically heaped on her by most of the media had little resonance with the people with whom he associated. They largely thought of her as a narrow-minded, dogmatic, patronising bully without charm and humour let alone compassion and humanity. Lest he be accused of moving in overly narrow social circles, he would add that she regularly received very low ratings in the opinion polls which frequently placed her among the most unpopular prime ministers of the twentieth century. At one stage she was actually **the** most unpopular prime minister ever. For this reason there is a need to challenge what have become popular fallacies and the lies and distortions posing as 'facts' that have been deliberately created to support them.

The author believes that Thatcher exerted a malign influence in British and indeed in international politics. Her current physical and mental state is no cause for celebration but it should not be used to shield her from a critical analysis of the impact of the policies carried out in her name. She came to office at a particularly crucial juncture in British history. As Marx said: *Men make their own history, but they do not make it just as they please: they do not make it under circumstances chosen by themselves, but under circumstances directly encountered, given and transmitted from the past. The tradition of all the dead generations weighs like a nightmare on the brain of the living.*[3]. Had the circumstances in which she operated been different, Thatcher might well have been no more than a footnote in the history books. The post-war political consensus had been thrown into disarray by the conjuncture of the end of the prolonged post-war boom, the onset of a worldwide capitalist recession and the growing recognition of the UK's relatively dismal economic record. Thatcher's was one among a number of voices then expressing the opinion that twenty-five years of consensus and compromise amounted to a culpable evasion of responsibility by the country's politicians. It was the specific circumstances of the time which allowed Thatcher, with large-scale media support, to emerge as a tough-minded conviction politician who would put Britain back on the rails. She clearly believed that she was the person to reverse the damage perpetrated by the political leaders of the last thirty years and this was a task she absolutely relished and one that she would never be deflected from believing that she achieved.

The Conservative Party has enjoyed considerable long-term success in presenting itself as somehow standing for the interests of the nation as a whole. In practice it has never been anything of the sort. It has always been dedicated to advancing the interests of the better-off and more influential sections of society but it has very successfully managed to dupe substantial numbers of working class people into believing that by voting Tory, they will improve their own circumstances and prospects. Superficially, Thatcher's appeal, although she claimed that it crossed all the social divides, was a demagogic one largely aimed at the concerns, insecurities and prejudices of the middle classes and better-off workers and their families who aspired to upward social mobility and economic betterment. Classically, these were readers of the *Daily Telegraph*, the *Daily Express* and the *Daily Mail*. As she had single-mindedly worked her way to prominence up the greasy pole of the Tory Party, she often referred to her relatively humble social origins which she claimed gave her an understanding of the concerns of the 'little people'. This was humbug. Her marriage to a millionaire effectively distanced her from having to share the worries of those she patronised as 'her people' because the reality was that she had put as great a distance as she could between herself and them.

It is worth bearing in mind that Mrs Thatcher was an extremely lucky politician. She was lucky to have become Leader of the Conservative Party before the general election of 1979 by which time the Labour Government had not only lost any sense of purpose but had been made to look ridiculous and impotent on account of its inability to hold back the wage demands of the public sector workers. Then from below its cold and murky waters up gushed the bonanza of North Sea oil and the revenue which it fortuitously generated for the Treasury. This unearned income greatly widened the options available to Thatcher's governments. Meanwhile and coincidentally, inflation was reined back by a fall in international commodity prices, the exact opposite of what had happened to her hapless predecessor Edward Heath when he was Tory Prime Minister.

Thatcher was lucky to escape the bomb planted by the IRA which blew up the Grand Hotel in Brighton where she was staying during the Tory Party Conference; lucky to survive the Westland Affair; lucky that the SDP appeared on the scene to split the vote among those who opposed her politically and lucky that the anomalies of the British electoral system allowed her to win three successive elections when on all three occasions far more people voted against than for the Conservatives.

Most of all she was lucky when, at the height of the unpopularity of her inept and unpopular first government, Galtieri, leader of the tyrannical Argentine military junta, decided to create a diversion from his own economic and political toils by invading the Falkland Islands, using as an excuse his country's longstanding claim to sovereignty over the 'Malvinas'. A war followed which Britain won, albeit with help from some unsavoury friends such as General Pinochet, every bit as much a tyrant with blood on his hands as Galtieri himself. The happenstance of the Falklands War provided an enormous boost for Thatcher's political career. It enabled her to enlarge upon the programme of neo-liberal reforms which did so much to alter social and economic life in Britain and which were continued by her successors in John Major and especially Tony Blair and Gordon Brown.

The period we will be looking at was a turbulent one of profound changes and new directions in economic, social and political policy. Inevitably, by force of her dominating personality, Thatcher has taken centre-stage in the events of the 1980s. It would be unwise to underestimate the personal influence she exercised during that and subsequent decades. Equally, care needs to be exercised so as not to make too much of the carefully created cult of personality surrounding her because there were economic and other processes at work which were much larger than Thatcher herself and which dictated the circumstances in which she operated and which influenced the responses she made.

1. The keynote points in this speech are either a deliberate or an unknowing misquotation of a prayer by St Francis of Assisi (c.1181-1226). What this is purported to have said was: *Lord, make me an instrument of Your Peace; Where there is hatred let me sow love; Where there is injury, pardon; Where there is doubt, faith; Where there is despair, hope; Where there is darkness, light; Where there is sadness, joy.*
2. Marx, K & Engels, F. (1845), *Theses on Feuerbach*, Selected Works, Vol.1 Moscow, 1969, p. 47.
3. Marx, K. (1852), *The Eighteenth Brumaire of Louis Bonaparte*, K. Marx & F.Engels, Selected Works, op.cit. Vol. 1, Moscow 1968, p. 398.

2. ECONOMIC DECLINE – A VERY BRITISH DISEASE

Before 1939

The relative decline of British capitalism had deep historical roots. In 1851 Britain proudly staged the Great Exhibition in Hyde Park in London. This was an international trade affair, partly the brainchild of Prince Albert who rather naively thought that if international trade could be encouraged and developed, amity between the nations of the world would naturally follow. The Great Exhibition was a huge success. British exhibits totally dominated and supported Britain's justified boast that she was 'The Workshop of the World'. The British Empire, at its peak, covered one-fifth of the earth's surface and controlled one quarter of its population. Britain in the middle of the nineteenth century looked economically and politically invulnerable. The Conservative Party evolved through the century to become the main political expression of the ruling class and its material interests and ideology. The British ruling class, simple to caricature for its posturing arrogance, snobbery, and blatant pursuit of self-interest, was easy to underestimate. It proved flexible enough to move with changing times and demands. In the nineteenth century it accepted the enfranchisement of working men and the consequent raised expectations for social reform. Later, in the twentieth century, it came to terms with Keynesian economic practices and what was called at the time the 'mixed economy'.

Britain's once unquestioned supremacy in manufacturing proved to be transient and even before the 1900s the economy was experiencing serious problems. In 1870 she had produced as much as one-third of the world's industrial goods; by 1914 she was producing only 14 per cent although of a considerably larger total output. The head start that British capitalism had enjoyed was threatened by the development of an increasingly militant organised working class and competition from countries with high technology industries, vigorously entering markets once monopolised by Britain's own manufactured products. Britain's record in reinvestment in new means of production was a dismal one even by 1900.

During the First World War, some British industries, especially those associated with supplying the needs of the war effort, enjoyed a boom in demand but, like other industries, did so at the expense of investment in the new plant and machinery which was required in order to be competitive on international markets when the war was over. The War marked a crucial watershed for Britain. When it was over, the USA emerged as the world's leading economic power. British capitalism was never to recover the seemingly unassailable position on international markets that she had once enjoyed. Britain was now shown to be dangerously dependent on a number of heavy staple industries which were extremely vulnerable to competition from companies overseas that had invested in the latest technology. Many of these consequently had higher productivity and lower costs than their British rivals.

The inter-war years were characterised by severe difficulties and setbacks for those industries on which Britain's past supremacy had been based. Coal-mining, shipbuilding, textiles and heavy engineering, for example, all underwent painful contraction. In 1929 world capitalism entered what up to then was the most serious crisis in its history. This hit the UK unevenly, some newer industries such as electrical consumer goods and motor vehicle manufacturing actually doing very well. Parts of England south of a line from the Humber to the Severn prospered as these industries attracted labour in huge amounts, much of which was supplied by workers moving from the areas hardest hit by the changed circumstances of the time. For the cradles of Britain's mining and heavy manufacturing industries these were desperate times indeed. It could be argued that parts of Lowland Scotland, West Cumbria, Tyneside and Wearside and South Wales never fully recovered from the body-blows they received in the inter-war years. The image we have of hunger marches and mass unemployment and of the deprivation and despair that occurred in such places as the shipbuilding town of Jarrow on Tyneside, may not be the whole picture but nationally, unemployment in 1933 reached a figure of 23 per cent of all insured workers. In some districts it temporarily hit figures of over seventy-five per cent. An economic upturn began in 1934 but it was weak and patchy and another slump was looming when the economy was let off the hook by the approach to the Second World War.

For most of the 1930s, a Conservative-dominated Coalition government was in office. Faced with a crisis of overproduction, government policy centred on restricting output and reducing capacity. Farmers were paid to destroy agricultural produce and cotton mills, coalmines and shipyards were closed in large numbers in the areas of old-established heavy and extractive industry. Britain came to rely increasingly on trading with the countries of its Empire which at this time were still a largely captive market for her manufactured products and a source of cheap food and raw materials. It was unhelpful to Britain's international competitiveness that British investors tended to export capital to the countries of the Empire rather than using it for modernising productive processes at home.

Britain – the Sick Man of Europe?

The period from about 1950 to the late 1960s was characterised in the western world by relative political and social stability based on an economic boom punctuated only by minor slumps. Worldwide gross output increased threefold between 1948 and 1973. By the early 1970s however it was evident that this phase had ended, being replaced by a new era much more typical of capitalism, characterised by economic volatility and uncertainty, social instability and stresses in international relations. The commentators coined new, ugly words – 'slumpflation' and 'stagflation' for the appearance of phenomena not previously found in the economics textbooks. Little or no growth in the economy, falling consumer demand and a rapid increase in unemployment were accompanied by a sharp rise in inflation. Britain was not alone in the 1970s in experiencing these stresses although on the basis of some indicators at least, she was 'the sick man of Europe'. In 1966 for the first time the increase in earnings had exceeded the growth in output. Thatcher inherited a situation in which serious problems faced British capitalism and Britain's politicians.

Not only in Britain but elsewhere in the western states there was a feeling that the political leaders had run out of solutions. Large sections of the population were cynical and apathetic regarding politics and politicians. In Britain in the 1960s a mood of introversion and navel-gazing led many economic, social and political commentators to subject various aspects of British life to close scrutiny. They usually concluded gloomily that society in general had lost its way and that the politicians either cared little or even if they did care, had neither the will nor the means to do anything about the problems.

As Britain went into the 1970s, there was an almost tangible malaise and air of resignation, a widespread feeling that the good times were over and there really was not very much to look forward to except perhaps the pursuit of short-term pleasures. There was indeed much to be seriously concerned about. In 1971-2 fixed currency exchange rates on international markets had imploded. In 1973 the price of oil quadrupled. The capitalist world went into recession as if to contradict those pundits of the 1950s and 1960s who had 'explained' that such a thing would never happen again because capitalism had solved its tendency to cyclical booms and slumps.

An important indicator of a country's economic well-being is the interest rates banks levy on borrowers. For much of the post-war years rates were low. In 1962 the bank rate fluctuated around 4-5 per cent, figures that encouraged borrowing by business. According to figures published by the OECD in 1978, however, in 1976 the average bank rate reached a hitherto unheard of 14.25 per cent. The chickens were truly coming home to roost for the British economy for such a high rate played havoc with the exchange rates for sterling on international markets and led to a fall in the exchange value of the pound. This could have had catastrophic outcomes not just for the British economy had the Labour government not obtained a loan of £5 billion from the IMF. This, like all such loans, came with strings attached. These were the requirement that the Labour carried out austerity measures involving cuts in public spending. Yet another indicator of fundamental malaise was Britain's balance of international trade. Britain's share of world manufacturing had been falling for about a century. In 1967 the British trade deficit reached a peacetime record of £153 million. The overall record on the balance of payments reflected this gloomy reality and in 1974 according to the OECD reached a staggering £3,591 million.

As if this tale of woe was not enough, British business was characterised by the closely-related factors of low productivity and low profitability. The rate of profitability of British companies fell from 14 per cent in 1960 to 4 per cent in 1975.[1] Associated with this was Britain's comparatively poor record on capital investment. Over the period 1960 to 1979 the UK reinvested a lower percentage of its GNP than any other of the eleven other countries then in the EEC.[2]

Another dismal record was that of investment in manufacturing industry. The marked reluctance of British banks and finance houses to lend to the manufacturing sector compared very unfavourably with rival economies such as those of Germany, France, Italy and Japan. Rooted in the perception of the City of London was a sense that such lending carried intrinsic risks. In practice this meant a serious shortage of funds for modernisation of technical infrastructure, necessary research and development and also training.

The fragility of the fabric of advanced western capitalist society was thrown starkly into relief in this period. The descent into recession was accompanied by inflation and sharply rising unemployment. The new reality evoked responses from the government which largely contradicted the conventional policies pursued over the last twenty years. Now the control of inflation took priority over the maintenance of full employment, previously a sacred cow of economic policy; many aspects of public spending now seemed extravagant and were cut back while wages and consumer demand needed to be kept under strict control. Economic growth could no longer be guaranteed and so the whole basis of two decades of social-democratic consensus politics was being undermined by a turn of events which had taken most pro-capitalist economists by surprise.

Britain was a prisoner of its past. Its descent from world leader with a global worldwide empire to a second rate power created tensions with which she found it very hard to deal. The two world wars set the seal on her reduced status but delusions of continuing grandeur were present into the 1970s. The Marshall Aid extended by the USA to war-shattered Britain came with onerous conditions. She had to hand over valuable markets particularly in South America to the USA and also patent rights and royalties on important British technological innovations including radar, antibiotics, jet engines and nuclear power. Had Britain been able to hang onto the royalties from these key developments, her balance of payments would have been considerably healthier. When American lease-lend ended, Britain had to negotiate a loan from the USA which had a major impact on national debt repayments into the twenty-first century.

Britain's inability to come to terms with her new role in the world meant that she still felt the need to act as a world policeman. It was as if her politicians felt that would lose face if she did not undertake this role but it had immensely damaging effects on her economy. Her expenditure on what was euphemistically called 'defence' was disproportionately large and in inverse ratio to her investment in industry. It contrasted starkly with Japan, for example, at 5.24 per cent of GNP in 1974 as opposed to Japan's mere 0.83 per cent.

Has anyone got any Idea how to get out of this mess?

The recession showed the extent to which the British and all the other capitalist economies had become intertwined and largely interdependent. The development of capitalism internationally over three centuries had seen an extraordinary growth in the means of producing wealth, in economic demand and in international trade and communications – a genuine world market. At one and the same time the various national economies of the world engaged in increasingly complex trading activities and relationships while simultaneously seeking to raise their own position in the international trading league tables. A world economy was being created and yet its components continued to be fragmented along national lines. Organisations like the IMF and the World Bank existed to keep the economic wheels going round and they did this largely on behalf of the interests of the more powerful economies, especially that of the USA. What had become clear was that this complex system was neither proof against economic recessions nor unexpected initiatives with massive implications such as that which occurred when the oil-producing countries greatly hiked up the price of oil, the *sine qua non* of the modern economy.

The post-war boom had witnessed a huge expansion in output and markets based on mass production and mass consumption. However, the advanced economies of the western world found themselves on the horns of a dilemma. Ways had to be found constantly to expand demand if producers were to be able to realise profits from their businesses. They therefore had to expand in overseas markets or enlarge the domestic market. For the latter, growing consumer demand was a necessity but here was the rub. In the 1950s and 1960s, because of a largely buoyant economy, full order books and full employment, the power of the trade unions had been greatly strengthened so far as collective bargaining was concerned. This emphasised one of the inbuilt contradictions of capitalism. Each individual capitalist wants other companies to pay their workers high wages to provide demand for the goods and services his own business produces. At the same time he himself wants to maintain his profits by keeping his own wage costs down. Built into capitalism is a tendency for the capacity to create wealth to outstrip the means for consuming that wealth and this leads to periodic crises of overproduction and consequent economic slump.

In many industries the trade unions had become extremely well-organised during the post-war period and, often bargaining from a position of strength with the employers having full order books, they had managed to win increasingly favourable terms and conditions for their members. In doing so they had frequently agreed to increases in productivity by way of a *quid pro quo*. The result was that employers representatives and the senior full-time trade union officers engaged particularly in national negotiations tended to come to something of an accord, working together to enhance their respective shares of the rising the prosperity of the period. The cooperation of the trade unions was seen as vital to smooth industrial relations and the continued successful growth of the economy. The union leaders were wined and dined and flattered. Many fell for these blandishments hook, line and sinker. They were then required to use their skills to 'sell' the agreements they had made with senior management to their rank-and-file members, including convenors, shop stewards, fathers-of-chapel and other elected workplace leaders, many of whom could be depended on to see through offers that were not really in their members' interests.

Full-time trade union leaders increasingly became a part of the economic and political fabric and consensus of the post-war years, sometimes building lucrative careers for themselves and even on occasions becoming poachers turned gamekeepers by becoming 'industrial relations consultants' or joining the boards of rapacious capitalist companies with whom they had previously been involved in negotiations from the other side of the table. Even while still employed by trade unions, their incomes and lifestyles were such as to mean that they frequently lost touch with the everyday problems their members faced. Their function in effect became the policing and control of their members on behalf of capital although they tended to hide this task behind the weasel words to the effect that they were acting in 'the national interest'. They became bureaucrats engaged in building up their own careers and, like all bureaucrats, they wanted a quiet life. Workplace militancy became as much anathema to them as it was to the employers. They could not necessarily control it, however.

This was all hunky-dory while the possibilities for continued economic expansion and generalised prosperity seemed almost limitless. However the cosy consensus was put under considerable pressure and proved extremely fragile once the capitalist world found itself in a serious recession. Now it was each country doing what it could for itself. The UK's response matched that of other advanced economies and she embarked on deflationary measures particularly after the onset of the oil crisis of 1973-4. Falling demand intensified competition and highlighted those countries and particular industries or companies whose plant, processes and business methods were inefficient, obsolescent, or both. In a desperate attempt to remain competitive, many companies shed labour. The consequent return of mass unemployment had a further deflationary effect as those without jobs could not afford to buy the goods and services produced by other workers who still had jobs.

The capitalist economies were facing an international crisis of overproduction and saw a way forward through destroying substantial amounts of productive capacity, eliminating large numbers of jobs and introducing new technology. This was an immensely wasteful and painful process and one likely to meet with the opposition of the organised working class.

Measures such as these to combat the effects of the recession were bound to conflict sharply with the policies and programme that had constituted the social democratic consensus for the previous two decades. These had included full employment and extensive welfare programmes funded out of taxes. The consensus involved a substantial expansion in the size and activity of the public sector and the role of government. Some commentators in the generally expansive 1950s and 1960s had observed rather caustically that capitalism was no longer really free enterprise at all and that the welfare state, paid for out of taxes, acted to prop it up by smoothing over some of the most obvious social inequalities associated with it. Meanwhile the nationalised industries provided it with cheap goods and services. That elaborate welfare systems had to be developed to provide a minimum standard below which it was intended that no citizen should fall was an institutionalised recognition, they said, of the great disparities in income and opportunity which were inevitable under capitalism. Be that as it may, Britain had enjoyed around twenty years of rising prosperity and appreciable social stability on the basis of this new collectivism which was an integral part of the social democratic consensus. Unfortunately, far from the post-war boom heralding a change for the better in the essential nature of the economic system, the onset of recession had revealed that the beast was up to its old tricks again. The western capitalist countries, and Britain was right up there at the forefront of them, saw their political leaders dithering around, confused and not knowing how to respond to a situation they had confidently thought would never occur again.

The post-war boom changed expectations and attitudes

Another feature of the post-war boom was a considerable change in attitudes on such issues as civil, political and social rights. This occurred at least partly as a result of economic factors. The huge expansion of production in countries like Britain required unprecedented quantities of labour. Two main pools were tapped into: these were migrants especially from countries of the British Commonwealth, and women. Their arrival on the labour market coincided with, and also made a contribution to, the generalised growth in prosperity. The 1950s and 1960s saw the emergence of a consumer society in the UK based on the rapidly increasing spending power which was being generated. The range of new leisure and cultural services available grew hugely and the enhanced choices on offer to consumers allowed people to make new choices. Frequently these led to a new and very different lifestyle, aspects of which were markedly at odds with well-established familial traditions and sexual divisions of labour. It was only to be expected that this challenge to patriarchy would arouse opposition from many quarters including the self-appointed guardians of the family. According to such people these developments were likely to cause an explosion of crime and an implosion of respect for authority. They accused consensus politicians of both main parties of lacking moral fibre and undermining the work ethic and sense of personal moral responsibility which, they claimed, had made Britain great in Victorian times.

One of the ironies of history in view of subsequent events was that early post-war Conservative governments played an important role in encouraging migrants to settle in Britain and find employment. Britain had always been a significant ethnic melting pot but it now experienced the arrival of immigrants, predominantly from the Caribbean and the Indian sub-continent, in unprecedented numbers. Among those encouraging this inward migration of labour was none other than Enoch Powell when he had been Minister of Health. Later, in 1968 and without batting an eyelid, he was to make his famous speech predicting rivers of blood that would flow as a result of unrestricted immigration. In Powell's utterances can be seen ideas which were later central to Thatcher. The newcomers largely did unskilled and low-paid jobs and their presence was vital to keeping parts of the economy such as transport and the health service going. Issues around race began to feature prominently on the political agenda and consensus politicians were accused of threatening the integrity of the 'white nation'. All the old canards about immigrants being scroungers, dirty, oversexed and bringing crime and disease with them saw the light of day again. Who was responsible for allowing this flood to take place? Well of course it was the mainstream politicians – the same people who were soft on criminals, opposed to physical punishments and who derided and even undermined the sanctity of the family. And it was getting worse.

Women in employment started asserting themselves. They had the effrontery actually to demand equal pay with men for doing work of equal value. Black and other immigrants facing racial discrimination started their own organisations and campaigned for equal rights. Some became militant trade unionists. The world was turning upside down. However in the 1970s when belt-tightening was demanded by politicians, among those who felt the brunt first and hardest were, precisely, women and immigrants and their families. With drastic measures needed to restore the health of the economic system, the political right needed to isolate, discredit and even demonise vulnerable groups.

Now the aspirations of groups such as women and immigrants were made to look unreasonable. Another vulnerable group, the unemployed, were characterised as work-shy freeloaders. The existence of lengthening dole queues was consciously used to make those in work feel insecure and to moderate their wage demands. And so it went on. It was divide and rule. Its effect was to set the ordinary people, those who were bearing the burden of hard times, against each other. It had been done dozens of times before and with the enthusiastic support of the newspapers and various other sections of the media, it was done again. The problem was that they were allowed largely to get away with it. Most of the left in the Labour Party and well-meaning members of the Liberal Party, it they spoke up in opposition at all, usually did so ineptly and unconvincingly.

This was the ugly new orthodoxy that rose like scum to the surface in the 1970s. It was prefaced on the reappearance of all the old ills associated with capitalism in crisis. The smug assumption, swallowed by the non-Marxist left and by the political right in the post-war boom, that capitalism had buried its problems for once and for all, had been totally discredited. Without any major politicians of the Left arguing for a radical socialist alternative, the 'solutions' of the Right were able to pose as being the common sense way of dealing with the crisis.

1. Brittan, S. (1989), Treasury figures cited in *The Thatcher Government's Economic Policy* in Kavanagh, D. & Seldon, A. (eds), *The Thatcher Effect: A Decade of Change*, Oxford, p.14.
2. Brown, G. (1989), *Where there is Greed...* Edinburgh, p.37.

3. POST-WAR BRITAIN AND THE RISE OF THATCHER

The nature of the package of policies put into effect by Margaret Thatcher's governments was no accident. It was an attempt to give a much-needed new direction and vigour to the British economy which, by the 1970s, could be seen to be facing a number of serious structural problems. We will trace how this came about.

The Brave New World post-1945

To the surprise of most commentators, a Labour government was elected in 1945. This was the first such government to have a working majority and it was determined to implement policies which would counteract the damage done to the economic and social fabric of Britain not only during the war itself but in the inter-war years. In particular it was keen to continue and extend the large degree of state intervention in the economic and social life of the nation which had been essential to maximise the war effort. It sought to apply state involvement in tackling the many problems the UK faced in the aftermath of the war. Soon the new government was engaged in what seemed at the time to be an extremely radical programme. It included large-scale nationalisation especially in the transport, the utilities and mining industries and the creation of the National Health Service and the Welfare State. By any standards and despite detail criticisms that could certainly be made, this was a remarkable achievement. The names of John Maynard Keynes and William Beveridge are credited with the intellectual underpinning of this brave new world which involved a marked redirection of British peacetime public policy.

Although some of its most rabid opponents regarded the 1945 Labour Government as being hell-bent on carrying through a socialist transformation of society, nothing of the sort was being contemplated. In fact it could be argued that what was being done was the application of sticking plaster to many of the gaping cracks in the façade of British capitalism, evident even at this early date. The industries that were nationalised were mostly run-down and suffering from under-investment but necessary for the effective functioning of what was still predominantly a capitalist economy. Therefore it fell to the government and basically the tax-payer to bail them out and then prop them up. The Welfare State was institutionalised recognition that poverty and poor health, serious inequality in standards of living and expectations and capitalism were inextricably linked.

In foreign affairs, Britain and the USA developed what they thought of as a 'special relationship'. Although the first signs of what proved to be the rapid break-up of the British Empire were already evident, there was a feeling shared by most British politicians that there was still an imperial role to play, that Britain remained a major military power with the economic clout to support such a role. Russia was seen as a threat, relationships with Europe were not especially genial and it seemed to make sense to strengthen ties with the USA. The reality was that Britain was very much the junior partner in this relationship and the USA certainly the greater beneficiary.

Some leading 'One Nation' Tories like Harold Macmillan and R.A.Butler were happy to accept the sweeping changes brought in by Labour in the areas of health and welfare if perhaps less enthusiastic about the whole of the extensive programme of nationalisation. The Conservatives had suffered a very severe and largely unexpected electoral defeat in 1945 and, while licking their wounds, regrouped to work out the changes that needed to be made if they were going to get back into office in the foreseeable future. Even though Churchill returned as Prime Minister of a Tory government in the election of 1951, he and the party knew it was wise to moderate their right-wing views and be seen to endorse the continuance of the NHS and the Welfare State. They even had to accept that it was both necessary and right to consult the trade unions when economic policy was being made.

The Boom and the Politics of Consensus

From 1945 to the early 1970s, Britain had experienced the so-called 'post-war boom'. These decades saw a very real rise in living standards and expectations which was enjoyed by the vast majority of the population. The comprehensive state welfare and health systems were immensely popular and responsible for considerable improvements in the peoples' health. Increased real wages provided money to spend on an unprecedented range of goods and services. Televisions and other consumer goods, cars and overseas holidays, for example, were becoming available to wide swathes of the population. Through the medium of mortgages, increasing numbers were becoming owner-occupiers. For much of this period, inflation was at around 3% and unemployment 500,000 or less, misleadingly described as 'full employment'. This situation allowed a certain complacency to enter into party politics. After the 1959 general election Macmillan said: "The class war is over and we have won it." There was a consensus between the two main parties that basically things were going well, that there was a need to keep a steady hand on the tiller and that no drastic changes in policy were needed or should be contemplated. In industry, capital and labour had, at least superficially, largely arrived at a working compromise. Conditions were made favourable for profit-making while the trade unions agreed to accept limitations on their demands in return for a share in macro-economic decision-making. Large numbers of their members partook in the general rise of prosperity. As far as compromise and consensus in parliament was concerned, some called this 'Butskellism' after two leading figures in the Tory and Labour Parties respectively. Both Reginald Butler and Hugh Gaitskell had aspired to the role of Prime Minister and both failed to achieve it. In spite of that, they characterised the politics of their day. There was very little to distinguish the political outlook of one from the outlook of the other. The consensus depended on economic growth, full employment and rising living standards. Such consensus was bound to break down if and when the economy sank into recession.

One who did not partake of this 'Tweedledum and Tweedledee' politics was Enoch Powell. Always identified with the right of the Tory Party, he was probably more feared than admired by most of his party colleagues, not least because of his formidable presence and even more formidable intellect. He was as unpredictable as a loose cannon, however, and it was this quality and what he said which eventually consigned him to relative political obscurity and isolation. It is likely that Thatcher watched and listened to him closely while maintaining a discreet distance from him within Tory Party circles. Even in the 1950s he was lauding the benefits of the free market, condemning what he thought of as too much government intervention in the workings of the economy and expressing his concern about what, in his opinion, was excessive public spending, high taxation and ominous immanent inflationary tendencies in the economy.

His party was not ready for Powell's views on economic policy. Had he only been born a few years later he might have found a more receptive audience because these general views went on to become very fashionable. It is likely that Thatcher was secretly impressed by the fearless way in which Powell was prepared to voice those things which other politicians were too cowardly or too discreet, to say. The populism he embraced and the sensation he made in expressing his views on race gave her a kind of model that she could use when she later made unashamed appeals to some of the more selfish and mercenary aspects of the electorate's views. Powell's concern about the imperative need to preserve the identity of the nation was echoed by Thatcher. Powell's contempt for political correctness and for those in the media and various interest groups who he believed were telling the people how they should think and what they should say was matched by Thatcher although she was a trifle more discreet.

The 'feel good factor' that accompanied the arrival of a consumer society disguised a more sinister reality. Britain was undergoing a marked, if relative, economic decline. The UK's output of goods and services increased by something like two-thirds between 1950 and 1970. The cause for concern was that the output of rival nations was growing much faster and that Britain's economic performance by comparison was distinctly sluggish. In the period 1962-72, for example, France enjoyed an annual growth rate of 4.7 per cent whereas the UK grew by only 2.2 per cent. Britain slipped rapidly down the international table indicating Gross Domestic Product per head of the working population. In the late 1950s she was in the top ten countries but had fallen to fifteenth in 1971 and eighteenth by 1976. There were many attempts to explain this dismal performance. For politicians and economists of the right at least one part of the answer was simple: the trade unions had been allowed to become much too strong and the bargaining power they could weald was seriously eroding profits and standing in the way of increased productivity, thereby dragging the economy down. They pointed to figures which indicated that the USA had a productivity figure 50 per cent higher than the UK and West Germany one that was over 25 per cent higher. That the British trade union movement had in effect brought down the Tory government under Edward Heath in 1974 and after 'The Winter of Discontent' in 1979 had done the same to Callaghan's Labour Government was added evidence that, as far as the right was concerned, the power of the trade unions urgently needed to be curtailed.

Cracks in the Wall

Neither the political left nor the right had really expected an economic boom of such volume and duration after the war. The boom had instilled a widespread although false sense of confidence that capitalism had put behind it the kind of problems that had manifested themselves with such damaging effects in the inter-war years and indeed for much of the history of capitalism. It was therefore a serious shock to both left and right when it became obvious in the late 1960s that the boom was running out of steam, admittedly not just for Britain alone. As early as 1971 almost a million were registered unemployed in the UK where the proud boast of politicians so recently had been that the goal of full employment had been achieved. Keynesian policies were the current orthodoxy but they were being questioned because of their apparently inbuilt tendency to be inflationary. Inflation reached nearly 27% in 1975, albeit partly because of the oil crisis of 1973-4. The proud former 'Workshop of the World' was already suffering increasing import penetration when, during the 1950s and 1960s, the UK's spending power was sucking in cheap but good-quality manufactured goods from countries whose consumers had once rushed to buy British exports. Sometimes they had had little alternative. Now the worm had turned! An overseas trade deficit of £110 million in 1965 ballooned to one of nearly £1700 million by 1975. The value of the pound on international markets went into free fall. It lost 30 per cent of its value between 1971 and 1975. In 1971, Rolls-Royce, the flagship of the British engineering industry, had to be rescued from imminent bankruptcy by, of all things, a Tory government! They did the unthinkable and literally nationalised Rolls-Royce overnight! It was a doom-laden scenario. How were the toils of capitalism to be tackled?

The nationalised industries had gained a reputation for being inefficient and loss-making. This was not entirely justified but was useful propaganda against the whole concept of state-ownership. In December 1972 it was reported that a staggering £2,934 billion of debts accrued by these industries had been written off. Labour and Conservative governments alike had thrown money at ailing nationalised and private industries. Labour propped British Leyland up to the tune of £1.4 billion in April 1975 alone. In 1972 Heath's Tories had given a helping hand to the shipbuilding companies Cammell Laird and Harland and Wolff (£3 million and £49 million respectively) and the British Aircraft Corporation who received £225 million. This, despite talk of not helping lame dogs.

The Labour Government 1964-70

A Labour government in office under Harold Wilson from 1964 to 1970 had recognised that beneath the surface, there were serious signs that a deep malaise was afflicting the British economy. Wilson claimed to have the answer with a modernisation programme which he rather unwisely called the 'white hot technological revolution'. In reality the revolution never even got lukewarm. He restricted wages through an income policy, restructured (not very successfully) some major engineering companies, introduced a number of reforms in hallowed institutions such as the civil service and the universities, widened the tripartite approach to economic planning and began to move Britain towards what was then the EEC. Wilson's efforts were a dismal failure. Rather than launching an attack on the power of the big monopolies and the City of London, he attacked working-class living standards by deflationary measures, wage restraint and attempts to curb trade union power through legislation. These actions were early auguries of the tide of neo-liberal policy which was on its way and also an indication of the latter days of the post-war consensus.

Wilson echoed rather than challenged the view systematically put across by most of the media that the trade unions were largely responsible for Britain's economic woes. Day after day the media incanted their opinion that 'excessive' pay claims were a major cause of inflation and the frequency with which strikes occurred particularly in manufacturing industry was undermining Britain's ability to compete on international markets. Workers downed tools and walked off the job, it was claimed, for the most trivial of reasons, such as dislike of the new toilet paper in the conveniences! In 1969 the Wilson government produced a white paper *In Place of Strife* proposing major new controls on unions and how they conducted industrial action. This provoked a huge furore in the labour movement and pressure, especially from the rank-and-file of the unions, forced the government to abandon its proposals.

Wilson managed to alienate both Big Business and the working class vote and it was no surprise that the Tories won the 1970 election. In a wider sense, Labour's inability to apply a workable programme to deal with specific economic problems seemed symptomatic of the manner in which Britain was losing her way in the world. The confidence and the sure touch displayed by governments in the nineteenth century were now turning into desperate ill thought-out measures, impotent vacillation and gloomy introspection. A new sense of direction and a will to face up to and deal decisively with problems were desperately needed but Labour certainly did not seem to possess the necessary qualities. Nor for that matter did the Conservatives.

Post-war Conservatism

In the relative economic and political stability of the 1950s and to a lesser extent the 1960s, the Conservative Party put its shock defeat of 1945 behind it and resumed its traditional role as the natural party of government. It was tied in a thousand ways to the individuals and institutions who wielded most of the power to get things done in Britain, although what was done was often carried out effectively through informal networking. Members of the ruling class, the seriously rich and powerful, although by no means homogeneous, looked to the Tory Party to deliver what they wanted and it could normally be relied upon to do so when in office, often getting things done outside the normal parliamentary channels. After all, what is the point of having a political establishment if every damned issue has to go through the normal tedious and prolonged formal procedures associated with parliamentary democracy?

Historically, the Tory Party has been enormously successful as a machine designed to put and keep Conservative governments in office. It has achieved this by being able to persuade substantial sections of the electorate, including many of the poorest and most put upon, that their interests and needs are always best served by voting Conservative. Leaving aside the sheer effrontery of such a claim, the Party owes much of its electoral success to cleverly appearing not to be too dogmatic and to operating in a flexible and pragmatic fashion. This, for example, led Tory leaders from the 1950s through to the 1970s to accept and even to end up defending such popular Labour Government achievements as the NHS and the Welfare State, despite the fact that the Tory Party had been bitterly opposed to the legislation that brought them about. Even to this day when the NHS is being dismantled before our very eyes, Conservative politicians with an eye to the next election hasten to assure voters that the NHS is 'safe in our hands'.

In 1946, as leader of the Conservative Party, Winston Churchill addressed the Party's annual conference and summed up the philosophy of Conservatism very neatly. He said: *Our main objective is to uphold the Christian religion and resist all attacks upon it. To defend our Monarchical and Parliamentary Constitution. To provide adequate security against external aggression and safety for our seaborne trade. To uphold law and order...to support as a general rule free enterprise and initiative against state trading and nationalisation of industries.* What Mrs Thatcher did has to be considered in the context of these principles. She had the reputation of being a radical whose reforming zeal reached into every corner of life in the United Kingdom but her thinking was generally in line with the Tory orthodoxies outlined above but was rendered more acute by the manifest problems of the British economy. Reduced to essentials the Conservative Party's priority is the implementation of measures which encourage capitalist enterprise and protect the hierarchy of power and privileges that go with it. Thatcher stood four-square with those aspirations.

During the consensus years of the post-war boom, Conservatives made an informal agreement to support extensive state-sponsored welfare systems and full employment while, in return, Labour accepted the continuance of private property, of profit-making and of an economy dominated by private enterprise. In this deal, Labour was prepared to give away considerably more in principles than the Tories. It seemed a cosy accord but it could not be sustained once recession hit the UK economy showing up the extent of its degeneration and of the fragile foundation on which the post-war consensus had been constructed.

Heath's Government of 1970-1974

Mrs Thatcher was climbing up the slippery pole that was the Tory Party in Parliament after Edward Heath won the election of 1970 and became Prime Minister heading what was then the most radical and right-wing Tory government since the war. The political stance of this government, although mild compared to the later governments under Thatcher, was evidence that British capitalism had its back against the wall. There was no natural sympathy between Heath and Thatcher despite the fact that they came from similar social backgrounds. Like Thatcher, Heath came to office promising radical change. Events did not to allow him to implement that change and indeed he had only been in office a short time when he was forced to eat his words. He brought in statutory pay policy, did a complete U-turn and was forced to rescue 'lame ducks' such as Rolls-Royce and tried unsuccessfully to take on the trade unions.

The case of Rolls-Royce was symptomatic of the depth and extent of the British malaise. The company was the flagship of British industry but in the late 1960s the continuance of its leading role in the world depended on it finding a purchaser for its latest aero engine, an exceptionally advanced and sophisticated machine. Realistically a major American aircraft manufacturer was needed. An order worth as much as £1,000 million was received from Lockheed, the US aerospace giant. This engine was a triumph of British engineering expertise but the cost of its development escalated way beyond predicted figures and the company went bankrupt when it failed to get financial support from the government. This episode demonstrated that no matter how superb British engineering could still be, senior management was incompetent and out of touch with the requirements of the modern market. This, incidentally, was in a company with largely cordial industrial relations. The aero-engine division was nationalised under the name of Rolls-Royce (1971) and the other divisions were sold off.

Heath's government was bedevilled by troubled industrial relations and no fewer than five states of emergency were declared during its years of office. An attempt to clip the wings of the trade unions was made through the Industrial Relations Act. Among other regulations was the requirement for trade unions to register with the National Industrial Relations Court (NIRC). This body had the power to order strikers back to work for a cooling off period during an industrial dispute, to impose massive fines if they refused to do so and even to jail strikers. The Act provoked a serious backlash from the unions and a series of confrontations which battered and bruised the government, damaged its credibility and eventually brought it down. The gestation, brief life and ignominious death of this Act was viewed at close quarters by Thatcher and confirmed in her mind that the power of the unions had become intolerable, that they needed to be put firmly in their place and that she was the person to do it. She was not going to let them run rings round her in the way that they had outmanoeuvred Heath. In particular she had identified the National Union of Mineworkers as her *bête noire* and correctly worked out that to defeat them decisively would be to knock the stuffing out of the rest of the trade union movement. Overall, Heath's government of 1970-4 gave Thatcher a lesson in how not to run an administration. She was determined not to make the same mistakes.

However the 1970-4 government marked a qualitative break from the established manner of doing things. In a small way and obviously predating Thatcher, it eased aside interventionism in industry and tripartite planning and moved towards a more laisser-faire approach, stressing the primacy of market forces and reducing the role of the state. It also predated Thatcher in the attention it gave to trying to reassert authority and law and order, especially in areas such as industrial relations, crime and student unrest. Heath also made clear his determination that Britain should join the EEC, a policy about which Thatcher was later to have grave reservations. As noted, Heath's attempts to bring the trade unions to heel were a dismal failure. The imprisonment of five dockworkers, the 'Pentonville Five', for breaches of the Industrial Relations Act nearly led to a general strike. The Upper Clyde Shipbuilders sit-in and the miners' strike of 1972 respectively drove a double-decker bus through his prized policies of not helping 'lame ducks' and of wage restraint. Heath was forced to abandon his 'modernising' efforts and after the fiasco of the three-day week, was forced out of office.

The humiliating defeat which Heath and the Tory government experienced in 1974 led to widespread discontent within the Party. In this situation some impatient anti-Heath MPs, spearheaded by Sir Keith Joseph, set out to provide a body of alternative ideas and to get them accepted as party policy. These ideas had been quietly gestating for some years in little-publicised discussions within organisations like the Institute of Economic Affairs and the Bow Group. Thatcher found them a natural pole of attraction and was soon involved with the Centre for Policy Studies which was set up by Joseph as a right-wing think tank. .

Labour in Office 1974-9

The post-war boom was yesterday's news by the time that Labour won the two general elections of 1974. Labour remained in office under Harold Wilson and then James Callaghan until 1979 but by that time it was a clapped-out government, tired, bereft of ideas and credibility and dependent on the support of the Liberals. In 1974, Labour had promised that if elected it would be a government that would get on with the unions, totally unlike the undignified shambles that had become the Tory's relationship with them. A 'Social Contract' had been established whereby the government agreed to meet with the trade union leaders on a regular basis. The economic prospects were pretty dire but the 'Social Contract' would help to get the union leaders on board, it was argued. The government would discuss the pressing matters of the day with the employers and the unions and promised to listen closely to the latter's side of things. In return the union leaders agreed to try to control their members' demands, especially on wages. It was their failure to maintain this voluntary anti-inflationary incomes policy that ultimately brought the Labour government down in the notorious 'Winter of Discontent'.

This Labour government was only one among many which have cynically played on the basic loyalty extended to them by large numbers of working class voters and then gone on to implement measures which reduced working class living standards for the purpose of improving the profitability of capitalism. To its eternal shame the Labour Party leadership contributed to the development of an anti-union culture. When Callaghan accused strikers in 1978 of practising 'free collective vandalism,' he confused and disorientated tens of thousands who looked to the Labour Party to provide them with a way forward.

In 1978 the government had acted to implement recommendations that key employees in the public sector needed significant pay rises. The result was increases of over 30 per cent for senior civil servants, the heads of nationalised industries, brass hats in the armed forces and judges. The police received a 40 per cent increase. While these awards all exceeded the rate of inflation, lower paid public sector workers were subjected to pay rises not exceeding 5 per cent which with raging inflation constituted a wage cut. A wave of justified outrage swept through the public sector unions, sufficient, for example, to push members of the Fire Brigades Union to strike for the first time ever in pursuit of higher wages.

The accord with the union leaders was seen as a concrete way of tackling the bacillus of inflation. This phenomenon is often regarded as the single most important indicator of overall economic health. For much of the post-war period inflation was scarcely significant and in 1959 by way of example, it was a mere 1 per cent. It 'exploded', however, during the period of the 1974-9 Labour Government reaching a totally unprecedented 28.7 per cent in 1974 and little better in 1975 at 24.2 per cent.**1.** It was then considered an almost irrefutable fact that wage rises were a major or even the major cause of inflation This assertion was repeated a million and one times in the media and by journalists, politicians, industrialists and even some trade union leaders on the basis that if it was said often enough, it would penetrate the mass consciousness and become a self-evident 'truth'. It was, of course, a rather crude attempt to demonise the trade union movement and depict its 'greediness' as a major cause of Britain's economic problems. Only small numbers of socialists, some within the Labour Party and others outside, were arguing that the underlying causes of inflation could be found elsewhere. There were many countries abroad where unions were weak and inflation was actually higher. Inflation at the levels mentioned above left Britain's low-paid workers in particular with little option but to try use their collective strength to obtain settlements which represented rises rather than cuts in real wages.

It was by no means just relations with the trade unions that were problematical. The Labour government found itself staggering from one crisis to another with no overall strategy for dealing with the root-and-branch problems from which the British economy was suffering. The crisis which occurred in 1976 had major historical significance. A serious run on the pound persuaded Denis Healey, the Chancellor of the Exchequer, to make sizeable cuts in public spending, to maintain strict wage restraint and attempt to move towards a balanced budget. He followed this package up with an application to the International Monetary Fund for a large loan. Inevitably the strings attached to this loan meant further major cuts in public expenditure. Healey's actions prepared the way for Thatcher's later more concerted and doctrinaire attack on the post-1945 consensus and everything associated with it.

This crisis in 1976 and Healey's actions to deal with it made history. It cannot be emphasised too strongly that this was a Labour Chancellor presiding over the application of monetarist policies well before Margaret Thatcher became Prime Minister. Admittedly Healey stood on the right of the Labour Party but he got away with it because no convincing alternative policy was put forward either by Labour's centre or left despite Healey's action having provoked much controversy and verbal criticism in those parts of the party.

It was only to be expected that the Tories under Thatcher, by now Leader of the Opposition, made considerable political capital out of the government's economic mismanagement and the servile way in which they had prostrated themselves before the IMF and then rushed to do its bidding despite having no mandate for swingeing cuts in public spending. However, it was not clear that the Conservatives would have done anything very different given the concern of both parties to try to extract British capitalism from the mire into which it was sinking. Both Labour and the Tories tacitly agreed that as usual it was the working class who should bear the major brunt of the cutbacks and austerity measures they believed were essential in order to give British capitalism the kiss of life.

The decline of British manufacturing industry continued under Labour. In 1975 Ferranti and IRD Industries had received £15 million and £3.9 million respectively of public money. Labour wanted to do the right thing by maintaining a manufacturing basis in the UK, keeping jobs and placating the trade unions. It took failing companies into public ownership or revamped them as workers' cooperatives supported by government funding. Injections of tax-payers' money did not prove a magic bullet for badly managed private companies and Upper Clyde Shipbuilders and Norton Villiers Motor Cycles failed as co-operatives despite the high hopes entertained for them at least on the political left.

The Social Contract between the government and the trade union leaders had the desired effect on their part of restraining wage demands, at least for a period. However by 1978 the effects of tapping into the bonanza of North Sea oil led to a euphoric although ultimately mistaken sense that things were about to turn round for the British economy.

Surely, it was argued, the oil could give the economy a desperately needed fillip. Perhaps the UK might even become self-sufficient in oil.

With wild rumours circulating that good times were just around the corner, the trade unions began to argue that they wanted their share of the expected goodies and they rejected government calls for further wage restraint, this time a limit of 5 per cent when inflation was running at about 8 per cent. Obviously this meant further cuts in real wages in addition to those already experienced. This 5 per cent limit was supposed to apply to the whole economy but it quickly collapsed in the private sector after a long strike at Ford in the autumn of 1978.

The Labour Government's frosty reception of union wage claims led to an outbreak of strikes. This situation was then carefully and systematically exploited by the Opposition and the media, the bulk of which, as normal, was rooting for the Tories. Referring to Heath's government which had effectively been brought down by the unions, it was now claimed that the Labour Government was equally under the thrall of the unions and that the country was becoming 'ungovernable' once again. This was of course was the background to the 'Winter of Discontent' with its lurid tales of rat-infested garbage piling up in the streets and cadavers that could not be buried. The media omitted to mention that the low-paid workers doing essential jobs who were at the centre of the action were seeing their already meagre living standards eroded by high levels of inflation caused by factors over which they had no control. This had left them with little option but to take industrial action in order to try to improve their living standards. The media ignored the absurdity of the claim that a union revolt against the government's demands for wage restraint showed that the government itself was in the pocket of the trade unions which were on strike. It could be argued that the Social Contract was a cynical deal brokered by the Labour government and the trade union leaders without reference to rank-and-file trade union opinion and was intended to relieve pressure on employers by imposing wage restraint on their employees. Trade union leaders however, whatever their instincts, can never be wholly dismissive of the mood of their members and some found themselves on a crash course with the government reflecting the anger of their members about the declining value of their pay packets.

Callaghan's government could do nothing right at this time. It appeared totally impotent. It had earlier made proposals concerning devolution for Scotland and Wales. These it had failed to carry out which had angered the various minority parties in the Commons on whose support it was dependent. Such was the low standing of the government that it lost a vote of confidence on 28 March 1979 which cleared the way for a triumphant Margaret Thatcher to form a government and become the first British woman Prime Minister.

The Tory Party moves to the Right and Thatcher emerges

She had not been wasting her time while things crumbled around the Labour government. In the second general election of 1974, the Conservative share of the vote had fallen to 35% which was the poorest showing in the whole of the twentieth century. The Tory Party was extremely disillusioned and had seemingly lost its way, having been unable to move with the times in finding policies to deal with the new conditions following the post-boom period. The Party reeked of failure and much had to be done if it was to be turned round and rendered able to launch a meaningful challenge for office in the foreseeable future. Thatcher believed she could make a serious contribution to a revitalisation and redirection of the Party. Edward Heath was hanging on by his fingertips as Party Leader and in her opinion he constituted a significant barrier to the radical overhaul of policy and procedures that the Tory Party needed. In a turbulent party licking its wounds and looking round for individuals and policies that could be blamed for its abject showing, it is hardly surprising that many on the right of the party felt that their time had come.

Thatcher's luck was in. After the narrow defeat in the February election of 1974, Heath was convinced that another election was imminent and set about a shadow cabinet reshuffle. Thatcher's manner had made her unpopular with her former Cabinet colleagues but Party insiders felt that it would be beneficial for there to be a woman ready to step up into a senior post once the Tories were re-elected. Thatcher was the only one in the running and she took over with Environment as her portfolio.

One senior figure in the Party who Thatcher admired greatly was Sir Keith Joseph. He was one of Heath's most vehement critics and from 1974 made a number of speeches in which he argued that the Party needed to return to its liberal economic roots by developing a programme around monetarist and free market principles. In doing so, it should reject Keynesian economic practices, reduce state intervention in the economy and corporatist practices, cut public spending significantly and discard income policies. Increasingly Thatcher was drawn to the ideas of the alternative right-wing think tank, the Centre for Policy Studies, established by Joseph. How she loved it when Joseph said, "We are over-governed, over-spent, over-taxed, over-borrowed and over-manned."

Joseph may have been regarded as an intellectual or ideas man but he was no great shakes as a popular politician or potential party leader. He markedly lacked the popular touch and seemed evasive and very ill-at-ease especially when he appeared on television. He ruled himself out as a challenger for the leadership when he rather indiscreetly made a speech in October 1974 which was interpreted by many as suggesting that he thought that the best way of ending poverty and deprivation was to place a statutory limit on the number of children that lower-income families could have. This was a fairly kind interpretation of what Joseph said. He could also be construed as having said that the feckless and unintelligent lower orders were breeding so rapidly courtesy of the welfare state that there was a real danger that they would swamp the rest of society. If this interpretation of what Joseph said has any basis, what he was saying was hardly new. Fear of the 'unwashed masses' can be identified in the utterances of right-wing political thinkers right back to Victorian times and beyond.

However, Joseph's influence on Thatcher was very considerable. She had a real reverence for him. In a speech in 1974 he put forward the Tory Radical Right position very clearly and there was little with which Thatcher would not have agreed wholeheartedly:

…*our industry, economic life and society have been so debilitated by thirty years of socialistic fashions that their very weakness tempts further inroads. The reality is that for thirty years Conservative Governments did not consider it practicable to reverse the vast bulk of accumulating detritus of Socialism…Socialist measures and socialist attitudes have been very persuasive. We have overestimated the power of Government to do more and more for more and more people, to reshape the economy and indeed human society, according to blueprints. I argue that there are limits to the good which Governments can do to help the economy, but no limits to the harm.*[1]

While Joseph is clearly using the word 'socialism' in a pejorative sense and as a smear, it is impossible to escape the impression that he'd never looked the word up in the dictionary. The 'thirty years of socialistic fashions' that he talked about had not brought one single measure through Parliament to which the adjective 'socialist' could seriously be attached.

His views contrast sharply with those of Harold Macmillan, a Tory of the old 'One-Nation' School. On many occasions he made clear his opinion that on the grounds of morality, social responsibility and sound economics there was a strong case for government to provide a strong guiding hand rather than allow peoples' lives to be subjected to what he called 'the push-and-pull of competitive effort'.

The Joseph/Thatcher and Macmillan views on the role of government were clearly poles apart. Tories both but Thatcher and Joseph were speaking for a new generation of Conservative MPs coming into politics at a time when international capitalism was undergoing its first serious crisis for the best part of thirty years and the deep-rooted weaknesses of British capitalism were becoming very evident. No wonder the Right felt in the ascendant.

The disquiet in the Tory party about Heath's leadership made it highly likely that a challenge for the leadership would be launched sooner rather than later. Intellectual brilliance was not required by the MPs who constituted the Party's electoral college. What was needed was a strong leader whose views would strike a chord with large sections of the electorate and who could handle the media effectively. In 1974 no-one came immediately to mind. Heath still had a coterie of supporters, many of them senior in the party but none of whom were likely to launch a challenge. Thatcher was not a fan of Heath but was not considered to be in the running, except perhaps by she alone. Her only experience of ministerial office had been as Education Secretary where she was remembered in many circles as 'Thatcher the Milk Snatcher'. This image had stuck and was hardly one that the Party would want its Leader to take into an election. She was so relatively unknown that 'informed sources' regarded her as a rank outsider.

Heath's supporters persuaded him to submit himself for re-election if only in the expectation that because there was no other very obvious rival, his victory might bring some much needed stability to the Party. Rather unexpectedly, Thatcher emerged as the candidate of the anti-Heath right-wing. She was not well-known in the Party but, perhaps surprisingly, she had made relatively few actual enemies and she benefitted from the support at this stage of those who didn't think she could actually win but that she might gain sufficient votes to persuade Heath to stand down. Her supporters ran a clever campaign and she beat Heath on the first ballot. He stood down, huffily and grumpily and a second ballot was organised. She won this and became Leader of the Party and of the Official Opposition. It was a remarkable achievement although it probably had more to do with Heath's unpopularity than with the extent to which Tory MPs were enamoured of Mrs Thatcher. Her election did not mark a Tory turn towards feminism. There were many in the parliamentary party and the constituencies who were unhappy that the Party was now led by a woman. That in itself was bad enough but she had also been frequently caricatured as a suburban housewife. For the snobbier elements, it did not help that she totally lacked a prestigious social pedigree. She had an abrasive style which called into question whether there was much intellectual substance behind the façade. Being intellectually-inclined is certainly not a requirement for a potential leader of the Conservative Party or any other British political party for that matter. However, the Tory Party owed much of its undoubted historical success to having produced over generations many intelligent, flexible and pragmatic leaders who were highly skilled in persuading substantial sections of the population that they stood for the interests of all sections of society – that the Tories were a truly a national party. This may have been a lie of monumental proportions but if the Conservatives had told the truth about what they really stood for, they would never have won an election. Was this all to be thrown away by someone regarded by many party members as a political parvenu, and a woman to boot?

Thatcher may have been seen as something of an upstart in the more patrician Tory party circles which was usually where most of the 'wets', the old-style 'one-nation Tories', were to be found but the reception to her rise was a mixed and contradictory one. In her memoirs Thatcher wrote that her winning the leadership of the Party was a 'shattering blow delivered to the Conservative establishment. I felt no sympathy for them. They had fought me unscrupulously all the way'. However, in the constituencies, the Tory Party rank-and-file had always contained backwoodsmen who had no truck with those Tory MPs who suppressed their own views in order to avoid controversy and not rock the boat in any way. They had had a bellyful of the class collaborationist consensus and tripartite way of doing things in the 50s and 60s although they might not have used those words to describe them. As Thatcher established herself at the head of the Party these people felt that here was a red-blooded new leader who they could do business with and who would not be afraid to speak out and act on her evidently strongly-held convictions. They warmed to the way she put across populist ideas which were actually of a highly reactionary nature but posed in a way that suggested they were simple common sense. Later, in the Falklands War and the Miners' Strike, Thatcher found causes around which she could bring together just about all the dissident tendencies within the Party. For all that, there were many Tories who simply never took to her. She was that kind of person.

'Thatcherism' begins to take shape

She had a big job to get the Party back on the right tracks. It had lost its way, was demoralised and seemed to have shed its self-belief that it was Britain's traditional ruling party, the party favoured by the really rich and powerful and tacitly pledged to ensure that this tiny minority of fat cats would still be able to enjoy most of the cream. In the period 1964-79 it had been in office for only four of those years compared with 37 out of 46 between 1918 and 1964. This figure includes coalition governments in which the Conservatives were the dominant party.

Large numbers of Heath's supporters remained at parliamentary and constituency levels and Heath himself, greatly embittered at his fate and virulent in his dislike of Thatcher, took every opportunity to attack her publicly within the Party and in the media. It was an unseemly sight. For her part, she made it clear that she would have no truck with 'more of the same', more of what she thought of as the consensual pap which had made up the politics of the last two decades. She laced her public utterances with references to the virtues of the market, of robust competition, of the benefits of freeing up individual initiative and the liberating effect on the economy and on people's lives of reducing the role of collectivism, state intervention and bureaucracy.

For years large sections of the printed media had been systematically orchestrating a mood of fear among their readers, telling them day after day that authority and law and order were collapsing; that Britain's pride and national identity were in danger of disappearing, swamped by alien influences (i.e. immigrants); that the trade unions were greedy, undemocratic and too powerful; that morals had become too permissive; that the role of the family was being undermined and that feminists had become too assertive in arguing their case. These and other topics were pursued relentlessly, portrayed in a totally one-sided way which was then dinned into readers as if it was facts rather than opinions that were being expressed.

Thatcher took these points up and used them, thereby giving them further credibility. Her argument was that the workings of free enterprise were being strangled by the relentless rise within the welfare state of a dependency culture, of a creeping, insidious egalitarianism throughout public life, and by militant trade unionism. Those she claimed were the wealth producers no longer got a just reward for their efforts, being obstructed by bloody-minded trade unions, bureaucratic red tape and excessive taxation. The trade unions would need to be tamed, statist restrictions on business freedom be abolished, public sector spending controlled, nationalised industries privatised and resources directed instead to the world of business. A revolution in public morale and morality would follow. Understandably Thatcher made little of the low-paid, insecure jobs that would be the result of her policies but argued that when it was known internationally that there was a 'flexible' and 'realistic' workforce in the UK, investment would flow in from overseas. This was music to the ears of the media moguls, especially the likes of Rupert Murdoch who in return, gave the maximum publicity to Thatcher's every utterance and set about creating the image of a determined woman of strong principles and morals who alone was the person who could save Britain from the morass into which it was sinking. Through his growing media empire, Murdoch was a major contributor to the farrago of myths that were invented about Thatcher's steeliness, her integrity and her determination to lead Britain to the status of a great nation once more.

Although Thatcher was a person of historical importance, her stature has been greatly exaggerated given the general mediocrity of the politicians around her and the fact that few, in her party and elsewhere, had the balls to front her. They might not have found her as formidable as 'The Iron Lady' image suggested. She was allowed to get away with far too much. That again was 'Thatcher's Luck'.

In her years as Leader of the Opposition, she produced one or two blockbusters. The first was a speech at Kensington in 1976 where she vociferously attacked those who wanted *détente* with the Soviet Union and she argued in favour of a much more proactive attitude - building up the weaponry of NATO and also launching an ideological assault on 'communism' and all it stood for. It benefitted her image when the Russian media responded by dubbing her the 'Iron Lady'. She revelled in her new nickname. Subsequent events were to prove that she was far from actually being an 'Iron Lady' and the Chinese phrase which was rather more applicable to the person who made so many U-turns was

'Paper Tiger'.

Thatcher made clear her belief that Britain should cleave to the USA as her natural ally. She believed that Britain could regain the leading position in the world that she had once enjoyed and which she thought had been belittled and allowed to fritter away especially at the hands of successive Labour governments. A natural corollary of this was an aversion to the idea of a united Europe of which Britain was only a part. From seeming indifference on the question of Europe, Thatcher moved over the years to an increasingly unenthusiastic and later openly hostile stance, sharply breaking with Heath's views and helping to foment an issue which has been a running ulcer in the Tory Party ever since. Thatcher believed that Britain's historical and political development gave her a special role to play in the world. As Prime Minister, one task of her government would be to administer just the kind of shake-up that would make the British people keen to resume their natural position of authority in the world.

On economic matters, she made it clear that the floundering Labour Government's sudden conversion to monetarist-type policies was forced on it by urgent necessity rather than conviction and that it was probable that these measures would be abandoned by Labour at the first opportunity. Thatcher argued that if the British economy was to be restored to anything like its former glory, tough policies had to be applied immediately and maintained until such time as the UK economy was out of the wood. Ironically, the Labour government had almost fortuitously managed to cobble together a set of measures which kept inflation and unemployment down, maintained an income policy and reduced the number of strikes. Even the prospect of revenue from North Sea Oil somehow still did not make the Labour Government look as if it could effect a permanent improvement in Britain's economic prospects. In spite of this, by 1978 they had the Tories genuinely concerned as to whether they would be able to win the forthcoming election.

Basing herself on the logic of capitalism, Thatcher was justified in arguing that such was the atrophy of British industry that the economy could indeed not afford existing levels of public spending and did need to reduce trade union power. At the same time the aim had to be one of restoring business profitability by balancing budgets, encouraging free markets and reducing tax levels. To achieve these aims, to remove obstacles to a free economy and dismantle the corporatist way of economic management which Labour was committed to and Heath's government had embraced, a deep-seated change in the economic and political culture was required. For those that did not concur, there were going to be some bloodied noses along the way.

One of the noses that would be badly blooded in the near future was that of the trade unions. Until the Social Contract broke down and the Labour Government and the trade union leaders lost control of the membership, the Tory's pronouncements on the unions were low-key. However their theoreticians and strategists had worked out that a confrontation, while inevitable and indeed necessary, was unwise until a future Tory Government could be sure that a battle was winnable. In the end the Labour Government did much of their hard work for them. The Tories were able to capitalise on the so-called 'Winter of Discontent' with frenzied assistance from the media. The aim of this outpouring of media filth was to portray the public sector unions as totally irresponsible and the Labour Government as completely unable to control them. Against a chorus of media support, Thatcher and the Tories declared that now was the time for a change and a new, far more resolute hand to be placed on the tiller to cut the unions down to size and address all the other urgent things that needed to be done if the UK economy was to be restored to a healthy state. This was the public message. What was really intended was a reduction in the share of wealth going to the working class and the transfer of resources to the private business sector in order to boost profits, induce investment and stimulate greater productivity and competitiveness.

Not the least of Thatcher's lucky breaks was to be around at a time propitious for the development of a body of ideas which probably seemed naturally congenial to her and on which she drew but to which she could also be said to have contributed in her own inimitable way. The dominating ideology of the late 1970s and of the 1980s was often known as that of the 'New Right'. While it was by no means simply a British creation, it would not be unfair to say that Thatcher consciously set the pace and the style in the implementation of policies which went on to be emulated elsewhere in Europe and indeed, across other continents. It was an uneven process as different countries adopted those aspects of New Right ideas appropriate for their own needs and in their own particular ways. It was part of a significant move to the right throughout the advanced economies of the world and it later spread with baleful results to many of the countries which were formerly part of the Communist bloc. Changes in political ideology and policy never simply drop from the skies, they are never accidental. This rightward shift was a response to certain organic difficulties in the capitalist world which had been at least partially disguised by the prolonged economic boom of the 1950s and 1960s. It was no accident that Britain should set the pace in the development of new ideologies and practices because it was perhaps the UK of all the advanced economies which was exhibiting these difficulties most clearly.

This is not the place for a detailed study of the ideas of the 'New Right'. The ideas touted around by those happy to be associated with the New Right were by no means homogeneous. It would be possible to identify two main strands: the Neo-conservative New Right and the Neo-liberal New Right. Thatcher was eclectic, taking a piece here and a bit there from these ideas and enjoying being seen as the standard-bearer of the New Right, adding a nuance of her own but also acting entirely pragmatically when she thought the situation needed it. From the Neo-conservatives she took, for example, a strong sense of nationalism, of national identity and of 'traditional values'. From the Neo-liberal wing she selected among others, the concepts of the free market, anti-corporatism, 'freedom' and the need for monetary control. She drew on both when avidly denouncing what she thought of as socialism.

Some idea of New Right thinking was encapsulated in a book edited by the Conservative MP Patrick Cormack.[2] The roll call of contributors to this volume is itself fascinating. Topping the bill is Reg Prentice. He was a man of exceptionally reactionary views and a poor record as a constituency MP which caused him to be deselected as a Labour MP. He then briefly flirted with the Liberal Party, realising that there was no future for him there before calmly crossing the floor of the House and taking the Tory whip! The other contributors, like Prentice not necessarily men of principle, were mostly ex-members or supporters of the Labour Party including Lord Chalfont, the author Kingsley Amis and the journalist Paul Johnson. Common themes were how Labour, from once valuing and emphasising humanity and individuality, had drifted into collectivism and humourless zealotry. Instead of recognising merit, it had moved towards a stifling egalitarianism, in education for example. The Labour Party, it was alleged, had become too tolerant of criminals and soft on the need for a strong defence policy. Leading Labour figures were condemned for refusing to condemn violence on picket lines during industrial disputes. Likewise they were charged with refusing to denounce Labour councillors who were defying the law over local authority spending. Additionally, and probably most unacceptable to our eight wise men, was the marked move to the left which had seen the Labour Party national conference actually debating a resolution for nationalising the commanding heights of the British economy! These were the kind of concerns which struck a chord with substantial numbers of Tories, both in the Parliamentary Party and at constituency level and resonated with Thatcher. She was happier with the populist nature of what these contributors were saying than with the more intellectualised neo-liberal views emanating particularly from the USA at this time.

Not that the thinkers of the New Right were necessarily correct in their analysis of what was wrong and what needed to be done. They characterised the public sector as an unproductive burden on the wealth-creating world of private business and commerce. In the post-war mixed economy, the private sector could not have functioned without the goods and especially the services provided by the public sector. Teachers, for example, are needed to educate and train the next generation of workers and nurses and doctors to keep them fit for work. Why did they not turn their attention to the growing armies of workers in service industries such as advertising who were also not directly productive? The UK was merely following the trend in the advanced economies for a reduction in jobs in manufacturing while employment in the service sector increased.

The New Right contended that public spending in the UK had reached a level which was burdensome on the taxpayers and was diverting resources away from productive industry and destroying incentives to business enterprise .However, in 1975 public spending in the UK was 46.9 per cent of GDP, just less that the 47.1 per cent of West Germany and markedly less than the 55.9 per cent in the Netherlands. Outlay on welfare in Britain at 7.7 per cent of GDP was significantly lower than the average for the other members of the then Common Market at 10.6 per cent. Taxation was higher than average but well below that of prosperous Norway and Sweden. The luminaries of the New Right were also mistaken about Britain's record on days lost as a result of industrial action. This was around the average for the advanced western economies and consistently less than Canada, Australia and the USA which, however, enjoyed higher productivity.

Nationalised industries were held up by the New Right as being examples of bureaucratic, inefficient, unprofitable 'socialist' practice. They conveniently forgot that they provided the private sector with subsidised goods and services while also carrying out the kinds of business activities that were often intrinsically unprofitable. Railways were an example. They chose to overlook the fact that some state businesses were highly profitable. Examples in 1977 were the Post Office (£392 million profit) and the Electricity Council (£206.5 million).

The New Right were never happier than when ranting on about 'dole-scroungers' and the so-called 'dependency culture'. Those who were in receipt of benefit, especially on a long-term basis, were a soft target and newspapers like the *Daily Mail'* thoroughly enjoyed bullying them, knowing that they couldn't fight back. For the New Right, fuzzy-minded do-gooder politicians of both main political persuasions had hijacked the idea of a welfare state, laudable enough in itself, and been responsible for the creation of a sizeable subclass of workshy freeloaders who, by manipulating the system, could enjoy incomes and benefits, courtesy of the honest, hard-working taxpayer, which were often higher than the earnings of those in full-time work. This, it was alleged, was having a harmful moral effect, not only on those who were milking the system but also on those whose taxes were underwriting it. Why go to work at all?

As they warmed to their theme, New Right theoreticians chose to ignore the fact that while fraudulent benefit claims cost the country £40 million in 1980-1, the value of the benefits that went unclaimed because people either did not know they were entitled to them or were perhaps too proud to claim, was of an altogether greater magnitude at £400 million. A discreet veil was drawn over the scandalous situation whereby tax avoidance cost the Treasury something in the order of £4,000 million. The rich freeloaders who could hire fancy accountants to cook their books for them were not a soft target and the *Daily Mail* was markedly more reluctant to regale its readers with lurid stories about their immorality and lack of social responsibility.

The collapse of fixed exchange rates and mercurial currency movements in 1971-2 and the steep rise in oil prices in late 1973 sparked a recession of varying severity in the advanced western industrialised countries. It came as a shock for many as crisis hit the capitalist system once again when some so-called 'experts' had consigned such problems to past history. Fordism as an economic philosophy in the western world suddenly plummeted from the height of chic to scorned obsolescence and obscurity. No longer was there talk about a high wage, high profits, high prosperity economy as pro-capitalist thinkers everywhere cast around desperately for some other magic bullet which would make the return of recession go away and remove the possibility of it ever returning. Having been consigned, so they had thought, to the pages of the history books, here, once again, was rising unemployment, inflation, declining productivity, balance-of-trade crises, lack of investment and industrial unrest. The New Right stepped into the void left by the discarding of Keynesian economic practice. In the event, the New Right's nostrums were to prove no more of a panacea than those of Keynes for the inherent problems and contradictions of the capitalist economic system.

---

1. Joseph, Sir Keith, Stockton Lecture, *Monetarism is not enough*, 5 April 1976.
2. Nevin, M. (1983), *The Age of Illusions*, London, p.179.
3. Cormack, P. (1978), *Right Turn: Eight men who changed their minds*, London.

4. THE IDEOLOGY OF THATCHERISM

When the bogey of inflation re-emerged as a major problem in the 1970s, Keynesianism came to be seen, certainly among those on the political right, as being a major contributor to the new and highly undesirable reality of economic instability. Inflationary tendencies were believed to be endemic in Keynesianism and consensus political policies were considered as too indecisive to be able to tackle the problem effectively. The sacred cow of full employment which had enjoyed almost universal support for two decades was sacrificed on the altar of expediency – the kneejerk reaction that if one set of policies had failed, now was the time to put opposite ones into effect. But what policies and who was to implement them?

Was there such a thing as 'Thatcherism'?

Some care has to be exercised when considering economic policy and relating it to the term 'Thatcherism'. Just about everything that Margaret Thatcher did seems to have attracted controversy and hyperbole. However it must be remembered that the economic crisis that replaced the post-war boom began several years before she was part of the government let alone before she was able decisively to influence national economic policy through holding the office of Prime Minister. She preened herself proudly when she was referred to as 'a conviction politician' pursuing 'radical' and 'bold' policies. It has already been made clear that Labour Chancellor Denis Healey paved the way for severe attacks on public spending when accommodating the demands of the IMF on the loan made to prop up the pound in 1976. The policies carried out when she was in office, although undoubtedly far-reaching, were a continuation or intensification of a process already in motion.

Does she actually deserve the plaudits of those that thought she was brave, single-minded and innovative politician in breaking with generations of pusillanimous politicians and taking decisive and necessary, although unpopular, decisions to restore Britain to a deserved position towards the top of the league table of world powers? Did her style of political leadership and the ideas and policies associated with her justify being dignified by the invention of the proper noun 'Thatcherism' as if there was something uniquely distinctive about them? If the historical circumstances had been different, would her particular personal traits and attributes have propelled her to such prominence? Was it her good fortune to be around at a unique time when historical factors not of her making came together to create a vacuum into which she could step and which she was able to exploit and, at least in her own mind, for which she could virtually take the sole credit?

These are complex questions which have already exercised many minds and do not permit a quick and simple answer. Any attempt at an explanation has to start from the fact that Thatcher was a Conservative politician attempting to address the concrete problems of an economic system to which she was totally committed. She was incapable of even considering that there could ever be an alternative, let alone a better way of creating, exchanging and distributing wealth than the capitalist economic system. A not very dissimilar view of capitalism is found not just among Conservative but also among Liberal-Democrat and large numbers of Labour MPs, past and present. What distinguished Thatcher was the absolute single-mindedness which she brought to her mission of putting British capitalism back on its feet.

As she wrote, 'not every capitalist has my confidence in capitalism'.[1]

Thatcher was very strongly influenced by the post-war boom and the politics of consensus in developing her view of the world and decision to become involved in politics. In these formative years, it must have looked as if capitalism had at last managed to iron out any serious internal issues and was on its way to providing prosperity for all, at least in the advanced western economies. By the early 1970s, however, cracks were beginning to appear in the façade of western capitalism. Thatcher watched, unimpressed and fulminating with impatience, as Heath for the Tories and then Wilson and Callaghan for Labour tried to apply policies to offset recession and get the economy back on an even keel once more. A major problem, as she saw it, was that Britain's political leaders had simply grown soft during the years of 'having it so good' and had become incapable of taking the necessary bold decisions and implementing tough, unpopular policies to deal effectively with the issues facing Britain. While Thatcher may have thought that consensus politicians were culpably indecisive and evasive so far as policy-making was concerned, some of her most strongly-held ideas were themselves straight out of the post-war consensus. Strong links with the USA, a British nuclear deterrent and emphasis on continued 'great power' status were examples.

For his part, Nigel Lawson, her long-time Chancellor, was convinced that Thatcherism was or had been a reality:

> *Thatcherism is, I believe, a useful term, and certainly was at the time. No other modern Prime Minister has given his or her name to a particular constellation of policies and values. However, it needs to be used with care... The right definition involves a mixture of free markets, financial discipline, form control over public expenditure, tax cuts, nationalism, 'Victorian values' (of the Samuel Smiles self-help variety), privatisation and a dash of populism.*[2]

Cards on the table

In an interview with 'The Times' in 1984, Thatcher outlined her general intentions. *I came into office with some deliberate intent: to change Britain from a dependent to a self-reliant society – from a give-it-to-me to a do-it-yourself nation; to a get-up-and-go instead of a sit-back-and-wait-for-it Britain.*[3] A typical politician's statement, it says a lot without actually saying anything specific but the gist is clear. She continued by saying that she intended to eliminate 'socialism' from British politics and, by reversing the trend towards collectivism so evident since the Second World War, she would bring about an economic and moral reinvigoration of the British nation. She went on record as saying, *Economics is the method. The object is to change the soul.*[4] We were told with remorseless repetition that there was no alternative. She argued that a moral and social regeneration was urgently needed. It would require an all-out assault on the mores of the permissive 1960s. She believed that it became fashionable in the 1960s to mock and dismiss what she described as 'the old virtues of discipline and self-restraint'. This statement is interesting given that she had voted for the legalisation of gay sex and of abortion-on-demand.

The author tends to the view that Thatcher certainly had some of the personal attributes that make for success in modern politics. This is not intended as a complement but is simply a statement, albeit a subjective one. He finds little to admire in at least 95 per cent of modern professional politicians. Thatcher was not plagued by the self-doubt that assails many of those with a more analytical and intellectual frame of mind. She tended to see things in very stark 'black-and-white' terms, was single-minded and extraordinarily energetic and hard-working in pursuit of her aims. She was ambitious, ruthless, egotistical, intolerant and narrow-minded. These latter characteristics scarcely distinguished her from most other politicians but they seem to have been far more highly developed in her. Having such strong opinions and being absolutely convinced of her own rightness made her inflexible, unsympathetic and poor at listening and responding, especially when hearing what she did not like and of which there was no shortage. She hectored those she felt to be weak and she was a consummate bully who, typically of her sort, was shown up on occasions as well able to hand out the browbeating and domineering but proving very fragile when faced with someone perfectly capable of standing up to her. She appeared to have a chip on her shoulder about being a woman from a relatively humble background making her way in the Tory Party. This was still the party of the ruling class in twentieth-century Britain, a male-dominated party epitomising the continued existence and importance of the class system, the deep roots of which have had such a divisive and debilitating effect on the country's economic and social development. All this constituted a volatile mix in a Prime Minister coming to office at such a crucial time in British history and facing the urgent need to reverse the long relative decline of the country's economy.

Thatcher had a visceral, irrational hatred of what she understood by 'socialism'. In her political memoirs, writing about the period after 1983, she said:

…there was still too much socialism in Britain… (it) was built into the institutions and mentality of Britain. We had sold thousands of council homes, but 29% of the housing stock remained in the public sector. We had increased parents' rights in the education system, but the ethos in the classroom and the teachers' training colleges remained stubbornly left wing. We had grappled with bringing more efficiency into local government; but the Left's redoubts in the great cities still went virtually unchallenged. We had cut back trade union power; but almost 50 per cent of the workforce in employment was still unionised.[5]

The Powell Influence

Thatcher's many biographers have dug deep in an attempt to identify the events and the ideas which most influenced her during her political apprenticeship and later when she was in office. A presence that was impossible to ignore was that of Enoch Powell. Here was a man for whom the word 'maverick' might have been coined but he had a massive presence in the Tory Party, ultimately too big and too hot for it to handle. Powell was very insistent from the mid-1960s onwards that Conservatism needed far more clearly to distinguish itself from social democracy. Powell probably remains best known for his 'rivers of blood' speech in 1968. He spoke in metaphorical language about the River Tiber 'foaming with much blood' as a consequence of large-scale immigration. Most of his then party colleagues hastened to disassociate themselves publicly from Powell's sentiments, whatever they may have thought privately. Powell, however, gained a receptive audience for his views on race from among the least politically sophisticated sections of the middle and working classes, especially those who read such newspapers as the *Daily Express, Daily Mail and Daily Telegraph*. This would have been noted by Thatcher who realised that considerable political capital could be made from appealing to the worst sentiments and desires of these layers of society. In her economic policies and elsewhere Thatcher displayed an unerring ability to tease out ideas which met this criterion. Some of her critics have called it 'authoritarian populism' and trace its origins to Powell. She achieved this with some skill while astutely distancing herself from Powell as he increasingly came to be seen as a political pariah.

From back in the mid-1960s, Powell had been taking every opportunity to denounce the social democratic census and to call for a reduction in the role of the state, reductions in direct taxes, a free market economy and warning of the inherent tendency to inflation of Keynesian economic policies. He was a monetarist before the concept became temporarily fashionable. However his was virtually a cry in the wilderness until he sprang to the forefront of the news with his anti-immigration views.

Thatcher and Victorian Values

Few politicians, even those who take the major decisions influencing everyday life, think dialectically. They do not consciously see history as a process of continuous change, of movement through contradictions and conflict, of the impossibility of being able to rewind the film of history to return to the same place. They ignore or refuse to consider the lessons that can be gained from studying the past and applying them to influence the present and the future. Modern capitalism is the perfect example of how this attitude is carried over into the world of economics and wealth creation. There is little concern about where we have come from and what we can learn from history since the point of capitalism is the making of profit. Its efforts are concentrated on the here-and-now or, at best, the very short-term future. History, as Henry Ford said, is 'bunk'.

Thatcher was something of an exception. She did indeed look back to the past and drew on it to perpetuate a very one-dimensional view of the nature of Victorian society in Britain. This concentrated on the unquestionable dynamic energy, confidence and optimism exemplified in the most successful projects of British engineers, scientists, entrepreneurs and others at this time in Britain itself, the Empire and elsewhere across the world. It chose to ignore, for example, the large number of unsuccessful projects, the brutal suppression of native resistance in the colonies, the racism associated with the concept of empire, the stifling and frequently hypocritical morality, the institutionalised and informal discrimination against women, the exploitation and abuse of children, the blighted environment and all the other issues that remained ignored, unaddressed or unsolved.

No reference was made in Thatcher's speeches to the massive collective struggles of innumerable, largely unsung, ordinary men and women for a healthy environment, for safer working conditions, for universal elementary education, for the vote, for the right to organise in trade unions and so on. Yes, these and other vital reforms were partly achieved in the Victorian era but they had to be fought for – they were never conceded willingly. Working people became better organised, more confident, educated and assertive during the nineteenth century and there existed a fear in the minds of the ruling class that if the masses weren't granted some bread, it might be far worse and, as the phrase goes, they would come for the bakery. Additionally, the ruling class came to be aware that to be prosperous capitalism needed a continuous supply of reasonably healthy and at least partly educated workers. They somewhat grudgingly came to accept that the state had a role to play in ensuring that this requirement was met. These considerations were not part of the Victorian reality that Thatcher chose to refer to in such roseate terms. Her Victorian values were extremely selective. She deliberately distorted history in an attempt to promote what she regarded as economically and morally desirable attitudes and behaviour. The press followed along obediently, simplistically portraying the Thatcher project as the struggle of order against chaos, good against evil and civilisation against its opposite. 'Victorian' was never equated with 'Dickensian' because of the latter's negative associations with squalor and want.

Deeply rooted in Thatcher was the sense that the 'Great' in 'Great Britain' had criminally been allowed to wither almost to nothingness. Perpetrators of this misdemeanour were generations of unprincipled career politicians of all parties; cautious, complacent bureaucrats, jobsworths and woolly-minded liberals and socialists with no pride in being British. Thatcher despised the mindset that had allowed this to happen and she believed she spoke for millions of British people when she took upon herself the task of trying to restore the country to its former position of pre-eminence. This was always going to be a task doomed to failure simply because of far-reaching organic and structural changes in the British and worldwide economies which made it impossible to bring back the conditions which had existed a century earlier. These had provided Britain with uniquely favourable conditions for a period of three or perhaps four decades which in historical terms is really little more than a snapshot in time. Those conditions could never be repeated.

There was nothing very innovative in Thatcher's views concerning Britain's departed greatness. Similar sentiments were regularly expressed at Tory Party conferences and with some frequency in the Letters to the Editor pages of papers such as the *Times* and, usually more crudely, the *Daily Telegraph* and *Daily Mail*. Thatcher was never noted for the originality of her ideas or for their measured and reasoned intellectual content. What she said, however, was always delivered in such a manner as to forestall any possible questioning or criticism. For all that, style took precedence over substance.

As so often with Thatcher, she unconsciously wrapped herself in a cocoon of contradictions. The crying shame was that few on the political left were able to challenge her effectively, not only in terms of ideology but through campaigns against her reforms. Those equipped with the best theoretical critique of Thatcherism tended to belong to small revolutionary socialist groups who did not have the resources and the numbers to mobilise an effective fight-back on both ideological and practical fronts. Therefore monetarism for her was a radical and brave new policy although those who knew their history of economic thought construed it as merely a return to old-fashioned laissez-faire and she was fond of quoting John Stuart Mill on the perils of over-government. Her prudish and somewhat anachronistic denunciations of permissiveness and gratuitous violence on television did not prevent her from licensing cable TV, a green light for continuing the process of debasement and dumbing down. Her admiration for the enterprise of the nineteenth century did not prevent her from telling the Institute of Directors that Britain was in danger of 'living in the nostalgic glories of a previous industrial revolution'.

Seemingly her first public mention of 'Victorian Values' was in an interview with Brian Walden on *Weekend World*, 10 January 1983. She was obviously pleased with her performance and before long most of her public utterances were laced with references to 'Victorian Values' although she was also fond of references to the Puritan work ethic which she seems to think of as being synonymous with the Victorian ethos. She told an *Evening Standard Reporter*:

> I was brought up by a Victorian grandmother. We were taught to work jolly hard. We were taught to prove yourself (sic); we were taught self-reliance; we were taught to live within our income. You were taught that cleanliness is next to godliness. You were taught self-respect. You were taught always to give a hand to your neighbour. You were taught tremendous pride in your country. All these things were Victorian values. They are also perennial values.[6]

As late as the 1970s, 'Victorian' was frequently used as a word of opprobrium for most things associated with that period. Thatcher was able to capitalise on and even give expression to a widespread sense of disenchantment with Britain's uncertain and reduced role in the post-war world. The formal empire had gone and after the post-war boom, Britain, we were constantly told by papers like the *Daily Mail*, seemed to be drifting along rudderless, losing pride and gaining a reputation for lack of enterprise, for moral laxity, for crime, welfare dependency and general cynicism. A yearning for a renewed sense of purpose led to a look backwards and in a largely uninformed and uncritical way gratefully seizing a fairly recent past period and endowing it with having had all the qualities that were needed to put the 'Great' back in front of Britain. It may have been a kind of highly selective amnesia but it struck a chord and Thatcher bled it white.

The result for the British working class was that for ten years, Britain was presided over by a Prime Minister who, while emphasising the need to restore the work ethic, carried through economic policies which led to the destruction of jobs on a scale unprecedented in the twentieth century. Thatcher would probably have included the dignity of work in her list of Victorian virtues. By the 1990s the proud individual and collective skills of huge numbers of working people in manufacturing industry had been decimated, lost for ever. There were new jobs in the service sector. These were largely low-paid, unskilled, non-unionised with low status and poor prospects and increasingly macho management regimes. A return to Victorian Values indeed!

Supply-side economics

The author suggests that there were three major components in Thatcher's economic theory. The first saw the public sector as an unproductive and expensive burden. It needed drastic pruning and the taking over of many of its activities by the private sector to ensure better value for money. Such a transfer of functions would allow tax cuts to be made, free up resources to be used productively by business and encourage family and individual responsibility. She omitted to mention that there might be parts of the public sector which, when privatised, offered the prospect of profitable pickings for the private sector. Secondly, prices should be stabilised by firm control of the money supply. This required limits on government borrowing and also on private credit. The state's efforts should be directed towards safeguarding a free economy and not propping up idleness and dependency. Thirdly, every obstacle to prevent markets functioning fully should be eliminated, if necessary by government intervention. Policing the economy to ensure smooth operation of markets required a strong state. A strong state was also needed for internal and external security. These policies, Thatcher said, would change Britain from a 'dependent to a self-reliant society'.

The theories put across by the emergent right-wing in the Tory Party and voiced most stridently by Thatcher marked a distinct move away from general twentieth-century Conservative economic policy towards the ideas of classical liberal political economy. Traditionally the modern Conservative Party had presented itself as the party of the national economy and state, the party of the community rather than the market, as the party of protection, imperialism, paternalism and intervention rather than a party committed to free trade, self-help and laissez-faire. On the other hand a very traditional Tory strand in Thatcher's thinking was the need for greater discipline and higher moral standards and the importance of the family. For her, order in society was essential for the effective and efficient running of the free economy.

Thatcher was never averse to claiming the moral high ground. She believed that her moral vision was grounded in Christian values but religion for her was a matter of individual spiritual redemption not of practical social reform. She loudly declaimed that Christianity was an absolute force for good although the briefest survey of the history of Christianity and the actions of its self-proclaimed practitioners would quickly disabuse anyone but the most obtuse of the notion that Christianity and goodness are synonymous.

She made abundant use of Biblical quotes to back up her moral precepts. She was particularly fond of the parable of the talents and used this as to justify the efforts of entrepreneurs. "Those who traded with their talents, and multiplied them, were those who won approval. And the essence of their performance was their willingness to take a risk to make a gain." [7] When several senior prelates of the Church of England offered up even muted criticism of Thatcher and her economic and social ideas, they were basically told to shut up or put up. She expected the Church, as a pillar of the status quo, to be on her side. Bishops were expected to support her moral crusade; after all, Nanny knew best. Biblical quotes concerning a camel and the eye of a needle or the renunciation of worldly goods by the disciples cut no ice with Thatcher. As Antonio says in 'The Merchant of Venice', *The Devil can cite Scripture for his purpose.*

Where was the Left?

No credible or convincing alternative to Thatcherism was put forward by mainstream politicians and in its absence she was able to portray what she said as common sense and even to make some headway in winning support for these policies. Thatcherism was even able to find support among those sections of society who would gain absolutely nothing material from her policies and whose social exclusion was only exacerbated by those policies. That Thatcher managed to gain even the minority support of the electorate says as much about the enfeeblement of Britain's Left at the time as it does about any virtues in her policies themselves. The leaders of the Labour Party and of the trade unions have consistently devoted more energy (and enthusiasm) towards vilifying, isolating and, preferably, expelling the revolutionary socialists on their left than they ever have given to developing an effective critique of capitalism and campaigning for a socialist alternative to it. Had they led a concerted fight against Thatcher and put forward convincing alternatives, they might well have found that she was not nearly as tough as she wanted people to believe.

Much of the blame for allowing Thatcher to get away with what she did must be placed on the leaders of the labour movement with their intellectual laziness, contempt for economic and political theory and lack of ideological commitment to fighting for better conditions for the working class. Most of the leaders of the labour movement throughout its history have sought solutions to the problems thrown up by capitalism only within the framework of capitalism itself. They have done so in the name of 'the national interest'. This has always been and remains an illusion, a metaphysical concept, a chimera, because there can be little commonalty of interest between a billionaire banker and the mass of the population who, while not necessarily being on the breadline, nevertheless has no hope of ever accruing that level of wealth which simply attracts more wealth. The conflict of interests is even truer of low-paid workers, unemployed and others living in very real poverty who feel that they have absolutely no control over the impersonal economic forces which exercise so much influence on their lives. In practice the labour leaders have traded on the tremendous loyalty of the working class in order to control them and restrain their demands. Worse, they have seen no alternative at times of economic crisis to destroying reforms won in the past and carrying out measures to reduce the share of wealth consumed by working people in order to boost the profitability of capitalism. Even the so-called 'left' leaders, who have retained a sentimental but pious hope that the rough edges might be rubbed of capitalism, believe that counter-reforms have been necessary to try to get capitalism back on its feet once more. Thatcher used this political pusillanimity and lack of principle to give some plausibility to her declarations that by contrast she had a radical and populist programme which would be able to turn things round and which had something to offer every section of society.

An end to consensus

Thatcher argued that the gutless politicians of the 1950s and 1960s had allowed the power of government to be eroded as they had consistently failed to stand up to the power of trade unions and other narrow sectional interests (She did not include employers' organisations in this category). The growth of material prosperity and its accompanying freedoms needed to be restored and this could only be done by bolstering the authority of the state, so the theory ran. It was this insistence on the restoration of a strong state that united the 'New Right' which was otherwise quite disparate in the various strands it embraced. It led to something of a contradiction when handled by Thatcher who boasted about rolling back the boundaries of the state when in practice the state became considerably more centralised and interventionist during her period in office. This paradoxical shifting between libertarianism and authoritarianism was a feature of her policies – sometimes unashamedly populist when selling off council houses, for example, but when putting paid to something she did not like such as the Greater London Council, simply draconian and authoritarian.

Another curious juxtaposition is that of the free economy with the strong state. A free economy presupposes business transactions carried out voluntarily by self-interested individuals but benefitting wider society because in theory they operate according to agreed rules to create and disseminate wealth. The argument is that it is necessary to have a strong state in order to ensure that all citizens play according to the rules. Since no national economy is self-sufficient and all nations need to engage in international trade, the New Right generally favoured substantial spending by the state on so-called defence in order to ensure that the rules are observed internationally as well. In the case of Mrs Thatcher, a strong state was also required in order to coerce, with force if necessary, any internal groups whose activities threaten what she thought of as being for the general good of the community. In particular Thatcher thought that during the years of consensus, society had been allowed to become too pluralistic and the state had become soft and unwilling or unable to limit the activities of minority groups whose interests she regarded as conflicting with those of society as a whole.

To break with consensus politics while dealing with the effects of recession, the government would need to cut taxes (popular) and public spending (likely to be less so) and roll back the state by a programme of privatisation. If public assets could be sold off to enable 'small people' to become shareholders this was likely to have considerable popular appeal. Money raised through such sales might help to defray tax cuts. Cuts in what are now called 'quangos' – regulatory agencies - might also be popular because they could be portrayed as reducing unnecessary and expensive red tape. Although it was considered that substantial parts of such a programme would enjoy public support, there might be opposition from employees in the public sector and various interest groups including trade unions and the state would have to be prepared to take on and defeat such opposition by any and all means available.

A strong state was also required to implement policies which were intended to encourage the 'enterprise culture' and make British business more innovative and competitive. With a stress on efficiency and modernisation in order to achieve these aims, it was highly likely that the government would run into opposition from the trade unions. The Right was united in its agreement that the unions were an example of an interest group that had been allowed to become far too powerful. Education, training and research would need to be extensively modernised to become an instrument of economic revival but reforms in these areas would be certain to arouse the ire of academics. The New Right had little time for the majority of academics, seeing them as an entrenched and privileged minority instinctively opposed to disruption and change. The Conservative Party has long been associated with tradition, the maintenance of sectional privilege and the upholding of the status quo but in championing New Right ideas, Thatcher's governments inevitably came into conflict with various individuals and many groups who found their interests threatened or who simply did not like her style and what she stood for. Thatcher, however, was able skilfully to present a raft of policies which played on prejudices, insecurities and various baser human attitudes to win considerable but by no means ever overwhelming popular support.

It was regarded as essential to boost the competitiveness of British business. Firms that were outdated or otherwise inefficient would either have to go to the wall or pull themselves up by their own bootlaces. They were not to be given financial assistance by the government. Those businesses that were prepared to move with the times would be assisted in being more competitive by the government stepping in with legislation to reduce the ability of the unions to defend their members – this would help by basically cutting the wages bill. At the same time expenditure on welfare programmes would be reduced to deter dependency on benefit. On an individual basis workers would be encouraged to make private provision against hard times through such means as private pensions. These measures were part of a strategy to fragment the working class, reduce collective bargaining power and increase profits at the expense of wages and conditions of employment and the social wage. The existence of a cowed, fragmented, low-paid working class was intended to make Britain an attractive place for investment from overseas. Those companies that survived the inevitable shakeout would be leaner and hungrier and more able to compete on international markets. That, at least, was the theory.

What then was the basis of Margaret Thatcher's popular appeal or populism? A theme which was bound to resonate was that of making Britain great again. This was pure rhetoric. It had the great merit that while it sounded really good, few people were going to ask awkward questions about what a revived Great Britain would actually be like. Great for whom? It had also had hints or undertones of nationalism, imperialism, racism and xenophobia, sentiments which had put down very deep roots in the British working class particularly in the days when the British Empire bestrode the world and which had not been entirely eradicated by time and changed circumstances. Thatcher appealed to those who wanted a break with Britain's not very auspicious recent past and a programme of modernisation to repair damage that had been done. Simultaneously she appealed to a largely illusory vision of the past when people had apparently respected those who had been put in their place to rule over them, when the authority of the male head of the family and the institution of marriage were sacrosanct, when Britannia ruled the waves, when people had been proud to be British and all other nations and races were thought of as being lower down the food chain and, not least, when workers had been happy to do a fair day's work for a fair day's wage.

Although the 'Guardian' newspaper rather surprisingly told its readers that it was 'one small step for Margaret Thatcher, one great step for womankind' when she became Prime Minister, this proved to be a woeful misjudgement. Thatcher had no interest in or sympathy with issues of specific interest to women or to other more general matters which were also of concern to them. She made this clear when she said: 'Some of us (women) were making it by our own efforts long before feminism was even thought of'. This gross solecism can only be attributed to complete ignorance on her part of a long history of women fighting the corner for their sex and class, in Britain and elsewhere.

For Thatcher, the woman was crucial in the monogamous heterosexual marriage and home that she valued so highly. The woman was the domestic goddess, the home builder and the mother. Here was one of Thatcher's many contradictions. She argued that women should have the same opportunities as men in the wider world outside the home. At the same time she also argued that the nuclear family and the woman's place in it was the best and the natural order of things. She could not, however, be consistent by fronting up a campaign to get women back into their domestic role because that would have deprived business of a valuable source of cheap labour, a strategy which, as has been noted elsewhere, was essential to a dynamic capitalist economy so far as Thatcher was concerned. This essential contradiction was encapsulated in a speech she made in 1988:

> ...*the family is the building block of society. It is a nursery, a school, a hospital, a leisure place, a place of refuge and a place of rest. It encompasses the whole of society. It fashions our beliefs. It is the preparation for the rest of our life. And women run it.*[8]

Creeping Socialism

Two associated concepts which Thatcher made use of as focuses for demagogic incitement to hate were 'The Nanny State' and 'Creeping Socialism'. It was an undeniable fact of post-war Britain that the state had grown significantly larger and become more interventionist in everyday life. The origins of this process can be traced back to the special requirements of managing the war effort and then the unique historical conditions under which the NHS and the Welfare State had been created just after the war. While these measures were a huge step forward, they were not, despite what the political Right said, socialism, nor were they ever intended to be. The perspective of the Labour Party was not a socialist transformation of the economy and society. At best it was to carry out a programme of limited nationalisation in a mixed economy to prop up ailing but necessary industries and a programme of reforms to tackle some of the worst examples of social and economic inequality and exclusion that were the inevitable product of the capitalist system. This strategy presupposed the long-term continuance of capitalism and was based on the idea that capitalism could be controlled or managed so as to achieve a greater accord between its interests and those of wider society, particularly its most vulnerable citizens. If capitalism would not police its own most aggressive or acquisitive instincts, then reformist social democracy would do it through the state on behalf of wider society. Labour governments in particular had presided over a great extension of the activities of the state. In the 'prosperous' 1950s and 1960s, expectations about what a civilised society consisted of grew in an unprecedented fashion and the state found itself trying to meet these expectations by becoming involved in wider and wider aspects of the country's social and economic life. As it did so, faceless government agencies sprung up overnight like fungi in a damp autumn wood and the number of bureaucrats increased exponentially while the cost of this social engineering could easily be portrayed to spiralling out of control.

A prominent influence in Labour Party political thinking had long been the Fabian Society concept of collectivism whereby increasing parts of the functioning of a capitalist society were to be brought under the management of the state via the civil service. By the 1960s this approach was being defined in some circles as being synonymous with socialism. In practice, Labour governments were using the state as a medium to implement reforms for ordinary people but with two important provisos. One was that the reforms did not cost too much and thereby detract from the ongoing process of capitalist accumulation. The other was that these reforms were carried out on behalf of rather than collectively by ordinary people. The right-wing reformist tendency in the Labour Party has always been repelled by the idea that the working class should organise and use its own immense potential power for the purpose of bringing about political and other forms of change. This view of how or how not to bring about change is deeply imbued with elitism and implied contempt for ordinary people who, it presupposes, need 'responsible', 'educated' people to guide them or, preferably, to do it for them.

In fact statism or state bureaucracy has little to do with a genuine socialist perspective on how to bring about meaningful economic and political change. In the period under review Labour managed to shoot itself in the foot. The corporate state which it did so much to create was originally intended to be a way to bring about beneficial change but it had become something of a Frankenstein's monster. As it had increased the scope of its activity it was being encountered by citizens in some very negative situations. It was met when spending hours waiting for attention in an outpatients' department or painfully when on a list waiting for an operation. It was met when signing on the dole and trying to deal with the intimidating regulations that that frequently involved. Again it was met when attempting to make sense of complicated and off-putting forms needed for the claiming of benefits. It was encountered when grappling with the mysteries and complications of a tax return. It was easy to see the government agencies concerned as bureaucratically top-heavy, expensive, unfriendly and unhelpful and an easy target for anyone who wanted to attack them.

A concept and set of practices which should have been a real benefit to the people could easily be perceived instead as a growing bureaucratic imposition. This played straight into the hands of the New Right. The state could be portrayed as a nosy, repressive busybody building up a self-perpetuating hierarchy and gorging itself at the expense of the tax-payer. It was encouraging a dependency culture in which tens or even hundreds of thousands of 'spongers' preferred to live on overly generous benefits rather than work. Lurid stories appeared in the media about families with no one in employment and a dozen or more children living in luxurious accommodation and receiving far more in benefits than the average worker received in wages. All this generosity to the feckless was paid for by the thankless hard work of others. It was also alleged that this dependency culture was eating into the inventive genius and talent for innovation which had been synonymous with 'Great' Britain. On occasion it was even claimed that civil servants and local government mandarins were accumulating power and developing an apparatus with sinister similarities to the state bureaucracies in 'socialist' Russia. Here were some of the themes around which Thatcher was able to assemble her populist rhetoric about the need to roll back the boundaries of the state and give people back their 'freedom'.

Playing on fears

Education proved to be a subject out of which Thatcher was able to make populist capital. Rancorous exchanges had taken place earlier between political lefts and rights about the virtues of comprehensive schools versus selective grammar schools, the left claiming the 'progressive' ground and the right eager to defend what was 'traditional'. For her part, Thatcher while Minister for Education presided over the disappearance of more grammar schools that any Education Secretary before or since. Without becoming involved in arguing the merits and demerits of educational change, we can say that by the mid-1960s many concerns were circulating about falling educational standards, about illiterate school-leavers, about politically-motivated teachers using the classroom to indoctrinate innocent pupils with socialist or 'alternative' ideas and about schools in which the kids ran amok while teachers either did not dare or were not allowed to apply disciplinary sanctions – if indeed there were any they were allowed to use. It was also said that there were inner-city schools which had such large intakes of the children of immigrant parents that the needs of the children of indigenous parents were being scandalously neglected. Thousands of children were being spewed out of secondary school and proving incapable of obeying the simplest of instructions or of acting in any purposive way in a place of employment.

It was a doom and gloom scenario of the sort that was meat and drink to unprincipled and mischief-making, alarm-spreading newspapers like the *Daily Mail*. With others, it kept up a systematic daily barrage of propaganda and disinformation masquerading as fact aimed at gullible readers and seeking to ignore, minimise or undermine any achievements that could be ascribed to the influence of progressive ideas in education. A climate of opinion was created which regarded it as an indisputable fact that standards were seriously declining in education. This decline was impacting gravely on the productivity and efficiency of industry, or so we were told. Scapegoats needed to be found among the liberals and lefties who were responsible and they should be called to account for their crimes. Thatcher was thoroughly at home with such sentiments and was able to make them part of her repertoire, sure in the knowledge that there was a ready reception for them in the constituency at which they were aimed. This was because substantial sections of the population had already been softened up with much of the media constantly regurgitating a limited number of themes knowing that if the ideas were repeated often enough they would come to be accepted as true, no matter how absurd or untrue they actually were.

Other examples of areas that Thatcher was able to exploit for her own purposes were law and order and race. Deep concern about the breakdown of law and order was a hardy perennial at Conservative Party Conferences but Thatcher found it a vote-winner by shamelessly playing on fears and insecurities – many no more than the product of spin and mischievous agitation but not necessarily implausible just because of that. Again she was the cheerleader with the right-wing press providing the chorus in the form of a conditioned response. The streets were no longer safe, muggings took place in broad daylight and no one intervened, more 'bobbies' needed to be seen out on the beat, ready and willing to cuff a youngster round the ears and they needed to know and be a part of the communities for which they were responsible. Tougher sentences were urgently needed. There was too much emphasis on the 'rights' of the criminal and too little attention given to the rights of the victim. Prison conditions resembled those found in 4-star hotels and needed to be made far more austere and demanding. Prison was, after all, supposed to be a punishment, not a respite from the cares of the world. Respect for authority, be it in the family, school or wider society, was declining with dire effects for all to see. Crime rates were going out of control… and so it went on. Such views were put across as if things had never been worse and this was the price that society was having to pay for allowing liberals and lefties to entrench themselves in so many influential positions in the post-war consensus society.

Not only were ordinary, decent people going round their respectable everyday lives in danger of being swamped by the sea of rising crime but they were also fearful of being overwhelmed by a tidal wave of immigrants of alien cultures, languages and religions. They were flooding into the country in such numbers that the British identity and 'way of life' was seriously under threat. When tighter immigration controls were mentioned, some audiences responded with great enthusiasm. Those cheering loudest were frequently from the leafiest and most affluent suburbs or from idyllic villages located in the depths of the countryside where no immigrants could afford to live and none were ever seen. The fact that Britain had long had one of the most multi-cultured populations of any country in Western Europe and that some of her greatest politicians, artists, engineers, intellectuals and others were immigrants or the offspring of new arrivals cut no ice when Thatcher and her ilk were playing on the fears and petty hates of what were often the most poorly educated and insecure layers of society. The uncertainties and difficulties they faced in their everyday lives were primarily caused by the nature of the society and economy in which they lived and not by immigrants.

Thatcher carefully chose the issues around which to mount her crusade and ignored others that were every bit as serious. Low pay, homelessness, the problems associated with old age and women's issues, for example, were just some of those which clearly ticked no boxes for her. Thatcher, like any politician, was constantly looking for issues which offered quick political gains for her and the Tory Party. She was not morally fastidious as to which issues she chose to campaign around and preferred those that appealed to the lowest common denominators – of personal self-interest, greed and acquisitiveness, contempt for the weakest and most vulnerable sections of the population, sexism, racism and xenophobia, for example. Although she made references to the past – to the days of Britain's former supposed greatness, she did so confident in the knowledge that those who listened to her were not going to go to the history books to check out the facts. Her appeal was a demagogic one and although she imbued her speeches with a certain moral fervour, the sentiments to which she appealed were not likely to have been the sort of which Jesus of Nazareth would have approved.

One of Thatcher's many biographers discourses on Thatcher's breathtaking rigidity and reductionism:

> *She viewed the world through Manichean spectacles as a battleground of opposed forces – good and evil, freedom and tyranny, 'us' against 'them'. The overriding global struggle between capitalism and Communism was reflected at domestic British level by the opposition of Conservatives and Labour, and more generally in a fundamental distinction between, on one side, 'our people' – honest, hard-working, law abiding, mainly middle-class or aspiring middle-class taxpayers, consumers and homeowners – and, on the other, a ragtag army of shirkers, scroungers, socialists, trade unionists, 'wets', liberals, fellow-travelling intellectuals and peace campaigners. All these anti-social elements had to be taken on and beaten to make the world safe for Thatcherism.*[9]

The author continues:

> She divided the country frankly into 'our people', who were to be encouraged, protected and rewarded with tax cuts, mortgage relief and all sorts of hidden subsidies to keep them voting Tory, and the rest whose votes she did not need, who were told to stand on their own two feet and stop whingeing.[10]

Nor was Thatcher too fussy about those she chose to do much of her dirty work. She had high hopes for Cecil Parkinson, who despite his determination to look and sound every inch a 'toff', hailed from a not dissimilar social substratum to Thatcher. He let the side down badly when she found out that he had made his long-standing mistress pregnant. Norman Tebbitt was another from a humble background. He was a saturnine-looking individual notorious for his contemptible observation that the long-time unemployed of Tyneside should get on their bikes and pedal off in search of work. Nicholas Ridley was a toff but didn't look it. Seemingly forever dangling a cigarette from his lips, in March 1990 he said, "Every time I hear people squeal, I know that we are right." The French have an expression to the effect of 'Show me who your friends are and I will show you who you are.' Thatcher's friends were awful. Ridley, of course, made sure that it wasn't he and his class that did the squealing.

That Thatcher was allowed to get away with what she said and did speaks volumes for the ideological bankruptcy, gutlessness and general ineptitude of much of the so-called political left at this time. A serious critique of capitalism in crisis and of Thatcherism and the posing of alternative economic policies was confined largely to the revolutionary socialists of what was frequently dismissed by the media as the 'loony left or 'hard left'. Describing someone as being a loony left was a way of dismissing them with contempt and thereby avoiding the need to examine and counter their ideas. They gathered in a number of small groups which, by their size, lack of resources and sometimes by the nature of their tactics, found it hard to get their views widely heard or taken seriously. Some Marxists such as those who supported the 'Militant' newspaper were active within the Labour Party. The media took their presence much more seriously and campaigned for their expulsion from the Party. This was taken up with enthusiasm by reformists of the right, centre and even of the left of the Labour Party. We were then treated to the sight of a Tory government tearing the guts out of vital reforms won by the past struggles of working people while the right-wing of the Labour Party, eagerly egged on by the media, devoted almost its entire energy to the witch-hunt of a few thousand Marxist Labouy Party members. The right could not answer the political arguments put forward by the Marxists and so had recourse to what such people have always done – the use of organisational methods and manoeuvres to shut them up and, in many cases, to expel them. Neil Kinnock in particular threw himself with frenzied enthusiasm into the ensuing witch hunt. As leader of the Labour Party he was, however, virtually useless as someone to front a vigorous attack on the Government. Senior Tories treated him with a contempt they had never extended to Foot and Healey, and simply swept aside his windy but feeble utterances. Within the Labour Party there was a widespread feeling that while he was leader, no general election would be won. This belief proved to be correct.

1. Thatcher, M. (1993), *The Downing Street Years*, London, p.44.
2. Lawson, N. (1983), *The View from No.11. Memoirs of a Tory Radical*, London, p.64.
3. *The Times*, 9 February 1984.
4. Quoted in Ridley, N. (1991), *My Style of Government: The Thatcher Years*, London, p.83.
5. Thatcher, M. (1993), ibid. p.281.
6. 'The Good Old Days'. *Evening Standard*, 15 April 1983.
7. Quoted in Raban, J. (1989), *God, Man & Mrs Thatcher*, London, p.48.
8. Speech at Conservative Women's Conference, 23 May 1988.
9. Campbell, J. (2004), *Margaret Thatcher. Vol. Two: The Iron Lady*, London, p.351.
10. Campbell, ibid. p.352.

5. THATCHERITE ECONOMICS – THE THEORY

Monetarism

Strict control of the money supply was a central tenet of New Right economic thinking. Monetarism as a concept was perhaps most closely associated with Chicago where both Friedrick Hayek and Milton Friedman had been professors. The latter in particular made the necessity for sound money an essential part of his critique of Keynesian economic policies. The apparent inability of governments in the 1970s to control inflation while at the same time presiding over serious rising levels of unemployment tempted some politicians to welcome monetarism as a timely new panacea. A programme of free-market measures borrowed from the 'Chicago School' was applied by the government in Chile which, with US backing, had overthrown the democratically-elected left-wing government of President Allende in 1973. It was like a miracle to embattled capitalists everywhere when a tranche of economic reforms was implemented by Chile's police state which brutally suppressed all opposition. The share of wealth going to the working class was slashed and a huge cash boost to business and the better-off was put into effect. Right-wing governments across the world cast an envious eye on the 'Chile Effect'.

The overthrow of democracy and the savage destruction of human rights in Chile were of little concern to the 'Chicago Boys'. They coolly viewed Chile as a laboratory in which innovative economic and social experiments were taking place. For them the 'success' of the Chilean experiment was the creation of a model which could be applied elsewhere to pump new life into tired old capitalism.

Influential economic theories never emerge and gain support by accident. They owe their influence to encapsulating the material needs of particular classes in society in certain specific historical conditions. So it was with the ideas of the eighteenth century Scottish economist Adam Smith and the concept of the free market associated with the classical political economy of Britain's heyday as the 'Workshop of the World' in the nineteenth century. These ideas had always retained an attraction for some of the more intellectual elements on the right of the Conservative Party even when the tide seemed to be running strongly against them during the post-war boom. However free-market and neo-liberal theories came into their own with the end of that boom. Economists of the right unexpectedly found themselves trying to explain the confounding of orthodox thinking as capitalism across the world once more plunged into crisis. Such a situation, they had recently been arguing, could never recur because capitalism had finally solved its tendency to cyclical boom and slump. No wonder then that monetarist theory and neo-liberal practice was eagerly seized upon by pro-capitalist economists and politicians as providing a solution to problems that they previously thought had been finally consigned to history.

Especially germane to any explanation of the impact of monetarism was the role it played when the system of fixed currency exchange rates ended in 1971/2. With fixed exchange rates closely controlled by the central banks it was possible to control demand in the domestic economy and also in the money supply. The agreement on fixed rates had provided a useful degree of stability during the two decades of the post-war boom. What brought about the end of fixed exchange rates was the basic weakness of the US economy at that time.

Potential disaster hit the western economies in late 1973 when the OPEC countries suddenly quadrupled the price of oil. This intensified both the incipient recession and the inflationary tendencies and threatened a possible breakdown of the international economy. As so often happens when there is a serious crisis with international implications, the nation states involved found themselves in a state of disarray and disunity. Under these conditions a return to fixed exchange rates was out of the question. A new means of controlling inflation was required - and urgently. The expedient proved to be monetarism. Here was a set of measures which, if adopted and carried out by national governments, could satisfy the international financial markets that they had the economy under control and that their currencies had integrity.

The adoption of monetarist policies involved the government making it clear to the international money markets that a strict control was being kept on the money supply and that extensive public spending cuts were being implemented. The priority given to the need to keep inflation down meant that one of the central tenets of consensus politics, the maintenance of full employment, was sacrificed. It would also not have gone unnoticed that the official renunciation of full employment would be a blow to the bargaining power of the trade unions. Nothing makes workers keep their heads down more than the threat of unemployment!

The right-wing economists who were on the ascendant from the late 1960s and who it is convenient to describe as 'monetarists' were not actually a homogeneous grouping nor were they were necessarily peddling a totally new set of ideas. This is not the place for a detailed examination of monetarist thinking or the different emphases among individual supporters of the general ideas. The two names that come most quickly to mind when monetarist theory is mentioned are F.A. Hayek, who didn't even like to be called a monetarist, and Milton Friedman. Even in the 1970s, the Austrian Hayek was an old warhorse, having first come to prominence decades earlier since when he had been continuously involved in tussles between pro-capitalist ideas on the one hand and socialist and collectivist theories on the other. His seminal work was *The Road to Freedom* published in 1944. It was utterly uncompromising in its attack on socialism in all forms and it even accused the meekest socialist measures such as selective nationalisation of being a Trojan Horse disguising an insidious conspiracy by communism to win control of the world. Such assertions were sweet music to the Thatchers of this world.

In 1981 Hayek had visited Chile and was hugely impressed by what he saw. So carried away was Hayek that when he got home he wrote a letter to his friend Margaret Thatcher in which he lyrically extolled the privatisation that was taking place in Chile, the inward investment from global business corporations and the evidence of new wealth in Santiago's glittering shop windows, full of luxury goods, and visible on its streets with towering new office blocks and swanky cars cruising by. Profits were booming for Big Business in Chile and Hayek suggested that Chile offered a model of economic policy that Britain would do well to follow. Thatcher's reply was a cordial one but she pointed out that replication of the

Chilean model of shock therapy was unfortunately not necessarily applicable given Britain's socio-economic and political orthodoxies. A military dictator or a junta of brass hats were just not the vehicle through which free-market economic policies could be introduced in the UK. The existence of obstacles to the introduction of a full free market economy may have been very regrettable so far as Thatcher was concerned but it does help to explain the patchy and inconsistent application of monetarist policies by her governments. It is no coincidence that Thatcher always regarded Pinochet, leader of the Chilean coup, as a friend and perhaps even a role model.

How extraordinary that Thatcher could equate the brutal suppression of democracy in Chile with any kind of notion of freedom. Except perhaps the freedom of capitalism to maximise its profits through the destruction of democracy and the infliction of misery, terror and sometimes death on those who opposed Pinochet. It is worth pointing out that the Chilean experiment reduced inflation from around 1,000 per cent in 1973 to a more manageable 30 to 50 per cent. The social consequences were disastrous. Around 50,000 medium-sized and small businesses went bankrupt, unemployment rose to 35 per cent, earnings fell, public expenditure was cut by well over 50 per cent, poverty spread like wildfire, dissidents were tortured and many simply disappeared. The justification was that the wealthiest 10 per cent of Chilean society became much better off. That thought made Thatcher purr.

For Friedman, inflation was the enemy. His view was that inflation could only effectively be tackled by means of a reduction in the rate of growth of the money supply. Such action would cause a temporary economic recession and care was needed by government to achieve a fall in inflation while keeping the likely hostile response from both capital and labour within controllable bounds. A period of severe austerity would be inevitable before inflation would be brought down to an 'acceptable' level and economic growth resumed.

Explaining, preventing and controlling inflation has always been a headache for pro-capitalist economists and monetarists with their obsession particularly with controlling the money supply and slashing public expenditure. However monetarists were no nearer reaching an ideal model for the UK economy than any other school of 'experts'. There is no necessary causal relation linking increased money supply to rising inflation as was shown by other countries who, while boosting their money supply, did not suffer with the excessive levels of inflation that the UK endured in the 1970s. These economists were like a doctor treating a patient covered in unsightly and painful green spots. Medication is prescribed and taken and it gets rid of the green spots for a while but no serious attempt is made to diagnose and treat the underlying problem which is causing the spots in the first place. In due course the spots, or in this case, inflation, returns. The economists are largely impotent because they dare not, they cannot, admit that inflation is an ultimately incurable symptom of capitalism.

Thatcher professed scorn for economic theory. Whereas Joseph had something of the intellectual about his Conservatism, with Thatcher it was instinctive. She never bothered to get seriously to grips with monetarism but she was swept along on the wave of misplaced euphoria which, for a short time, claimed that it had found the answer to one of the irritating little niggles that seemingly popped up from nowhere to interrupt the workings of the capitalist system. If it is accepted that a key to monetarist economics is strict control of the money supply, then it would be difficult to categorise Thatcher as a monetarist for that control is something her Chancellors never actually achieved and in due course they even gave up trying.

Thatcher's first government contained ministers sympathetic to monetarism in key roles such as Geoffrey Howe at the Exchequer, Keith Joseph at Industry and John Nott at Trade but she also 'bought in' expert advisors. One of them was Terry Burns who was a monetarist from the London Business School. Another was Alan Walters, an academic economist who had worked for the IMF and he became her personal economic guru and friend. Such unelected advisors may have had a significant influence on government policy but Thatcher while being a neo-liberal never fully embraced the monetarist agenda and made it clear who was in charge when it came to making and implementing policy. If pragmatism rather then theory was the order of the day, so be it. From 1981-2 monetary control was gradually ousted by supply-side policies involving reductions in personal taxation and a freeing up of the labour market.

Essential to any understanding of monetarist theory and practice is its aversion to the public sector and this was certainly a concept which struck a chord with Thatcher. It sees the public sector as a monstrous incubus, self-perpetuating, self-interested and essentially parasitic, leeching wealth out of the productive efforts of the business community. Monetarism makes a sacred cow of the virtues of the 'market' in economic matters. While it could be argued that the 'market' is an example of reification or trying to make a concrete reality out of something which is essentially abstract, monetarists argue that market solutions are in virtually all cases superior to those where goods and services are provided by public bodies. Some even extend this conviction to the provision of health services, wider social services and to education. They argue that any good or service is bound to be provided more efficiently by entrepreneurs responding to the spur of competition and free of outside, i.e. government interference. This argument ignores the tendency of capitalism which, far from promoting competition, ultimately tends towards monopoly or at least oligopoly. The purpose of capitalism is the provision of goods and services from which profits can be made rather than necessarily the supply of those things which are most widely needed and at affordable prices. It is evidence of capitalism's essential nature and its inefficiency and inequity that, for example, in Britain it has never been able to provide sufficient good housing for people on low incomes. A housing crisis of varying intensity is a continuing feature of life in Britain.

'Freedom of choice' is bandied around as one of the benefits of the free market but such claims sound hollow with regard to the utility companies privatised by Thatcher's governments where public monopolies have predictably been replaced by private ones which have been able to hike prices up with almost total impunity. Now the consumer can buy gas from an electricity supply company and electricity from the gas people but prices rise inexorably and there is no real freedom of choice.

The views being put forward under the general banner of monetarism were evidence that after the unprecedentedly long post-war boom, capitalism once more had its back against the wall. With Keynesian ways of managing the economy having revealed their serious shortcomings, there was a desperate scramble to find some other way of overcoming the tendency to crisis that is inherent in capitalism. Monetarism was a reactive response which promised a new set of solutions, rejecting Keynesian ideas which were now debunked as outdated and ultimately unworkable. Monetarism was gleefully seized upon as the new panacea for all capitalism's ills. It proved no more efficacious than Keynesianism.

Monetarism and morality

At the time, the monetarists not only claimed the high ground as far as economics was concerned but also on the issue of morality. With some justification they were dismissive of elections every few years as providing a meaningful yardstick by which the public could comment on how they felt about what governments claimed to be doing on their behalf. For them the smooth everyday workings of a market economy efficiently bringing consumer and producer together in a mutually beneficial manner provided abundant evidence of the morality of a good society. Individuals, university departments and think-tanks galore sprang up to spread the good word and give it an intellectual veneer. To question or criticise the new orthodoxy was to be a no-hoper, a Luddite. For the monetarist, the entrepreneur was the great wealth creator and the good society was the one which gave him his head and allowed him the maximum freedom to innovate. The results of the entrepreneur's enterprise, even if not shared out equally, would benefit all. This view, which it is hard to believe that anyone could put it forward seriously, is euphemistically known as 'the trickle down theory'.

Thinkers of the right were by no means homogeneous in all their views. Some believed that the growth of the public sector and increase in state intervention since the Second World War had an erosive effect on the freedom of the market and therefore of the individual. Others, further to the right, were more concerned that the growth of pluralism had undermined the authority of the state and that this needed to be restored as a matter of urgency. No blame was ever put on the beast itself, on capitalism, because its inescapable internal contradictions could not be recognised nor admitted. Instead the blame was always placed, for example, on the power of organised labour and the growth of the welfare culture. These factors were hindering the working of the so-called free market by stifling initiative and reducing profitability while simultaneously raising unrealistic popular expectations and fomenting discontent.

Enemies are always needed

Hanging over the West in the post-war years was the perceived threat from Russia, of China to a lesser extent but certainly of something conveniently called international communism. This created a cultural climate inimical to socialist and collectivist ideas. It certainly forced those holding left-wing views, be they in political parties large or small or simply individuals, into a defensive stance and it labelled them as 'extremists' while allowing those with right-wing views to masquerade as 'moderates'. This attitude even extended to those holding radical or liberal but non-socialist views. It caused the supposed left to be fragmented and demoralised and even in many cases to become unconvinced of the case for socialism given capitalism's long-drawn out boom. This meant that its leadership in Britain and elsewhere was unable to launch an effective fight-back when Thatcher's government went on the offensive against the gains working people had made in the past. Because they felt that they did not have a convincing case to make for a socialist alternative, even a mild reformist one, the leaders of the Labour Party tried to convince an imaginary 'middle England' that they were statesmanlike and responsible and were a safe set of hands when it came to dealing with the problems caused by the return of economic crisis. In this situation it was natural for them to turn on the left-wing and revolutionary socialists who had a critique of capitalism and an alternative programme. Where such socialists were in the Labour Party it became imperative to expunge their influence by expelling them. At the same time the trade union leaders sought to minimise their influence at rank-and-file level. They were eagerly backed in these efforts by the Tory-dominated media hypocritically asserting when it suited them that they were concerned for the health of the labour and trade union movement.

Some of those on the right believed that the consensus days of the 1950s and 1960s had bred a 'rights-for-all culture' of permissiveness and excessive tolerance which had undermined respect for authority and was subverting the fabric of a free society. Lumped together as the 'enemy within' were people of dubious loyalty particularly in such places as schools and universities, parts of the media, particularly the BBC, the trade unions and even the churches. Belonging to sinister small groups or acting on their own initiative, these people shared a desire to destroy a free society in every way they could but most of all by belittling and undermining 'authority' and the ethics of business. As Thatcher explained:

> *And nowhere is this attitude* (opposition to wealth creation) *more marked than in the cloister and common room. What these critics apparently can't stomach is that wealth creators have a tendency to acquire wealth in the process of creating it for others.*[1]

The argument of the right was that such people might think of themselves as libertarians but in reality were they to succeed in their intentions, the outcome would be the destruction of 'freedom' and the imposition of an authoritarian state. Of course it all depended on what you meant by 'freedom'. The people who saw conspiracies to subvert 'freedom' were anxious to defend a society in which the financial rewards were shared out with grotesque inequality and unfairness. Birth still conferred privilege and the Tories fully supported that idea and the lack of equality of opportunity which went with it. Substantial numbers of the wealthiest lived off unearned income. Many who were well off did work that could not seriously be construed as benefitting society in any imaginable way. Those whose work was vital to the economy and society and without which civilisation would grind to a halt were generally paid in reverse ratio to their actual usefulness. They had to make do with what was left after the rich and powerful minority had had the lion's share. In reality the conspiracy theorists saw 'the enemy within' as anyone who dared to criticise or question the status quo.

Thatcher and Freedom

But what is the reality of 'freedom' in the late twentieth and early twenty-first centuries? There are indeed many valuable political and civil freedoms although most of these were only gained after heroic struggles in the past by those prepared to challenge the existing order. The freedom of assembly, freedom of speech, freedom to belong to independent trade unions, freedom from arbitrary arrest and freedom of the press, to cite just five.

It would not be unfair to say that most if not all of these have frequently been observed in the breach in modern Britain. During the Thatcher years, for example, police prevented striking miners from travelling across the country to meet other strikers or lend them solidarity and support. Certain picketing miners were deliberately targeted for arrest during the 1984-5 dispute and often later released without charge but not before they had been on the receiving end of verbal and physical abuse from the constabulary. The right to belong to trade unions was withdrawn from civil servants at GCHQ.

Freedom of the press has long been a total mockery. It is projected as meaning the right of citizens to express their views publicly. The reality is that most of the media is in corporate hands and strenuously defends the existing economic and social order. It can print more or less what it wants when it attacks 'greedy' workers or those involved in strikes, for example, knowing that it can give a totally one-sided account and that there will be little or no opportunity for those involved to have an equal chance to put their side of things. The owners and managers of the media decide which people, which facts, even which version of the facts and which ideas will be allowed to reach the public.

The much-vaunted freedoms are not necessarily an everyday reality. Bulging dossiers exist on those citizens known to hold dissenting political views or to belong to organisations whose beliefs do not meet with official approval. Even those dissidents who work hard and have undoubted talent may struggle to gain the rewards their efforts merit. Despite the strictures of the law, women do not necessarily have the freedom to enjoy equal pay with their male colleagues.

Even the absence of coercion does not guarantee freedom. The mere fact that no law prohibits you from doing something does not mean that you are in a position to do it. Everyone has the right to buy a Ferrari or stay for a month in a five star hotel surrounded by every expensive luxury. However you are not really free to do either of these things if you do not have the money to pay for them. What use is the freedom to do something if you are unable to exercise it? It is no real freedom at all.

Freedom is much more than the mere absence of restraint. Freedom means the ability to be able to live life to the fullest – not only the material ability to satisfy the needs of the body in regard to adequate food, clothing and shelter but also the effective opportunity to cultivate the mind, to develop the personality and to assert each person's unique individuality. By any criteria, it is evident that everyone does not have equal freedom to buy the Ferrari or even to live in a decent home. As the writer Anatole France (1844-1924) so aptly put it: *The majestic equality of the law forbids the rich as well as the poor to sleep under bridges, to beg in the streets and to steal bread.*

Ruling class ideology usually defines freedom in terms of non-interference with established legal and political rights but most people measure freedom less in terms of abstract rights and more on material matters such as the ability to pay the bills, to enjoy economic security, to provide a decent future for the children and to live in reasonable comfort in old age. Is a school-leaver without a job and with few prospects of getting one, free? Is someone living in rack-rented slum accommodation free? Is someone working all the hours God sends on the minimum wage and who still cannot pay the bills free in any meaningful way? Is a worker constantly living in fear that his job will disappear, free? Only the better-off are able to enjoy freedom in this broader sense of access to abundance, security, leisure. It is only they and not the poor that have the freedom to make choices.

When Thatcher talked about 'bringing freedom to the people', she meant 'her people' - the better-off minority of the population for whom freedom in the material sense was a reality.

Economics and morals converge

Some time has been spent considering these ideas because Thatcher's economic agenda can only be understood in the context of her determination that it was necessary to break from practices which she believed were dragging the country down. She was adamant that a strategy urgently needed to be implemented that would put British capitalism back on its feet and thereby reverse many years of relative economic decline. But her economic policy was by no means simply about economics. It took on the form of a wider moral crusade. The public and private lives and mores of the British nation and its people had been allowed to degenerate. Economic revival was unsustainable, she argued, without a drastic change in direction and thorough overhaul of its social culture. What Thatcher's governments did can only be understood against the background that the woman herself believed she had a moral mission as well as one that was economic and political.

She was fond of claiming that she was restoring the Conservative Party to its true principles. Most of what she said publicly was delivered in speeches which of course had been researched and written for her. What Thatcher and those she employed were able to do between them was ingenious. It was to convert a complicated set of economic theories into an idiom with a popular appeal to large numbers of the electorate across the classes. The economics was made to look simple; to be common sense but Thatcher also managed to infuse what she said with the air of it being a moral mission, morality being a dimension of which little had been heard during the consensus years. Thatcher had the enthusiastic backing of the bulk of the news and comment media which happily created and then disseminated an image; creating an 'ism' as they went. 'Thatcherism' was born and packaged, actually first mentioned in the 'Sun' newspaper. It was made to look new, radical, brave and even moral. All this was 'spin' before the term had been invented. Her economics, in so far as it had a theoretical base, was derivative. What made her economic policies distinctive was the moral fervour she brought to rationalising and implementing them. As one of her biographers wrote: *She used the deliberately homely language of housewife economics to lead the most ideologically driven government of the century, giving her name to a distinctive political philosophy in a way that none of her predecessors had done.* [2]

Thatcher's speeches contained seemingly innocent and artless phrases like the need 'to balance the books' and 'you cannot spend more than you earn'. These homespun phrases sounded like simple housewifely common sense and were eagerly seized on as such but they frequently obscured unpalatable neo-liberal intentions. These phrases were glib and misleading. They might be applicable to the limited budgets on which most households operate but were nonsensical when applied to government expenditure. Governments frequently spend more than they receive in income and often find that if they reduce expenditure they lose revenue from taxes and end up having to pay out increased benefits.

Thatcherism drew on the long-standing Tory themes of freedom, the nation, the family, duty, respect for authority, the maintenance of standards and respect for tradition but added an aggressive edge, drawing on neo-liberalism to add concentrated self-interest and anti-statism. It also named and shamed those institutions, especially the trade unions, which it considered stood in the way of repairing the damage that had been done to the economic and social fabric of the UK over a period of decades. It gave notice of intent to these institutions that hard-hitting changes were on the way. Thatcherism claimed that it was going to put the 'Great' back into Britain. In reality, leaving aside such mystical abstractions as 'duty' and 'freedom', the mission of Thatcherism was to try to restore the health and profitability of British capitalism.

If war was needed to achieve this aim, then war was what they would have, even if the enemy was not foreign. One of the most obnoxious adherents of the new militant brand of Toryism associated with Thatcher and indeed one of her close associates, Peregrine Worsthorne, is reported to have told *The Observer* in June 1983, "Old fashioned Tories say there isn't any class war. New Tories make no bones about it; we are class warriors and we expect to be victorious." Worsthorne also argued in *The Sunday Telegraph* in 1977 that if a left-wing government was elected, the duty of right-minded citizens was to act treasonably. By her friends shall we know Thatcher.

---

1. Speech at Newcastle-on-Tyne quoted in Kavanagh, D. (1990), *Thatcherism and British Politics. The End of Consensus?* Oxford, p.292.
2. Campbell (2004), Vol 2.op cit. p.395.

6. THE TORY GOVERNMENT 1979-83

This chapter looks at the first of Margaret Thatcher's three administrations and considers and assesses what this government did. The criteria this writer is applying in evaluating events are very different from those that a hardened admirer of Thatcher would use. Political information in a capitalist society is overwhelmingly provided by private businesses and presented by people largely chosen for their support of the capitalist economic system. Despite what is so often claimed, it is impossible to approach political issues in a disinterested fashion (using this word in its correct sense as meaning 'unbiased'). Those commentators and historians who claim that they approach all political phenomena without fear or favour are simply deluding themselves. This is even truer when what is being considered is as controversial as were so many of Thatcher's activities.

The previous Labour Government went out with scarcely a whimper. It was tired and unloved and the prospect of another four years of Labour had little allure. However the 1979 election results were hardly a ringing endorsement for the Conservatives because they had received the lowest share of the poll of any post-war Conservative government. Thatcher had a lot of work to do to pull the Party together and she had even more to do to stamp her imprimatur on the incoming government and on the wider electorate. Here was Britain's first woman Prime Minister. All eyes were on her and no one knew quite what to expect. Inflation was growing at an ominous rate. Desperate measures were needed.

On 5 May 1980 a number of hostages were seized and held in the Iranian Embassy in London by Iranian dissidents who were armed to the teeth, bristling with high-powered weaponry. A force of SAS troops stormed the building, rescued the hostages and killed all but one dissident. This strike was gung-ho and ruthlessly efficient and it made a strong impression across the world which is precisely what it was intended to do. It sent a wake-up call that Mrs Thatcher had arrived as Prime Minister of the United Kingdom and that she wasn't going to stand for any nonsense. It was a cleverly choreographed media event which made Thatcher look decisive and courageous without having had to endanger herself personally. It seemed out of the question that any of her three predecessors in the office of Prime Minister would have given the orders for such an action. It was a crucial date in the creation of an image of the 'Iron Lady'. Much more was to follow. It was also the first public showing of the love affair between Thatcher and the SAS. This elite fighting force was the creation of one Colonel David Stirling. Some years earlier when Britain's relative decline was becoming increasingly obvious and governments showed themselves totally incapable of reversing the process, he was one of a number of the brass hats from the armed forces who argued in favour of determined right-wing governments using military force if necessary to stop the slide. The trade unions were identified as the main villains and Stirling thought it would be justified to use the military to bring them to heel. Such a view naturally endeared him to Thatcher and he was eventually rewarded with a knighthood.

59

The siege worked wonders for Thatcher's public relations but there wasn't much else to enthuse about in the first three years of this government. Unemployment rose sharply and so did inflation in the early days. There were hunger strikes in prisons in Northern Ireland and destructive urban riots in several British cities. Thatcher was besieged by critics both within and outside the Conservative Party. Among the most eminent critics was a group of no fewer than 364 economists, mostly from the world of academe, who were signatories to an open letter in 'The Times' predicting dire consequences from the government's deflationary measures as outlined in the 1981 budget. Thatcher squared up to those who were calling for her head on a plate and this assisted the creation of the image of the principled leader prepared to sweep aside opposition to unpopular policies certain in the knowledge that she would eventually be vindicated. Those who supported her were fond of military analogies when making reference to her courage (others thought of it as intransigence or mere bloody-mindedness). Making an imaginative leap, supporters of Thatcher recalled the bravery in the face of those caught up in the 'strategic withdrawal' at Dunkirk and the heroics of the mainly young men who risked and often gave their all in the Battle of Britain. These events were recalled to reinforce the idea of Thatcher's bulldog, backs-to-the-wall spirit. It was conveniently forgotten that Dunkirk, bravery aside, was a disastrous military defeat and that while the Battle of Britain was won, it was on a wing and a prayer, an extremely closely-run thing, far too close for comfort.

Economic measures make a bad situation worse

Once the IMF loan negotiated by Denis Healey in 1976 had been paid off, the Labour Government breathed a sigh of relief and started spending with some abandon once more. This meant that the public finances were again in disarray when Thatcher took office. They soon became worse despite swashbuckling statements she had made about how she was going to apply monetarist policies. The Tory Government honoured promises to increase pay in the public sector and money had to be found for this and for increased defence spending and pay rises for members of the armed forces and police officers. Deflationary government economic policy led to large-scale joblessness and an increased burden of benefits to be paid out of the social security budget. At the same time rising unemployment obviously led to a fall in government revenue from taxes.

In October 1979 the government had abolished exchange controls as part of a deliberate tactic of boosting the City of London's role as an international centre of the money markets. This critical measure demonstrated Thatcher's belief in the virtue of freedom of the international money markets. Restrictions to the movement of capital which had been in place since 1939 were swept away. The pound sterling became strong which made things very difficult for British businesses trying to export goods that became considerably more expensive overnight. The effect on British industry was devastating. Literally hundreds of medium-sized and small businesses went to the wall. Even industrial giants like ICI were badly affected. Terence Beckett of the 'boss's union' the CBI went so far as to call for 'a bare-knuckle fight with the government'. The high pound did, however, help to bring inflation down which was a more important priority with the government than assisting the interests of British manufacturing industry. It is not unfair to say that the hammering which industry took at the time did not just 'shake out' hopelessly inefficient companies but it also inflicted damage on many other, more robust, companies. Unabashed, Thatcher prattled on about how the service industries needed to be encouraged because they would provide what she called 'tomorrow's jobs'.

Unthinking enthusiasts of Thatcher's every action (and there were some), would probably like her to have had the credit for the fact that oil had been found in the North Sea and that it started flowing in 1980. Let us say that it was her good fortune to be around when this bit of nature's largesse came on stream because it significantly brightened the short to medium-term prospects for the British economy. It occurred, fortuitously, just when oil prices were reaching an all-time high on international markets. Now, however, there was the prospect of the UK becoming self-sufficient in oil, possibly even becoming an oil exporter and the government garnering a bonanza of revenue for the Exchequer. It would help the strength of the pound and would, hopefully, lessen the country's dependency on coal and thereby weaken the bargaining power of the National Union of Mineworkers. The pound did indeed rise sharply on world money markets because of the oil and other factors, so much so that the price of British exports increased rapidly and, as mentioned, Thatcher was lobbied by the indignant bosses of various British manufacturing companies complaining that they could not sell overseas. Their pleas fell on largely deaf ears.

After Howe's budget of 1981 which had made further cuts in public spending, increased taxes, reduced public borrowing and held down interest rates and which even Howe himself described as the 'most unpopular budget in history', the economy started showing some definite signs of recovery. The Thatcher glee club used this as a vindication of their heroine's bold stance against the odds and declared that it was the long-awaited turn round in Britain's fortune. It was nothing short of a miracle and could not have happened had anyone other than Thatcher been at the helm, they crooned. Critics were less willing to ascribe what they said might be no more than a short-term reversal in a continuing long-term downward trend, to anything that Thatcher had masterminded. They argued it was largely due to various extrinsic factors. Thatcher and her acolytes used the recovery, however, to kick sand in the faces of those academics who, earlier, had made such gloomy prognostications about the impact of her policies and had said, 'there is no basis in economic theory…for the government's present policies'. Over the years Thatcher availed herself of every opportunity to have a pop at the world of academe, contrasting her hard-headed 'housewife's common sense' with the airy, fairy theories of those who dwelt in ivory towers rather than in the real world.

The Role of the Trade Unions

Way back in the late 1940s Thatcher had apparently stated that the trade unions were too powerful and she carried this opinion with her during her entire political career although before she gained high office she had gone on record as encouraging Tory Party members to join unions and become active in them. ('The enemy within' although in reverse). Under the growing influence of the resurgent Right, however, she took a far more aggressive stance concerning unions. With her self-appointed task of restoring the profitability of British industry, she came simply to loath the idea that working people could organise and use their collective strength to bargain with capital sometimes on equal terms and on occasion even from a position of superior strength. The author would argue that the interests of labour and capital are diametrically opposed. Profit is the unpaid labour of the working class. Profit is what capital takes for its share in an unequal relationship. Profit is the difference between what the worker is paid and the value which his or her labour creates for the employer. Capital is always seeking ways of increasing profit by making the labour force work longer or faster, by increasing its productivity or cutting its wages. For its part, labour is always looking for shorter hours, longer holidays, better conditions and pay rises.

Trade unions stand in the way of capital maximising its profits and that is what Thatcher and her ilk really objected to. The 'freedom' which she made so much of in her speeches as something that Britain needed in order to restore its economic well-being meant the freedom of employers to sack at will, pay starvation wages and in other ways browbeat, bully and intensify the rate of exploitation of the workforce while enhancing their own profits. 'Freedom' did not extend to workers combining to use their collective strength to defend jobs or to win improvements in their terms and conditions. The balance of forces in society, however, meant that although she went on to launch a frontal attack on the unions, she backed away from trying to abolish them altogether.

At this stage Thatcher did not move too far or too fast with respect to the unions. She was mindful how pathetic they had made her predecessor Heath, look. The Employment Acts of 1980 and 1982 introduced compulsory ballots over closed shops, provided government funds for union ballots and reduced a number of legal immunities enjoyed by trade unions, especially with regard to secondary picketing. Privately Thatcher agreed with those of her backbench MPs who wanted more draconian measures against the unions but she knew that this was not the time. Yes, she would do battle with the unions but at a time of her own choosing when she felt certain that she would win. That is why the miners received a generous pay settlement in 1981 – the government was not yet ready to take them on. The award to the miners, while a tactical move, was one of Thatcher's many u-turns.

While rising unemployment may have been deliberately used as a weapon to deter workers from taking industrial action, its success as such a ploy is difficult to establish with certainty. The existence of lengthening dole queues certainly sends a message to those with jobs that it would be wise to keep their heads down because there are unemployed workers only too keen to replace them and possibly prepared to do so on poorer terms and conditions. At the same time, fear of being made jobless can have the effect of stimulating industrial action in order to fight job cuts. This was definitely the case with the miners in the 1980s. They fought to prevent the decimation of their industry and massive job losses. Such was the location of many pits and the age of many of the workers in the industry that many miners knew that large numbers of them were unlikely to work again. They fought the good fight although they lost. The threat of unemployment may have deterred certain other key workers from taking industrial action to support them.

Union organisation was frequently very strong in nationalised industries as Thatcher found out in the steelworkers' strike of 1980. This lasted for four months and involved the loss of 8 million working days. The British Steel Corporation was desperately in need of investment. Much plant and equipment was outdated, productivity was low, costs were high and large amounts of cheap imported steel were flooding into the UK as a result.

A series of planned closures was announced in 1979. The major union in the industry, the Iron and Steel Trades Confederation (ISTC), was led by Bill Sirs, a right-winger, virtually a fifth columnist for the establishment. He gave his career ambitions and personal aspirations for political honours far greater priority than leading the fight of his members against the most serious threat the industry had ever faced. The members fought a hard battle, in spite of and not because of Sirs. Their tactics included the use of 'flying pickets' in an attempt to prevent supplies of imported steel reaching various consumers. The mettle of the steel-workers (no pun intended) was not in doubt but the dispute was lost. In retrospect it can be seen as something of a dress rehearsal for the miner's strike that was looming.

Not all in the business world were wholly enamoured of Thatcher, her government and its measures. The recession of the early 1980s hit manufacturing industry particularly hard and the CBI demanded lower interest rates and a lower pound. Remember that Terence Beckett, the belligerent head of the CBI, promised his members that, if necessary, he would take on the government in a 'bare-knuckle fight'. It did not come to this and donations to the Tory Party from Big Business which had faltered briefly, soon picked up. The fact that the government had reduced tax rates for high earners may have helped to bring them round. It was said that one particularly highly-paid captain of industry had gained so much because of the tax cuts that in two years he in effect pocketed the same very generous amount that his company had donated to the Tory Party to help them fight the 1979 election.

Unemployment – the growth industry

The deflationary measures carried out by Thatcher's first government inevitably resulted in a substantial increase in unemployment. Before they were in office, some of what were to become Thatcher's ministers and close lieutenants had mused over just how much unemployment was likely to be caused by the policies they wanted to put into effect and what the social and political response would be. It was generally thought that no figure above two million unemployed would be politically sustainable. It was fine in theory to say that unemployment was a price that was worth paying if it had the effect of keeping inflation down. Fine, that is, if it wasn't you that was going to lose your job. In the event no one had expected that unemployment would reach the levels that it rose to in the 1980s. Even Keith Joseph, Thatcher's rather sinister economics guru, had said in the 1970s that there was no possibility of unemployment reaching a million if policies he favoured were carried out. Late in January 1982 unemployment reached over 3 million for the first time since the 1930s. Joblessness stayed around this figure until 1986.

As early as May 1980 Thatcher had wept crocodile tears about unemployment. In an interview with a Sunday newspaper she said, "I couldn't live without work…that's what makes me so sympathetic to those people who are unemployed. I don't know how they live without working." [1] Later in the year at the Tory Party Conference she returned to the theme when she said unemployment was: "…a human tragedy…Human dignity and self-respect are undermined when men and women are condemned to idleness." The sentiments expressed above do not fit with her oft-repeated statements that the unemployed should move to where there were jobs and that they were somehow morally reprehensible for being unemployed in the first place and doubly so if they did not go in search of work. It probably never occurred to her that what she considered as 'the jewel in her crown' – the selling off of council houses – was a serious deterrent to labour mobility because it considerably reduced the availability of accommodation in the rented sector.

Mass unemployment became one of the realities of the 1980s, 'the Thatcher Decade'. It entered deeply into the culture and the collective consciousness of the British people, reflected, for example, in theatre, film, television and pop music. Unemployment blights everything it touches. It is one of the most heinous aspects of capitalism, criminal in the waste of economic and human resources that it represents. It creates the absurd situation in which huge numbers of people who want to work are prevented from doing so while those in work are taxed in order to provide the unemployed with some income for not working! Unemployment is also heinous for the damage it does to people's well-being, self-esteem and potential to contribute to society. It is particularly a crime for it to be used coolly and dispassionately as an instrument of macroeconomic policy.

Thatcher doggedly refused to accept that it was government policy with the high pound that was creating unemployment and pointed instead to the lack of competitiveness of British industry. The implication she drew from this was not that it was capitalism's continuous failure to reinvest profits in updating the means of production that was to blame. Rather it was the excessive wage demands of workers, insisting on outdated work practices, who were pricing themselves out of jobs and causing the problem. She was supported in this view by 'The Economist' which argued: *Wages are too high. 'Too high' means the level of wages relative to profits…wages in the five largest capitalist economies are now between 8 per cent and 24 per cent higher than they ought to be if profits are to regain the share of national income they held.*[2]

Labour let's Thatcher get away with it

How did Thatcher's first government get away with launching such an attack on the share of wealth going to the working class, encouraging unemployment on this scale? The answer is both simple and complex. It lay in the nature of the Labour Party and its inability to organise effective opposition around a credible economic alternative. That is the simple answer. More difficult to explain is why the Party was incapable of giving a lead to the enormous resentment that Thatcher's policies generated at this time. Opinion polls consistently indicated that her personal unpopularity was even greater than that of her government.

To answer these questions fully would involve examining the processes that contributed to bringing the Labour Party into being. This would need to be followed by a survey of the Party's history and the evolution of its theory and practice in response to events and the opportunities with which it was presented. The writer would contend that the Labour Party leadership, although it has had electoral successes, has never put forward and campaigned seriously around a socialist alternative to the capitalist economic system. At best, Labour has been equivocal on what kind of economy and society it wanted compared to the Tories who have always stood totally and unequivocally for the preservation of capitalism while in the 1950s and 1960s being happy enough to live with a 'mixed economy'. There have been, and still are, substantial numbers of ordinary Labour Party members who believe that socialism is a necessary, urgent and indeed the only alternative to the regression and barbarism that seems to be all that capitalism has to offer in Britain and elsewhere. However the rules of the Labour Party have evolved in such a way that power is concentrated in the leadership and in the hands of the leaders of the biggest affiliated unions and progressively the rank-and-file have been excluded from policy-making and any real say in the direction of the Party.

Labour MPs have shown an increasing tendency to consist of university-educated middle-class men and women from professional backgrounds who have made second careers for themselves as politicians. Fewer and fewer Labour MPs are of working-class origins and have been employed as manual workers or in lower-paid employment. This means that Labour MPs are drawn from a narrow social elite and have little experience of the problems of those on low pay, pensioners and the unemployed, for example. The role of MP offers a lucrative, prestigious career and the possibility of numerous perks, official and unofficial. Many Labour MPs consider socialism to be unachievable, a fantasy, if they consider socialism at all. The development of their careers takes priority to airy-fairy ideas of changing the world. They do not believe there is any serious or viable alternative to so-called 'free enterprise' so when the capitalist system is in crisis, which it is frequently, they will take whatever measures they think are necessary to come to its rescue. This almost always involves trying to boost profitability by reducing the share of total wealth going to working people and their families. They do this without turning a hair, claiming that the pain of cuts will be shared by all when in fact the brunt of the pain always falls on that majority of the population which possesses little or no significant wealth. When times are better for capitalism, then a Labour government may be able to extract a few reforms of some benefit for ordinary people. These reforms will be graciously handed down to them through the MP's efforts in Parliament. The idea of mass political action in the workplaces and on the streets to obtain radical change is totally unacceptable in the eyes of Labour MPs and always has been. Like the official trade union leaders, Labour MPs believe that any movement even for the most cautious change must be strictly controlled by them.

This means that the Labour Party has generally had very little to offer the electorate that was distinctively different from the Conservatives, with the marked exception of the manifesto for the 1945 General Election. Even in 2010, so-called 'New Labour' agreed with the need for drastic cuts to rescue the British economy but was 'kinder' in the sense that had it been in office, it would perhaps have made the cuts over a longer period. Labour's limited political perspectives mean that if the capitalist economy is in crisis, it is prepared to impose such cuts and implement a programme of counter-reforms, dismantling the limited reforms made in the past. Although Labour has miraculously managed to keep a loyal core vote despite its record, that core has diminished since 1945 and working-class voters are markedly unenthusiastic about voting Labour. In the context of the 1970s and 1980s, Thatcher and the 'New Right' seemed to offer something much more dynamic and radical than Labour.

After the 1979 election Labour gave the impression of being world-weary and worn down, bereft of energy and direction. An inspirational new leader was desperately needed given that the former Prime Minister Jim Callaghan was a discredited and spent force. Denis Healey was a formidable Rottweiler-like figure on the right of the Party who might have been a candidate for the leadership but his abrasive and derisive manner won him few friends. In the event the leadership contest was won by Michael Foot. He was elderly for the job, a respected, decent old-fashioned socialist and fine orator but he somehow seemed too donnish to be at home in the rough-and-tumble of parliamentary politics, especially up against a street fighter like Thatcher. He quickly found that he was sipping from a poisoned chalice. Foot had been consistently identified with the left of the Party but on becoming Leader of the Opposition was to find himself at odds with two influences. One was a marked move to the left in the constituency parties where attempts were being made to deselect certain MPs of strong right-wing views, some of whom were also extremely negligent of their constituency duties and highly resentful of attempts by the party members to call them to account. Activists, predominantly young, were also campaigning vigorously for measures to increase the influence of the trade unions and the constituency parties on Labour's policy-making processes, particularly at the annual conference and to push party policy markedly to the left. The other tendency was from the right-wing. It was an attempt to prevent any tide of change, to maintain the existing rules and thwart the ambitions of those who, they claimed, wanted the party to adopt red-blooded socialist policies which they believed would be electoral suicide.

Foot therefore found himself between a rock and a hard place. It didn't help that the left had its own darling in Tony Benn. Although not party to any conspiracy to undermine Foot, Benn had a high profile and was busily active on issues such as anti-racism, feminism, Irish nationalism and opposition to nuclear weapons. His prominent stance on these and other issues made him the natural leader of the left at a time when significant numbers of new members were joining up, the economic situation having convinced them that Labour needed to adopt bold socialist alternatives. In Abraham Lincoln's words, "A house divided against itself cannot stand." Foot had to try to forge some unity in a party full of acrimonious divisions as well as to make a proper fist of acting as leader of the Opposition in Parliament. The rifts and confusion could be seen in the manifesto that Labour drew up, belatedly, for the 1983 general election and which was dubbed by some cynics as 'the longest suicide note in history'.

There were further ingredients in the heady brew that was the Labour Party at this time. There had always been small numbers of revolutionary socialists in the Party but now a vociferous and growing group of Marxists around the 'Militant' newspaper was making its presence felt, prominent in the moves for constitutional and political change in the Party and developing an influence in the affiliated unions. Back in 1976, a Militant supporter, Andy Bevan, had become the Labour Party's Youth Officer. The right-wing of the Labour Party and the right-wing pro-Tory media vied with each other as to who could make the bitterest denunciations of the presence of Marxists in the Labour Party and the direst predictions of what would happen if they ever gained a significant position in the Party. Those who were the most vehement in their attacks on Militant often had only the haziest idea of what Marxism was about but felt it was enough simply to utter the dreaded word 'Marxism' for them to have won the argument. Sworn enemies of the left like the 'Daily Mail' shed crocodile tears about the fate of the Labour Party should it fall into the hands of the Marxist 'extremists'. It would become 'unelectable', they wailed. This newfound but touching concern for the health of the organised labour movement was sheer hypocrisy coming from a paper that had for generations sneered at, belittled and attempted to undermine all those who dared to advance any serious critique of the Tory Party, pose an alternative to capitalism or suggest even the most modest redistribution of wealth in favour of the less well-off.

The end of the post-war boom and the onset of a period of severe economic turbulence and austerity was reflected in a marked shift to the left among significant layers of the more class-conscious workers while substantial numbers of people who had never before been involved in politics decided to become active as a result of their own experiences and what they saw around them. Of these, many joined the Labour Party. By no means did they all move towards the ideas of Militant but their presence assisted the general leftward move which was so unacceptable to the long-established and deeply-entrenched right-wing in the parliamentary party, the affiliated trade unions and the constituency parties. They had enjoyed having the Party largely sewn up for years and they strongly resented those new members or reinvigorated existing members who wanted the party to become more active and more political, actually campaigning around socialist ideas.

It is ironic that at the same time that the worldwide economic problems of capitalism were being refracted so starkly in Britain, causing significant moves to the left in the rank-and-file both of the Labour Party and the trade unions, gloomy and tortured soul-searching was taking place in certain elements of the political left, particularly among layers of intellectuals who were members of or had been associated with the Communist Party of Great Britain. They had been severely battered by revelations about the Stalinist regime in Russia and the Soviet invasion of Hungary in 1956 and had never fully recovered.

This feeling of this part of the left of being on the back foot was greatly exacerbated by the victory of the Tories in 1979. As far as they were concerned, a marked rightward trend was apparent in society. It was being evidenced by the growing influence of the New Right and was a result of the rising affluence of the working class because of the economic growth associated with the post-war boom. This had atomised society, they argued, reducing basic class awareness as blue collar manufacturing jobs had been replaced by white collar clerical and service sector employment. Massive housing clearance schemes had broken down close community ties and general aspirations and expectations had been raised in a society where consumerism was now a reality for large sections of society. The nationalised industries were widely viewed as inefficient and the welfare state and the NHS as bureaucratic monoliths. The election results showed that increasing numbers of Labour's 'traditional' voters were now disillusioned with what the Party stood for and this was particularly true of skilled workers and the growing number of those in non-manual occupations. It was a doom and gloom scenario.

The processes unfolding in the Party were too much for a cabal of senior Labour MPs curiously described in the media as 'moderates' but in reality extremely right-wing by any socialist standards. For years they had enjoyed a cosy existence in a party that was essentially undemocratic, much of the grass roots of which was largely inactive and in which political debate of any sort, especially if it was critical of capitalism, was discouraged to the point of having almost become non-existent. They strongly resented the changing mood and they had already seen how one like-minded colleague, Reg Prentice, had fallen foul of his constituency party and been deselected in 1975. Prentice had a history of studied contempt for party members and the decisions they reached democratically. When he was ousted, he further showed the contempt he had always had for the labour movement and for socialism by resigning from the Party, flirting with the Liberals and then realising that they had no realistic chance of forming a government in which he could play a leading role. He then brazenly joined the Conservatives and was quickly offered a role in the Government by Thatcher. Prentice claimed that he was hounded out of the Party by Marxists. This 'explanation' was eagerly taken up by the media and the Tories with the intention of inflicting the maximum damage on the Labour Party. Prentice was portrayed as a brave man of principle who stood up to the bullying 'bed-sit infiltrators' and paid the price. His subsequent political career showed what his opponents had always known, that he was a man without political principles.

The cabal mentioned above had four members. They were Roy Jenkins, David Owen, Shirley Williams and Bill Rodgers and early in 1981, while still members of the Labour Party, they called for a 'realignment' in British politics. If they had been left-wing rank-and-file members, they would probably have been expelled for going public on such an issue. Soon after, to a fanfare of applause from the media and grandiloquent predictions about their golden future, they left the Labour Party and established the Social Democratic Party. They took a small and motley collection of other Labour MPs with them. The manner in which they handled this 'realignment' was designed to inflict the maximum damage on the Labour Party and give succour to all those who opposed it. They left behind many like-minded MPs who decided that their careers would best be served by staying in the Labour Party. There they continued to fight against the move to the left and against changes in party procedures which favoured participation in open debate. It was not to be long before they were calling for the expulsion of Militant supporters and others on the left. Although the SDP peaked quickly and then became involved in internal wrangles and disputes with the Liberals, its creation was welcomed by the media and the Tories because it inevitably deprived Labour of many of the anti-Tory votes it might have otherwise have expected in the 1983 General Election.

We have devoted so much space to these processes and events in the Labour Party because they help to scotch one particular myth about Thatcher. This was that she was uniquely charismatic and displayed superb leadership qualities right from the moment she became Prime Minister in 1979. The economic record of her first ministry was fairly dismal and she personally was widely unpopular as consistently shown in opinion polls. However any leader worthy of the name would have been able to make capital out of Labour's utter disarray in these years. It was the internal struggles of the Labour Party and especially the machinations of Labour's right-wing that gifted the upper hand to Thatcher between 1979 and 1983. The 'Falklands Factor' and the arrival on the scene of the SDP were also gifts. Thatcher was a very lucky politician.

Evidence of the tensions building up in society, some of which can probably be ascribed to the policies carried out by the previous Labour administration as well as Thatcher's first government were the riots in the early 1980s in some inner-city areas such as St Paul's(Bristol), Brixton (London), Handsworth (Birmingham) and Toxteth (Liverpool). Anyone familiar with these districts before might have been surprised that it had taken so long for the riots to occur. The causes of such events are many, complex and inter-related. What the areas had in common were the tensions caused by high levels of poverty, despair, deprivation and exclusion, bad housing, a blighted environment, crime, unemployment and lack of opportunity. As such they were witnesses to decades of neglect by successive governments and the inequalities that were an integral part of capitalism, even during the relative prosperity of the post-war boom.

By 1982 it was evident that a partial economic recovery had taken place. Inflation had fallen to 8.6 per cent from its peak of 18 per cent. Some economic growth was taking place and mortgage rates were at their lowest levels since 1970. On the other hand, manufacturing output had fallen by 30 per cent in a decade and unemployment which was deliberately allowed to grow, was a standing indictment of the government. GDP in 1983 was 4 per cent lower than it had been in 1979. Public spending had risen from 41 to 44 per cent of GDP and what economic recovery had taken place was mostly in southern England.

The 'Falklands Factor' let Thatcher off the hook, as will be seen. Previously the auguries for her continuing in Parliament had not looked good. Late in 1981 her personal approval rating fell to just 25 per cent, lower than any previous British prime minister since political opinion polls had been invented. It was in the election campaign of 1983 that Thatcher appeared on the 'Nationwide' programme, being interviewed by Sue Lawley. Viewers were able to phone in and one who did so was Diana Gould. She asked her repeatedly for the truth behind the sinking of the 'Belgrano'. For once Thatcher had come up against someone who was not going to be browbeaten and the longer that Gould persisted, the more she made Thatcher first look evasive and then visibly disconcerted and uncomfortable. Thatcher was a bully and, as such, was good at handing it out but not so good at taking it. After this episode, Thatcher appeared much less frequently in media situations which might involve such confrontations and these tended to be handled by her senior underlings. Hardly the 'Iron Lady'.

The SDP had come along at just the right time and had predictably extracted large numbers of votes from Labour. The result was by no means a resounding endorsement of Thatcher's record and the Tories actually received 700,000 less votes than in 1989. For Labour, it was a disaster and they were relegated to the inner-city and de-industrialising areas of the North, the Midlands, South Wales and Lowland Scotland. They won only three seats south of a line from the Humber to the Severn, except for some in London. Thatcher had succeeded, as she so often did, in achieving the opposite of her stated aims – a country whose voting behaviour reflected the sharp and destructive divisions within society which she may not have necessarily created but which were made immensely more real by her policies.

1. Interview in *News of the World,* May 1980.
2. *The Economist,* 27 November 1982.

7. THE FALKLANDS WAR

A constant theme throughout this work is that Thatcher can be described as a lucky politician. On a number of occasions it seems that opportunities just landed on her plate without any particular effort on her part. Perhaps the most significant of these occurred in 1982.

The Falkland Islands are an archipelago of remote, bleak and inhospitable rocks in the South Atlantic. They supported hundreds of thousands of sheep, a small contingent of marines who must have wondered what they had done to deserve such a posting and a declining local population which in 1982 was down to about 1,800. The original 'British' settlers were mostly of Scottish birth, transferred there by the Falkland Islands Company to look after the sheep. The Islands stand about 400 miles off the South American mainland.

In 1816 after Argentina won its independence from Spain, it laid claim to the Islands. However, Britain, in triumphant mode after finally defeating Napoleon in 1815, was looking for territory across the world to add to its empire. A few years later the islands were seized by the British and officially taken under British sovereignty in 1833. Ever since that time, Argentina has claimed the islands as part of her own sovereign territory. In 1964, Britain and Argentina went to the United Nations over their concerns about the Falklands. Argentina argued that that the geographical position of the islands and the need to close the chapter of European colonialism in South America meant that they should be restored to Argentine sovereignty. Britain argued, somewhat hypocritically, that to hand the islands back to Argentina without the consent of their people, would itself constitute colonialism. All this was posturing considering that the Falklands seemingly had no strategic or economic value. Suddenly, in 1982, these obscure islands sprang to the forefront of world news.

The Falklands were a low-maintenance surviving part of what was once Britain's far-flung empire. Most of the territory belonged to the Falkland Islands Company who didn't really seem to know what to do with them. The annual visit from a Royal Navy vessel was being threatened with withdrawal and there was an airstrip from which flights could be taken to and from the South American mainland, about 400 miles away. The locals had gripes about the airstrip. It was poorly-maintained and getting worse by the year, but requests to London for its repair and modernisation fell on deaf ears. For generations the British government had been making half-hearted attempts to divest themselves of the islands by simply giving them to Argentina, hence the hypocrisy mentioned above. Even though the islands were cared for on the cheap, the expenses involved greatly outweighed the benefits, if any, they brought with them. The fly in the ointment was that the islanders didn't want to be given away. They were proud to be 'British' and they wanted to stay British. An emerging factor which received little mention at the time because it could have been embarrassing was the knowledge that exploratory investigations carried out jointly by Argentina and Britain had suggested that the seas around the Falklands possibly contained oil and other precious minerals and that they were also rich fishing grounds. The stated morality of going to war over matters of sovereignty or self-determination might have been spoiled if there was a hint that what was really going on was the usual reason why capitalist countries go to war – to gain economic advantage.

What thrust this ill-favoured part of the world into the limelight was the decision of General Galtieri, the leader of Argentina's military junta, to claim the islands for Argentina and invade them in pursuit of the long-standing territorial claim. The military had seized power in 1976 and Galtieri had become head of state in 1981. The Argentine economy was in a state of economic and political crisis and, just like Thatcher, was imposing severe public spending cuts. There was widespread opposition to the government's measures to which the junta responded with a brutal repression which had seen thousands of protestors imprisoned, tortured or simply murdered. Galtieri desperately needed a diversion; some quick, easy and successful stunt which would take the pressure off the junta and off himself in particular. Knowing that there was a strong anti-imperialist feeling among the Argentine population, he decided that the seizure of the Malvinas, as they were known, might just be the thing he was looking for. He did not think Britain would retaliate. Despite official statements to the contrary, Thatcher's sources of intelligence had already alerted her to the possibility of an Argentine invasion but she chose to ignore the threat because a larger British presence in the area would have been expensive to maintain. She had not taken the matter seriously until she had no option but to act. During the war, an opinion poll showed that 60 per cent of those questioned blamed Thatcher for having let the invasion occur. Such an invasion needed time to be planned and the British had known that such preparations were being made.

The irony is that Mrs Thatcher was also looking for something to boost her own situation. A general election was just around the corner and her prospects of winning were not looking good. Although the international economy was starting to pick up, Britain's response was somewhat sluggish and Thatcher's low standing was indicated in one political poll after another. The 'unexpected' landing of Argentine troops on British territory must have seemed like manna from Heaven and she feverishly grabbed the opportunity that had landed so fortuitously in her lap. Thatcher and Galtieri had a common reason for going to war – their political futures were both at stake.

We need not concern ourselves with the military details of Britain's victory over the invaders and her consequent retention of the Falklands except to say that severe tensions were revealed between the politicians and the top brass in the British armed forces and between the various components of the armed forces themselves. Additionally, considerable weaknesses came to light in the complicated communications systems needed for the conduct of a war 8,000 miles away. The Argentine war effort was generally inept and it was impossible to escape the impression that large numbers of the young conscripts that were involved understandably did not really have their hearts in the war. Failure brought about the rapid fall of Galtieri and the junta. Thatcher's luck lay not only in being able to exploit Galtieri's foolishness in embarking on the Malvinas venture but in the fact that with severe cuts in defence spending in the pipeline, this was probably the very last occasion on which Britain could have gathered together a task force to deal with a war situation of this sort. Labour MP Tony Benn commented, "It looks more and more as if what is at stake is Mrs Thatcher's reputation, not the Falkland Islands at all." T-shirts emblazoned with the words 'Ditch the bitch!' were now replaced by others proclaiming 'Up your Junta'.

For the two leaders involved, the results were diametrically different. Galtieri could not survive and the hated junta fell quickly, free elections being held in Argentina within a year. The majority of the media portrayed Thatcher's handling of the crisis as masterful, an undiluted success because of her gritty courage and determination. The war became a piece of theatre, a visual media event, a proof of Britain's (and Thatcher's) virility. Only the *Financial Times, The Guardian* and *The Observer* consistently questioned or criticised the whole venture. The posture of the *Financial Times* was probably based on its concerns about the heavy investments which the City of London had made in the Argentine economy. Parallels were drawn with Sir Winston Churchill although Britain in the Second World War was fighting far more formidable enemies than Argentina. While Britain had slipped down the league table of military powers, she was still a 'big boy' compared with Argentina and the British forces would have to have mishandled the situation very badly to lose the war. There was a distinct element of bullying on Britain's part but this went largely unmentioned. By no means was it the 'great thing' that Thatcher and her supporters in the media, with typical hyperbole, claimed it to be. Against a stronger enemy it might well have gone seriously wrong.

The victory gave Thatcher the best boost possible for her political career just when she most needed it. It was used to create the image of a leader of courage and integrity and a justification for her using her second and third administrations to carry out a far wider programme of what were euphemistically called 'reforms'. It led indirectly to later governments led by Tony Blair and Gordon Brown who continued and even expanded on many of the policies first implemented during Thatcher's time at No.10.

Thatcher basked in the glow of some of the most unashamedly chauvinistic jingoism and xenophobia that the British media had ever spewed out. She proved herself well able to extract every possible benefit for herself with a series of populist and triumphalist statements including one which started:

We have ceased to be a nation in retreat. We have instead newfound confidence-born in the economic battles at home and tested and found true 8000 miles away...we rejoice that Britain has rekindled that spirit which has fired her for generations past and which today had begun to burn as brightly as before.[1]

The media talked about how Britain had got the 'feel good factor' back. 255 British service personnel died and 649 on the Argentine side. None of those 900-plus people felt good about the war. Thatcher, for her part, felt extremely good. Her standing in the opinion polls was transformed and the Falklands episode ensured, despite unfavourable odds laid even a few months earlier, that she would win the 1983 general election with a sizeable margin. 'Thatcher's luck' had meant that the fracas occurred just before a series of stringent cuts in naval spending were due to be implemented. Had Galtieri moved a year later, it is highly likely that Britain would have been unable to despatch a force to win the islands back.

Thatcher even had the gall to declare that the war had been fought to defend the democratic rights of the Falkland Islanders. In fact successive British governments had turned a deaf ear to their many requests for improved facilities and resources and her administration was only the most recent of several that had been covertly plotting how to go about selling the islanders down the river and handing the Falklands back to Argentine sovereignty, albeit leasing them back, at least in the short term. That's how much she cared for their democratic rights. If democracy was so dear to Thatcher's heart, why had she never previously raised a word in protest at the junta's brutal methods of dealing with opposition? If she cared so much about democracy how was it that during the war she called in some favours from the blood-soaked hands of Pinochet in Chile? Also why had she been happy for Britain to engage in lucrative trade operations, including arms deals, with a government that denied its people fundamental democratic rights and murdered its opponents? This was sheer, unashamed hypocrisy.

Unanswered questions remain. Why were all diplomatic means not employed to prevent a resort to arms? What was the truth behind the sinking of the Argentine cruiser *Belgrano*? Had Thatcher realised that she was likely to lose the election and did she then decide that the deaths of substantial numbers of service personnel on both sides of the conflict was a small price to pay in order to create a wave of popularity on which she could ride to electoral victory? How come a government bent on cutting public spending underwrote the multi-million pound cost of the war without turning a hair? Why did Thatcher not comment on President Reagan's reluctance to get involved in the dispute? Was she just being ingenuous or did she prefer to gloss over US concerns that defeat for the Argentine junta might be followed by political revolution in that country? Was it true that Argentina, soon realising that it had embarked on an unsustainable venture, had tried to revert to diplomatic measures as quickly as possible and that Thatcher knew this but continued with the military effort because, for her, that was where glory lay?

The Labour opposition was all over the place with regards to the war. The support of the Labour Party and the trade unions was vital to Thatcher and it was readily given without any of their leading figures approaching the issue from the point of view of socialist internationalism. None of them put forward an argument unequivocally posed in terms of how the issue could best be solved in the interests of the British and the Argentine working classes. Foot made himself look ridiculous by supporting the despatch of the task force but, when it got there, arguing that it should not be used. Lacking a worked-out socialist analysis, Labour was unable to come up with a strategy to counter the militant chauvinism and xenophobia of the moment and so it largely followed along in Thatcher's slipstream, not wanting to be too critical for fear of losing even more credibility. As usual, Labour allowed Thatcher to make the high ground her own.

Thatcher was never one willingly to look as if she was assailed by self-doubt but her self-satisfaction and egotism rose to Olympian heights when the war was concluded to her satisfaction. Despite the fact that she had the effrontery to tell one reporter that she would not use the victory for party political purposes, she unashamedly made political capital out of it. She believed that the outcome was yet more proof, if it was needed, of her courage and soundness of judgement, even of her infallibility. Puffing herself up like a bullfrog, she reckoned that her 'success' put her among the leading statesmen of the world and she then started even greater posturing, attacking what she regarded as the centralising tendencies of the European Union and stridently echoing President Reagan's denunciations of what he described as Communism's plans to take over the world. Her name and style became synonymous with confrontation at home and overseas and she was proud of it. From then on she made increasing use of the royal 'we'.

An evil South American tyrant embarked on a military adventure which he lost, thereby paving the way for Thatcher to win the 1983 general election and to receive the green light for a full-blooded programme of privatisation and deregulation and her showdown with the National Union of Mineworkers. A sardonic Argentine commentator at the time described the Falklands War as being 'like two bald men fighting over a comb'. It was a sordid little war that reflected little glory on either of the protagonists but its indirect effects on British history were incalculable. We are living with some of the fall-out in the twenty-first century.

In all the talk about the Falklands War, the significance of the British Nationality Act of 1981 is rarely mentioned. This had been passed largely to prevent Hong Kong Chinese coming to settle in Britain after the colony returned to Chinese sovereignty. It deprived the Hong Kong Chinese of their British citizenship and did the same to the inhabitants of Diego Garcia in the Indian Ocean. They had been forced by the British to leave their island home which was earmarked for being taken over by the US and Britain for 'defence' purposes. At the same time it also deprived the Falkland Islanders of their British citizenship. The fact that she knew all about this did not prevent Thatcher from being transformed overnight into an ardent if entirely two-faced defender of their 'Britishness'.

One curious outcome of the war was the apparent sense of surprise and outrage when it was learned in the UK that the Argentine forces were using French-made Exocet missiles against British targets. This strongly suggests the existence of quaint illusions about the nature of defence industries, be they French, British, American or any other. The selling of weapons systems and other materiel of war is highly lucrative and those engaged in it do not allow moral considerations to influence their business activities. Defence industries are not in favour of international amity but they are in favour of making profits. A defence industry in one country will sell to a foreign power even in the knowledge that that power may later turn the weapons it bought on the very nation whose defence industry sold them in the first place.

Eric Hobsbawm, the left-wing historian, aptly summed up the Falklands War when he said it was 'as if we had won the world cup with guns'. For Thatcher it was the perfect war. It enormously boosted her position, it reasserted Britain's 'greatness', it generated a marked swing to the right in British society and it diverted attention away from the unpleasant reality that Britain's relative economic and political decline was continuing. She was to refer to it time and time again over the ensuing years. She saw it as her greatest triumph. She said little, however, about the cost on maintaining 'Fortress Falklands'. In 1987-8 this was approximately £100,000 per annum for each of its inhabitants.

She rewrote the history of the Falklands War. She vindicated her judgement by claiming that the war was won because she, personally, had not allowed Britain to disarm, being dedicated to a strong defence policy. This was nonsense. The British won the war because the Argentine invasion took place just before sanctioned swingeing cuts in defence spending had been implemented. Her memoirs omitted the fact that talks had been taking place with Argentina regarding the sale to them of certain Royal Navy warships likely to be made redundant by the proposed cuts.

Not the least irony of Thatcher's topsy-turvy career was that she had called for the nation to recover its pride and sense of purpose through an economic revival. In the event it was a piece of outdated imperialist theatre which, at least, for a period, gave many in Britain a sense of well-being they had not enjoyed for three decades or more They were not told the truth about the war.

Thatcher used the war as evidence of her omniscience and omnipotence and went on to launch an unprecedented assault on one aspect of British life after another. In doing so she showed that the implementation of substantial elements of a Chicago School economic programme could be achieved without the strutting military dictators and their brutal methods of eliminating opposition that the New Right and Thatcher so greatly admired for doing an exemplary and necessary job in Chile, for example. One of Thatcher's blue-eyed boys, Cecil Parkinson, as early as 1980, had said: "The British admire the efforts made by Argentina to reduce inflation and their achievements so far". It was another senior Tory, Sir Ian Gilmour, by no means at the top of Thatcher's Christmas card list because as far as she was concerned he was a 'wet', who made it clear that the Conservative Party did not worship democracy but regarded it only as a means to an end. What Gilmour was saying was that democracy was valuable because it was an economic way of ruling while all the time its real purpose was the preservation of the status quo.

1. Thatcher, M. (1993), op.cit. p.235.

8. THATCHER AND THE MINERS

Introduction

The events, the outcomes and the lessons of the miners' strike of 1984-5 shaped an epoch. The writer believes that the dispute was not about 'uneconomic pits'. Confrontation with and defeat of the National Union of Mineworkers was a crucial part of Thatcher's failed grand plan to make Britain great again by removing every possible obstacle to maximum profit-making by private enterprise. Although there might be rich pickings for Thatcher's capitalist cronies when a greatly slimmed-down coal industry with a tame workforce was privatised, that was only a minor consideration. Standing in the way of Thatcher's mission as she saw it was the organised labour movement and in particular the National Union of Mineworkers and the destruction of their power was what the dispute was really about.

The strike was a critical event in Thatcher's premiership because, in the words of 'The Godfather', this was 'not just business but personal'. Had the miners won the strike, it is highly likely that Thatcher's would have been the first head to roll. Still basking in the faux glory of the 'Falklands Factor' and with the blood on her hands scarcely dried, she famously declared, "We had to fight the enemy without in the Falklands and now we have to fight the enemy within, which is much more difficult but just as dangerous to liberty." [1]

Elsewhere, Thatcher continued the same theme:

The nation faces what is probably the most testing crisis of our time – the battle between the extremists and the rest. We are fighting, as we have always fought, for the weak (sic) as well as the strong. We are fighting for great and good causes. We are fighting to defend them against the power and might of those who rise up to challenge them. The government will not weaken. The nation will meet that challenge. Democracy will prevail.[2]

Speaking shortly afterwards, again to 'her people', Thatcher returned to the same general theme:

…these are the very dangers which we face in Britain today. At one end of the spectrum are the terrorists within our borders, and the terrorist states which finance and arm them. At the other are the hard left operating inside our system, conspiring to use union power… to break, defy and subvert the laws.[3]

In Arthur Scargill she faced an intelligent, articulate and determined leader who personified so many of the things she hated and a trade union whose members, while by no means necessarily left-wing, were known for their toughness and determination when they took industrial action, which was not very often. This was a fight to the finish in which the government, the state and the bulk of the media were prepared to use any and every means available to crush the miners. Although ostensibly the adversaries were the NCB on one hand and the NUM on the other and not the government, Thatcher was deeply involved because she knew a defeat for the miners would be a massive setback for the trade union movement and would provide the green light for her to proceed with the other policies she was hell-bent on implementing. No other result could be allowed. She used the dispute to show the world how much more macho, resolute and effective a leader she was than her predecessor Edward Heath who had been roundly beaten by the miners. Winning, for Thatcher, was an absolute necessity. It was also an obsession.

As miner's pickets faced the police, two different views of the world confronted each other. The miners had no option but to fight the threat to decimate the coal industry. They were fighting in defence of jobs, communities and a way of life dependent on the industry but symbolically they were also fighting for the ideas of working-class solidarity and collective action. The police represented a totally different set of values. With their batons and riot gear, they were the bodies of armed men; they were the fighting vanguard of the market-orientated neo-liberalism that Thatcher & Co were imposing on Britain. This new world of greed, individualism and selfishness was symbolised by those police officers who taunted the miners they faced by visibly thumbing the wads of paper money they were earning from their overtime duties of 'keeping the peace'. This was naked class war.

Isolating and vilifying the miners

The bulk of the media portrayed the dispute as virtually an anti-democratic insurrection, of miners steeped in the ways of the past violently, stubbornly and stupidly defying both the law and common sense in trying to keep alive a loss-making, outdated industry. At the same time, the bulk of NUM members, a few trade union national leaders, a handful of Labour MPs, many rank-and-file trade members of other trade unions and of the Labour Party, members of various small revolutionary socialist groups, a few journalists of integrity and a curious cross-section of what is most easily but not very accurately described as 'the general public', sympathised with and in many cases provided great moral and material support for the striking miners and their families.

An all-out attempt was made to isolate and defame the miners and their leaders and for this purpose the media poured out an unprecedented barrage of lies and smears with which to win the propaganda war. They personalised it by portraying Arthur Scargill as a scare-mongering, demagogic extremist for his warnings that the Tories were out to destroy the mining industry and the National Union of Mineworkers while also intending to deliver a mortal blow to the trade union movement as a whole. Some years later, when Scargill's grim predictions had been vindicated and John Major's government was about to close down or sell off what was left of the British coal-mining industry, an extraordinary campaign of vilification against Scargill was suddenly launched by the *Daily Mirror,* at that time owned by Robert Maxwell, a man who was by no means the epitome of moral rectitude. This campaign, eagerly taken up by the bulk of the media, alleged that Scargill had corruptly diverted large amounts of money sent from overseas to support the striking miners into his own pocket for purposes which included paying off his mortgage. Calls were made for him to be sacked from the union and banned from ever holding office again even when he came out of prison. The venal journalists who put this disgusting nonsense together acted as prosecuting counsel, judge and jury because as far as they were concerned, it was 'when' and not 'if' he came out of prison.

One allegation after another was proved to be nothing but a web of falsehoods only for another set of lies to follow close behind. While it was well-known that unscrupulous journalists never allow the truth to get in the way of a good story, rarely have they stuck so unblushingly to their task despite being revealed as liars time and time again. Small matters like the revelation that there was no mortgage that Scargill needed to pay off, were simply swept aside. It is said that the first victim of war is always truth. The sheer viciousness and unprincipled nature of this attack was evidence that there was a war going on - the class war. It was also an unintentional tribute to Scargill – the man they could not buy and whose fighting spirit they could not crush and the journalists knew, although of course they couldn't admit it, that even with their media millions behind them, he was bigger than they were. They didn't like that.

The miners lost the battle of 1984-5 but this dispute and its impact have had a curious habit of refusing to go away. Even soft landscaped green open spaces where once pithead gear stood and hundreds of men were employed cannot erase individual and collective memories and anger. In the 1990s, perceptions of the strike and its significance had altered somewhat. Scargill's warnings about the Tory's intentions to decimate the coal industry were totally vindicated by events. Films like *Billie Elliott* and *Brassed Off* expressed in vivid visual form the impact that Thatcher's politics of class hatred had in South Yorkshire and elsewhere. In late 2000 there was a rash of blockades by self-employed farmers, lorry-drivers and others protesting about the fuel-tax. They caused severe disruption but were treated with exaggerated indulgence by the police in a manner which contrasted totally with the battering the constabulary inflicted on the miners during the 1984-5 strike. In 2002 the fire-fighters were engaged in a bitter struggle against the Blair government. There were no depths to which Blair would not descend in his hostility to working-class militancy and it was typical of the man that he attempted to weaken their resolve by deliberately using 'Scargillite' as an insult when describing the fire-fighters' leadership. Result - more lost votes for Labour. The adjective 'Scargillite' warranted a badge of pride compared with the dreaded word 'Blairite'.

In 2004-5 on the twentieth anniversary of the miner's strike, the media decided to revisit the events of the 1980s and eminent, supposedly 'objective' but in reality right-wing, pro-capitalist historians were hauled out to pontificate about the greatness of Maggie and how right she had been to face up to and beat Scargill and his anarchic miners. The nadir was probably reached in a Channel Four documentary called *When Britain went to War* where the flying pickets were described as 'storm-troopers' and 'hit-squads' employing the tactics of 'blitzkreig'. They saw no irony in lumping together references to Nazi Germany with the activity of the 'Communist' Scargill. The author does not agree with all the tactics of the various Communist Parties in the 1930s but he knows that large numbers of party members died fighting fascism in Germany, Spain and elsewhere. The small-time gofers for Toryism and Big Business who dished up these disgraceful calumnies in blackening Scargill's name were seeking to discredit the whole idea of union militancy and, indeed, the trade unions as a whole.

And blacken Scargill was precisely what they set out to do. Was it just a coincidence when, in early 1990, the Tory Government was preparing to close down or sell off what was left of the nationalised coal industry, that the *Daily Mirror* spearheaded a campaign based on the alleged corruption of Arthur Scargill? This embroiled the NUM and diverted its attention at a critical time, but the biters got bit. In the course of subsequent litigation and further investigations, a farrago of dirty tricks was revealed. It became evident that during the miner's strike, the Tory Government through the medium of the security services and MI5 in particular had employed *agent provocateurs*, covert surveillance measures, bugged telephones, had provided cash gifts to strike-breaking miners and carried out a variety of other unethical and often illegal political tactics in order to beat the miners. *The Guardian* launched a counter-campaign to that of *The Mirror* and the rest. It was spearheaded by journalist Seamus Milne and was based on information from various sources including disaffected civil servants, some of them from GCHQ where the Thatcher Government had unilaterally and without warning banned trade unions. An in-depth analysis called *The Enemy Within: MI5, Maxwell and the Scargill Affair*, was published in book form along with a TV documentary called *Spy in the Camp*, broadcast by Channel Four. Written by Milne, the book was an instant success, its revelations causing one kind of outrage among those of a liberal and fair-minded outlook and another, very different one, among the forces of reaction throughout the UK. A third, expanded edition of this magnificent piece of investigative work came out in 2004 and it is recommended without hesitation to anyone who wants to know more about the lengths to which the ruling class will stoop to defend its system or who thinks that conspiracy theories are just the products of the minds of obsessive geeks.[4]

Milne showed that what Thatcher said publicly was very different from what she actually did. She boldly claimed to champion parliamentary democracy and the rule of law against the 'extremist' activities of the NUM and other 'subversives'. However she sanctioned the illegal abuse of power by virtually unaccountable security forces whose nefarious activities have continued to be the most secretive in the western world. It was revealed that the security services had a long tradition of suborning leading trade unionists and using them to obtain information about, for example, the activities of leading union militants. Those used in this way included Joe Gormley and 'Silver Fox' which was the code name for a leading NUM official who provided the security services with a mass of insider information during the 1984-5 strike.

Thatcher pretended that the dispute was between the NCB and the NUM and that the Government was deliberately keeping aloof. In fact she appointed Peter Walker to chair a 'war cabinet' which met daily and whose members included representatives of the NCB, the Home Office, the Energy and Transport Ministries. Its task was to oversee the defeat of the miners and she kept a close watching brief on what it was doing.

A Labour Government initiates the Attack on the Unions

Thatcher's government was not the first to attempt to deal with one of the central issues thrown up by the end of the post-war boom. An issue regarded very seriously in the changed, more difficult economic circumstances was Britain's troubled industrial relations record. Harold Wilson's government of 1964-70 was famous for proclaiming its 'white heat of the technological revolution' which was intended to reinvigorate sclerotic British industry and apply the latest technology in order to improve the output and productivity of manufacturing industry in particular. In the event it was a dismal failure, not so much 'white heat' as a damp squib. Wilson had approached this task from the standpoint of capital and clearly saw the unions as being the problem so far as industrial relations were concerned. For this reason the white paper *In Place of Strife* recommended outlawing unofficial strikes and compelling unions to hold ballots before strikes were sanctioned. The unions had no truck with these proposals and when Wilson lost the 1970 election, it might have been thought that they would sink without trace.

So it was not just the Conservatives who were concerned about the power, sufficient even to topple governments, which the trade union movement had accrued. Both Conservatives and Labour correctly viewed the National Union of Mineworkers as the vanguard of the organised movement. The second election of 1974 returned a Labour government with a working majority which soon revealed its desire to clip the wings of the NUM. In an extremely cynical move it introduced a so-called 'incentive' scheme whereby men in pits where the conditions allowed high output and productivity could enjoy sizeable bonuses. The accident of where a miner lived and which pit he worked in now had a significant bearing on the pay he got. This highly divisive scheme was imposed on the industry without consultation. The miners themselves had held a ballot in which the scheme had been overwhelmingly rejected. The men had obviously seen straight through its intention of undermining the unity of the workforce in the industry. Inevitably the scheme had a pernicious effect during the great miners' strike ten years later. The men in certain districts and even certain pits were encouraged to believe that their long-term job prospects were rosy and that influenced significant numbers who thought they had an assured future to cross picket lines and go into work.

The Ridley Report

In 1977 when in opposition, Nicholas Ridley, one of Thatcher's most willing lackeys and a staunch 'dry' or right-winger, even by Tory standards, drew up a report on the nationalised industries, the ostensible purpose of which was to identify ways in which they might be managed better and made more efficient. Ridley predicted that an attempt to modernise one or more of these industries might lead to major industrial action by the workers involved. He singled out the coal industry as the one where this was most likely to happen. He did not mince his words in outlining plans for dealing with such action. He made it perfectly clear that well organised workers in key industries had enormous potential bargaining power. The miners' strength lay particularly in their grip over the supply of coal to the power-generating industry. The issue therefore was how could that power be neutralised?

Ridley proposed that supplementary benefit would be cut for strikers so that the union would be under pressure to make up the shortfall in their members' income. He knew that the union did not have the funds to sustain payment to members over a prolonged strike. The police would be deployed in mobile semi-militarised squads in as large numbers as was necessary and ready to move instantly to sites where mass-picketing was taking place. Lessons from Northern Ireland had been absorbed and these hit squads would be trained and equipped to deal with large numbers of possibly very worked-up pickets. In addition, companies in the haulage industry would be encouraged to recruit non-union drivers who would be prepared to cross picket lines. Massive quantities of coal would be stockpiled. Oil and gas reserves would be built up to reduce the strategic importance of coal. A propaganda campaign in favour of nuclear and alternative sources of power would be launched. Facts and figures would be manipulated to make the cost of British coal contrast unfavourably with other power sources. Power stations would be adapted to use alternative fuel sources. One of Thatcher's constantly repeated mantras was the need to give primacy to market forces but this requirement was totally ignored when it came to using imported coal to reduce industry's dependence on coal mined in the UK. This coal was frequently more expensive than indigenous coal but the government was prepared to have recourse to any measures that weakened the position of the NUM.

Ridley may have sounded as if he was dying for a scrap but he was taking account of the dire results of Heath's confrontation with the miners a few years earlier. He was circumspect enough to see the need to avoid large-scale industrial action that could not be won. He suggested that a future Tory government would be wise to buy time and appease the miners by agreeing to meet their immediate pay claims. It was clear that he thought that a confrontation was likely or even inevitable but that it should only be embarked upon when the government was fully prepared and confident that that it would win. It was his opinion was that a national miners' strike would not bring the economy to an immediate and grinding halt unlike a strike by electricity or water workers and that the government might be able to hold the miners at bay in a national stoppage for around six weeks. The question was whether that would be long enough to break the will of the miners. Ridley argued that above average pay awards to workers in other nationalised would be helpful in isolating the miners and reducing the likelihood of solidarity action. Ridley was a clever and dedicated defender of capitalism and enemy of everything to do with the trade unions and the political left. The sense of purpose evinced by Thatcher, Ridley and company contrasted with the feebleness and lack of resolution displayed by most of the Labour Party and trade union leaders in the lead-up to the strike.

The Ridley Report was not for general circulation but as is so often the way, parts of it were leaked. The determination to fight but at a time of the government's choosing had considerable resonance with large numbers of Conservative MPs. Heath's humiliation in 1974 still rankled, even with those who regarded him as a wimp. Dislike of collective action by working people is a natural characteristic of Tory MPs. Thatcher had a particular bee in her bonnet about it, especially since trade unions had so recently brought down a Tory government, even though it had been headed by a man for whom she had ill-disguised contempt. It should be mentioned that this aversion of hers to unions did not extend to the activities of Solidarity in Poland. It was typical of her double standards that she approved of and encouraged trade unions and workers' collective action when it occurred in a country in the so-called Communist bloc.

In their considerations that the miners should not be taken on lightly, the Tories were not allowing their hearts to rule their heads. Unusually for them, they were learning from history, admittedly very recent history, and did not want to repeat the farcical scenario which engulfed Heath.

The Tories square up to the Unions

As part of its preparations, the Tory government introduced legislation which removed a number of established legal immunities from trade unions in such areas as breach of contract. This meant that if unions did not hold a ballot before a strike or if they engaged in secondary action, they would now be open to being sued in the civil courts. At this stage, the Tories preferred the 'salami' tactic to direct confrontation. They preferred to pick off groups of workers, to isolate and then beat them one by one. It was a softening-up process on a labour movement which over decades had build up its organisation and its confidence but with the downside that many of its leaders having grown complacent and flabby, cosily negotiating with the employers over brandy and cigars and living a lifestyle in which they had lost touch with the everyday issues faced by the membership.

In November 1979 the British Leyland bosses managed to sack Derek Robinson, the card-carrying Communist Party member and militant convenor at the huge Longbridge automotive plant in Birmingham. This destroyed one of the best-established shop stewards' organisations in the UK. Early in 1980 a thirteen-week strike took place in the then nationalised iron and steel industry. This was the first national strike in the steel industry for over 50 years and was in pursuit of a 20 per cent pay rise and an indication of concern over the continuing trend for the closure of plants, some which made a profit. This was a major strike involving 155,000 workers and the loss of over 8 million working days. The steel workers ended up with a 16 per cent pay rise but soon faced an escalating programme of closures and job losses. There was considerable evidence of bungling and misunderstanding between the management of British Steel and the government and within the government itself. Lessons were learned and applied to ensure more effective operations in the confrontations that were looming with the miners.

Preparing for the showdown with the miners

Early in 1981 the NCB, with the government behind them, and the NUM, had locked horns in the annual round of negotiations over wages and pit closures. The leader of the NUM was then Joe Gormley, a right-winger, who was vastly-experienced in negotiations and an obdurate man who tended to achieve his aims but usually without recourse to industrial action. Beneath his blunt exterior operated a very shrewd man who had become a close friend of Derek Ezra, then head of the NCB. That is how Gormley did his business. Gormley, incidentally, turned out to be a stooge working for the security services and being handsomely paid for it. The negotiations ended with a settlement favourable to the miners. The government had weighed up the situation shrewdly and concluded that they were not yet ready to risk provoking the miners into a strike. The government had decided to settle the hash of the miners once and for all and it then set about making the necessary preparations for the inevitable confrontation with great patience, determination and a large element of ruthlessness. Vengeance was going to be sweet!

Thatcher was clearly up for the fight but she kept a fairly low profile on the issue and put Nigel Lawson in charge of the preparations. He did this with great thoroughness. It was impossible to hide the government's intentions as vast quantities of coal were transferred from pithead to the power stations, largely by rail. The railway unions should have shown some solidarity and made this more difficult. Lawson was well-informed enough to know that there were tensions within the NUM and in particular that many miners in the East Midlands, especially in Nottinghamshire, were unlikely to support a national strike. They believed, mistakenly as it turned out, that the long-term prospects for most of the pits in this district were rosy. They did not see why they should put themselves out to support miners elsewhere working in pits with little or no economic future. In a classic ploy of 'divide and rule', Lawson announced that a great 'superpit' would be opened up in the Vale of Belvoir, enhancing the industry in the East Midlands and creating further divisions between local miners and those in other districts. Meanwhile the police underwent secret training in tactics for dealing with the expected mass picketing. His mission completed, Lawson was rewarded with a move to the Treasury and was replaced as Energy Secretary by Peter Walker, admired by Thatcher for his toughness, not least in standing up to her. The fact that he was a 'wet' on the left of the Tory Party was intended to show that there was unity across the cabinet with the 'dries' or right-wingers on the issue of the miners. He was also more expendable than most. Ridley became Transport Secretary charged with the job of ensuring that when the strike took place, the coal kept on moving.

The Central Electricity Generating Board would be a crucial player in the strike and its existing head was replaced by Sir Walter Marshall, a man of working-class origins drafted in not because he would be an effective long-term manager of a key nationalised industry but because he was extremely belligerent. As mentioned, the head of the NCB was Derek Ezra. Thatcher loathed him not least because he epitomised the spirit of post-war corporatism. He was a career mandarin who she thought had criminally failed to stand up to the miners during the dispute in the early 1970s. He was edged out in 1982 and after a brief interregnum, was replaced in September 1983 by Ian McGregor. Of Scottish descent, McGregor had compiled a fortune from business ventures in the USA. Described by Scargill as a 'Yankee steel butcher, waiting in the wings to chop us to pieces', his appointment was a deliberate provocation because he was known for his tough anti-union stance. Earlier he had smashed strong union organisation in a pit in Wyoming. He exhibited the same ruthlessness at British Steel and was proud of the fact that the number of steelworkers had fallen by 50% during his time there. However, he was something of a loose cannon and he was greatly disliked by the senior NCB management. It was widely and correctly believed that he had been taken on by Thatcher's government as a hit man with a list of pits which he was determined to close, come what may.

Arthur Scargill, the new miners' leader

Gormley retired in April 1981 and was replaced by Arthur Scargill, younger, highly energetic, combative and articulate, an intense man and a loner, a left-winger who knew his Karl Marx. His political views and some of his personal traits made him enemies in the labour movement, even among certain others on the left. However, he was hugely popular among his own members who had swept him to victory with an unassailable majority in the elections for the leadership, even before he was a nationally-known figure. He was a courageous leader from the front which was exactly where he had been when he and 15,000 miners acting as flying pickets with the support of a large contingent of Birmingham trade unionists had succeeded in closing down the Saltley Coke Depot during the miners' dispute of 1972. He never tired of referring to this as a great working-class victory, which indeed it was. Scargill was convinced that McGregor had a hit list of pits he wanted to close and that at least 20,000 jobs were at risk. McGregor's equal in belligerence, Scargill had held ballots on the issues of pay and pit closures in 1982 and 1983 but had failed to get the necessary majority for strike action.

Few trade union leaders have ever been on the receiving end of such poisonous vilification as that to which Scargill was systematically subjected. He became 'the Prince of Darkness'. This was not accidental. The government and the media realised that Scargill was tough and had large reserves of support among the miners who were seen as being the 'awkward squad' of the union movement. However, it was not his personal style that ultimately was seen as the problem. It was that he refused to play by the rules which had come to be used with so much success to inveigle and neuter generations of trade union chiefs. He would not be threatened nor flattered nor could he be bought. But it was more than that. Like them, Scargill was aware that this was a political strike. The capitalist class have had to learn to live with the existence of trade unions but they have always held strong views on what the legitimate objectives of trade unionism should be. The objectives as far as they are concerned do not include 'political' activity. This is an absurd distinction to make because, as has often been said, 'politics is only distilled economics'. The miners' strike clearly had the potential to challenge parliamentary and constitutional ways of doing things and so fell outside the official definition of what was legitimate. The government's misuse of the police, abuse of the law and attempts to use the security forces to subvert the NUM leadership in the strike also fell outside the arena of legitimacy but that, of course, was different.

Changing the law to fight the miners

The relationship between Thatcher and the trade unions in general is dealt with elsewhere. Here we look at issues that were raised during the miners' strike. Picketing had become a particularly contentious issue from the 1970s with the onset of economic recession and a hardening of attitudes in the class struggle. Industrial conflict intensified and unions resumed the use of flying pickets, a ploy used in the past but which had largely gone out of use. Just what mobile mass picketing could achieve was demonstrated with startling clarity at the Saltley Coke Depot in 1972 and it had enraged and terrified the ruling class. Labour's attempts to legislate on the issue were largely rendered impotent by rank-and-file industrial action. The Tories acting on behalf of the ruling class but sailing under the flag of the 'national interest' were determined to curb union power and as far as they were concerned, the gloves were off. However it was to be done, this was now one battle they were not going to lose.

The legal situation was clarified and beefed up by the 1980 and 1982 Employment Acts. The 1980 Act restricted picketing to small numbers attending the places where they themselves worked and who kept out of the way, not being allowed to discuss with those contemplating crossing the picket line or threaten them with words or gestures. This rendered pickets virtually impotent which, of course, was exactly the intention. Secondary picketing was made illegal. An extremely astute move was to make the law on secondary picketing enforceable through civil proceedings rather than through the application of the criminal law. This transferred the onus of initiating legal proceedings onto companies or individuals affected by picketing. It therefore absolved the government from being seen to be openly engaged in political activity against strikers.

The 1982 Act re-emphasised the role of businesses or private individuals in legal action where breaches of the law had taken place. This was intended to avoid the Heath government's earlier blunder whereby it created martyrs in the 'Pentonville Five' by imprisoning strikers who had refused to pay fines for breaking the law as it then stood. Sympathy strikes or other industrial activities which could be construed as 'political' were outlawed. This and other subsequent Acts were presented by the Government as being about 'democracy' and 'giving the unions back to their members'. This was hypocrisy blatant even by the standards of Tory politicians. Since when have the Tories been concerned about democracy? Thatcher as leader of the Conservative party was not elected by a democratic vote of the party members. Her government was not elected by a majority of the voters. MPs and local councillors were rarely if ever elected with a majority of votes cast let alone a majority of the potential electorate. She never asked for a democratic mandate concerning the location of American Cruise missiles on British soil or about going to war over the Falklands. While she constantly told us how she prided herself on speaking directly and saying what she meant, this was yet another example of her saying one thing while meaning something totally different.

It was perhaps the innovative changes in the use of the police which best exemplified the Thatcher government's determination to render strike action virtually impotent. Badly scared by the success of the mass picket at Saltley in 1972, the ruling class was determined that nothing of the sort would be allowed to happen again. Basically, the police were put on a militarised footing. Much experience of dealing with mass insurgency had been gained during the 'troubles' in Northern Ireland and later from the inner-city urban riots of 1981. Thatcher admitted as much when she said, "If we hadn't had the Toxteth riots, I doubt whether we could have dealt with Arthur Scargill." [5] The Special Patrol Group had actually been formed by the Metropolitan Police under the Labour Government of 1964-70. Similar units well trained in the use of firearms and riot control had been established elsewhere. Thatcher had seen to it that at a time when public sector spending was in general being reined in, money had been found to give the constabulary a substantial pay award. A Civil Contingencies Unit based in the Cabinet Office had earlier been set up to ensure effective liaison between the government, the Chief Constables and the military.

Shots across the bows of the Unions

Further anti-union 'successes' occurred when a small-time chancer called Eddie Shah egged on by the political right, successfully used the 1980 Employment Act to inflict a serious defeat on members of the well-established NGA union at the *Stockport Messenger* free newspaper in Warrington. This occurred in 1983 and was ostensibly concerned with the maintenance of a pre-entry closed shop and the introduction of new technology which threatened de-skilling and redundancies among NGA members. This was a test case and the dispute took on national significance when Shah went to court and obtained two interim injunctions. One restrained the NGA from lawful picketing, the other ordered the unions to refrain from blacking the Stockport Messenger Group of Companies. The Institute of Directors lent Shah their support and government ministers spoke on his behalf, portraying him as simply a decent entrepreneur just wanting to keep his business competitive by introducing new technology whereas the bully boys of the NGA were intent on maintaining current manning levels, come what may. Mass picketing of Shah's premises took place and then Thatcher emerged from behind the scenes where she had been helping to orchestrate the confrontation. She stridently denounced the NGA and with the co-operation of the media, a completely one-sided view of the dispute was presented as part of the process of creating an atmosphere of hate towards unions in general and the NGA and mass pickets in particular. The TUC stood by supinely and let the NGA take the rap to the tune of nearly £1 million in fines and legal costs. This was all the more disgraceful because it was clear that Thatcher and Co were seeing how far they could push the trade union movement and preparing for further action in the near future. Thatcher took great satisfaction from the outcome of this dispute.

Unfortunately the old truism that an injury to one is an injury to all carried little weight in top trade union circles. The trade unions were always being abjured to keep politics out of union business but were now being subjected to a political threat of unprecedented seriousness. The trade union leaders knew what was happening. Their response was to prostrate themselves before the tsunami of media propaganda which told them how unpopular unions and strikes were. Their defeatism made further defeats inevitable. Neil Kinnock had succeeded Michael Foot as leader of the Labour Party. Previously associated with the left, Kinnock was moving rapidly to the right and he quickly made it clear that he was both unwilling and unable to square up to Thatcher on the issue of the NGA or, indeed, anything else.

In January 1984 at Thatcher's personal behest, membership of trade unions at the General Communications Headquarters (GCHQ) at Cheltenham was banned without warning. Despite protests and questions about the legality of such an action, the government made it clear that it was prepared to bar unions from workplaces where their existence might threaten 'national security'. The implication of this action was the disgraceful one that trade union membership and activity was potentially treasonable. This was an indicator of the direction in which Thatcher wanted to go. They also show how relative was her use of the word 'democracy' where trade unions were concerned. She did not call for a ballot of union members at GCHQ on the issue of losing their fundamental legal right to belong to a union. She was trying it on and each small victory was a fillip making her feel surer of success when she went for the 'big one' – the miners. What Thatcher wanted was an emasculated movement incapable of preventing employers from forcing down wages and conditions. With unions entangled in legal fetters and liable to seizure of funds if the law was broken, their full-time officers were likely to make every effort to keep the membership strictly under control. Thatcher found a reassuring mode in the labour unions in the USA for the kind of trade union movement she would be prepared to tolerate in the UK.

Changes in Policing

Some senior police officers were concerned about the overt way in which the police were being deployed against strikers. It is not only Marxists who know that the state consists of 'bodies of armed men'. Some police officers expressed their concern that the systematic use of the police for political purposes might for once and all destroy the very precious myth that the police were impartial and just there to maintain law and order for everybody's benefit. In fact specialised units of police capable of intervening in industrial disputes had been in place for a decade or more and the history of the police being used against strikers is almost as long as the history of the police themselves. The National Reporting Centre had been created after the 1972 miners' strike and was intended to co-ordinate the activities of the then forty-three British police forces. It was the existence of this centre that enabled road blocks to be set up in Kent to prevent miners from that district heading off to a mass-picket in South Yorkshire, for example. This was done under the guise of the questionable argument that if the apprehended men had been allowed to proceed, they might have been involved in a breach of the peace at a later stage somewhere else. The officers engaged in these duties often threatened or used violence and even the immobilisation of the vehicles in which the would-be pickets were travelling. Bus companies were illegally intimidated into not accepting contracts to transport miners to sites where picketing was taking place (another intervention in the market place).

The violence employed by the police, very frequently unprovoked, all too often encouraged violent responses from those they were supposedly policing. The mere appearance of officers on horseback, of officers in riot gear rhythmically beating their shields and of excited police dogs could be enough to change a good-natured atmosphere into one pregnant with tension where the smallest incident could spark off bloody violence. In some districts, the police were like an army of occupation, specialist squads making regular patrols through pit villages, their presence deliberately designed to threaten and overawe. On occasions police officers forced their way into homes, destroying property as they went and assaulting anyone they clapped their eyes on, male or female, old or young, when they claimed they were in pursuit of pickets. Sometimes they appeared to do it just for the sheer fun of terrifying the people of the mining communities who they so clearly hated. Thatcher turned a blind eye to these illegal abuses of police power. So concerned was the European Parliament that it set up an enquiry into the police violence.

Although machinery existed to handle complaints against the police, Lord Scarman had pointed out even before the strike that no one had any confidence in the system because it involved the police investigating themselves. Any miners or supporters who found themselves in custody and announced their intention to put in a complaint were likely to be beaten up. Arrests were used, sometimes apparently at random but actually systematically and on a mass scale, to break the will of pickets. Many of those arrested were held for long periods without charge and denied their fundamental statutory rights. Police officers on occasion admitted that they were acting outside the law but proudly boasted that they knew they could get away with it. Old anti-union legislation which had fallen out of use such as the Conspiracy and Protection of Property Act of 1875 was revived to make a crime of the old offence of 'watching and besetting'. *Agent provocateurs* were infiltrated into crowds of pickets to stir up trouble. This was class war and evidence that the wealthy and privileged minority of society are perfectly prepared to unleash illegal violence and terror in order to maintain their power. Thatcher and the Tory government were complicit in these tactics, being determined to teach the miners a lesson they would never forget.

Thatcher had no truck with those senior police officers who expressed concerns about the use of their officers for militaristic purposes and she told them in no uncertain terms to get on with their job which was to implement the rule of law (or turn a blind eye when their officers infringed it). Picketing was an essential tactic for the commission of a successful strike but court decisions over recent years had established that there was no absolute legal right to picket. Striking miners may have seen picketing as both a legitimate and a necessary tactic but those who used that tactic risked falling foul both of the civil and the criminal law.

The Association of Chief Police Officers (ACPO) is a body with no statutory basis which exists ostensibly to act as a forum and think-tank for the country's most senior police officers. During the Miners' strike it took on a very different role becoming virtually the command post of a state police force implementing the deployment of officers widely across the UK. The directing of officers from different forces for duties across the country, often far away from the remit of the authorities which employed them, made a mockery of what was supposed to be a sacrosanct principle of policing, that they were responsive to the needs of local communities and were controlled locally .

There were many individual police officers who loved nothing better than beating up striking miners, members of their families, supporters and sympathisers, especially when they were on overtime rates for doing it. Many times officers went way beyond the operational requirements in their use of unnecessary or excessive force and in doing so with impunity drove a coach and four through the so-called rule of law. In fact the police did not necessarily rely on actual violence in every situation. A significant part of their tactics involved intimidation by sheer numbers and militaristic appearance. Nowhere was this carried to greater lengths than in autumn 1984 when over fifteen hundred police were used at Cortonwood Colliery to escort just one miner into work. People with no axe to grind gazed riveted with horrified amazement at their televisions as they watched news footage filmed at Orgreave Coke Depot near Sheffield. They were treated to the sight of what initially looked to be a re-enactment of medieval mounted warfare but which turned out to be hundreds of mounted, baton-wielding police charging largely unarmed pickets who were, of course, on foot.

Welfare as a weapon

Just as calculated and political was the use of the welfare system against the strikers. The Welfare State may have been imperfect but it was one of the achievements of which the British have every reason to be proud. It was an institutionalised recognition of the fact that in a wealthy and advanced capitalist society, there would inevitably be weak, vulnerable and otherwise needy people who should be assisted towards at least a minimum standard of life by welfare benefits of various kinds provided out of taxes. So far, so good. However during the miners' strike, another side of the welfare system was starkly revealed. What was then the Department of Social Security was harnessed to stand alongside a militarised police force as part of a coercive state apparatus intended to browbeat and bully miners and their families and to starve them back to work. This was done perfectly legally under the two Social Security Acts which had been passed in 1980, designed with just such a situation in mind.

This was from a Prime Minister who boasted of how she was increasing 'freedom' by rolling back the boundaries of an increasingly intrusive state. Like her pronouncements on many other matters, this was simply untrue. The 'freedom' she talked about was the freedom of a dog-eat-dog society in which every person was out for themselves. The already rich minority would have conditions made even more free and favourable to allow them further opportunities to enrich themselves. It was 'devil take the hindmost' for the rest. In the welfare system Thatcher found a weapon that she could turn on those she hated, like striking miners and their families, and she did so with unmitigated spitefulness. This meant was that no benefit was paid to most strikers and payments to their dependents were cut. A single man on strike would receive no benefit at all. Thatcher constantly stressed that the dispute was between the NCB and the NUM. She lied. It was her government that had passed legislation in 1980 which was ostensibly intended to reduce so-called 'benefit dependency' but which had the bonus that it could be used to starve strikers back to work.

Cortonwood, a Pit too far and the Question of the Ballot

In March 1984 it was announced that Cortonwood Colliery in South Yorkshire was to close. This enraged local miners who knew that there was still five years' worth of winnable reserves of coal and indeed that men were still being transferred in to work at this pit. Large numbers of miners across South Yorkshire and in Scotland responded by downing tools and marching off the job. Under the NUM rule 41 individual districts of the union could call their members out on strike without a ballot providing they had the permission of the union executive. Scargill decided not to hold a national ballot and instead a special national conference of all the districts was convened which voted to support a strike. The strike was called in the spring when demand for coal was falling rapidly from its winter peak. Not a good time for a strike but if they had not taken action then, 20 pits and 20,000 jobs would have gone almost immediately. Not all districts were in favour of strike action so the response was not unanimous. Support for the strike was weakest among pitmen from the East Midlands and especially the Nottinghamshire miners. To plaudits from the NCB, the media and the Tories about their 'responsibility', 'moderation' and 'courage', they mostly stayed at work believing their reward would be the long-term security of their jobs. They were cynically encouraged in this belief by the government and the media but it was a foolish delusion for which they later paid dearly.

For its part, the NUM executive, while acting entirely within its own rules, weakened its own case and almost certainly lost some popular support by not holding a national ballot on strike action. It is extremely likely that it would have won such a ballot but without it, the critics of the miners, including the government and the tabloid press and to their shame several Labour Party and trade union leaders, were able to make the NUM executive's action somehow look underhand and undemocratic. The proprietors and editors of mass circulation newspapers and their pet poodles in the columnists and journalists they employ were the last people to lecture the miners on the virtues of democracy. No one elects them to their positions of considerable power and influence. Democratic procedures are not evoked when it comes to the appointment of those in powerful and influential roles such as judges, top civil servants or senior executives in powerful multi-national companies. No British government in the twentieth century was elected on a majority of those who could have voted or even of those who did vote. Talk of democracy from these people was simply cant.

Traditionally in the NUM, important issues such as the taking of industrial action had been put to the membership at mass meetings held during working hours to maximise attendance. Approval or rejection of a proposal was decided on a show of hands. The law had been changed by the Tories and now required unions to hold a secret postal ballot otherwise any industrial action would be illegal. This was not done in the interests of democracy as the Tories claimed but to entangle the unions in legal considerations and to reduce the likelihood of industrial action. Filling in a postal ballot paper in the quiet and isolation of the home rather than voting in the hurly-burley of a mass meeting also made the members more open to outside influences such as what they had just read in the paper or seen on television where the union side of the case was unlikely to be given full coverage.

The right-wing media who hysterically denounced the NUM as 'undemocratic' for refusing to hold the national ballot were completely silent about the totally undemocratic way in which the incentive scheme mentioned earlier had been imposed on the mining industry back in 1974. Although every NUM district had balloted the membership and rejected the scheme that cut no ice with the media. During the strike what could have been more 'democratic' than the sight of working miners taking their own union to court for allegedly breaking the union rules and knowing that they could do this without any fear of being disciplined by the NUM? So much for Tory and media allegations about out-of-touch and autocratic militant miners' leaders manipulating a gullible leadership. What a contrast between prejudiced judges interpreting the union rule book from their own narrow and privileged class standpoint and the democratic procedures written into that rule book to ensure openness and transparency in union affairs. It was deplorable that working miners resorted to legal measures against the NUM, but that was their right under the rules and that right had to be upheld. They were given every encouragement to do so by the sworn enemies of the trade union movement. A lot of tainted money changed hands.

The NUM executive refused to budge on the issue of the national ballot even on advice from friends in the labour movement. To have done so would have made it appear that they were climbing down in the face of sustained hostile pressure. Scargill argued that those labour leaders who were most vocal about the lack of a national ballot were trying to throw up a smokescreen to cover the fact that they were not giving the miners the solidarity and support they should have done. Eric Hammond, the leader of the electricians' union, declared that he would have favoured bringing his members out had the miners held a national ballot favouring strike action. Hammond's curriculum vita gives the lie to this claim. His real attitude was shown at the Labour Party Conference in 1984 when he described the miners as 'lions led by donkeys'. Even if the issue of the ballot had not existed, the likes of Hammond would have found some other reason for not supporting the miners. It is hard not to conclude that most of the Labour Party and trade union leaders wanted the miners to be defeated to vindicate their own 'moderation'. A victory for the miners could have provoked a wave of militancy which they would not have welcomed and might have found hard to control. Failure to call a national ballot may well have been a serious tactical mistake, however, and it created a monkey on the backs of the strikers. The

NUM leadership acted as though it was a matter of principle whereas it was only a tactic. Miners who continued to work used the ballot issue as a justification. Scargill ought to have called their bluff by holding a ballot which the NUM Executive would almost certainly won and left these men without an excuse other than greed for betraying their brother-miners. By not holding the ballot, the NUM leadership allowed its critics to take the high moral ground and thereby divert attention away from the issues of 10,000s of job losses and the virtual destruction of entire communities.

On the receiving end of the law

The government pretended that the dispute was purely a matter between the NCB and the NUM but a cabinet sub-committee which was virtually a 'war cabinet' was established to monitor every aspect of the ongoing strike. Shrewdly Mrs Thatcher excluded herself from this body which was soon trying to ensure that laws which the government had just enacted against secondary picketing were not implemented against striking miners. These laws would have allowed for the NUM to be sued but Peter Walker persuaded McGregor that to use them might have a damaging effect because it could unleash a wave of sympathetic industrial action. Thatcher said, "This is not a dispute between miners and the Government. This is a dispute between miners and miners… It is some of the miners who are trying to stop other miners going to work." [6] This was sheer hypocrisy. Thatcher moved might and main to secure victory over the miners and she was involved at every level right through the dispute.

Use of the civil law therefore was shelved by the NCB but it was taken up enthusiastically by various companies whose business had been damaged as a consequence of the strike. The criminal law was also invoked with great frequency. It was a criminal offence to use or threaten the use of violence against anyone wishing to work during an industrial dispute. There were significant numbers of miners who wanted to continue to work and the police were determined to protect their right to do so. Striking miners rightly felt indignant that some of their workmates chose to cross the pickets and go to work and things did get heated on the picket line. It left a legacy of hatred which continues in some places to this day.

One of the many ironies in the situation was how Tory politicians and the media ranted on about the 'right to work'. This now became a reference to those miners who continued at work. They were not traitors to their class but were portrayed as brave, principled individuals who simply chose to exercise their right to cross picket lines and earn their money even though in many cases there was no work for them when they got there. This was sheer hypocrisy coming from a Tory government that was denying millions the right to work because unemployment was being deliberately used as a means of reducing the power of the unions. The crying shame was that they were allowed to get away with it.

The Propaganda War

A war was being fought and the first victim of war is always truth. Words were being used as weapons. The words 'moderates' and 'extremists' were bandied around by politicians and those in the media and in doing so they were continuing a long tradition in the selective use of words during industrial disputes. It was a bit like the conversation between Alice and Humpty Dumpty in *Through the Looking Glass*. It goes like this:

"When I use a word," Humpty Dumpty said in rather a scornful tone, "it means just what I choose it to mean – neither more nor less."
"The question is," said Alice, "whether you can make words mean different things."
"The question is," said Humpty Dumpty, "which is to be master – that's all."

The nature of the situation meant that the government and the media had the resources to pour out far more words in the war than did the striking miners and those who supported them. The former were able to portray themselves as being on the moral high ground. Those hostile to the strike and those miners who crossed the picket lines were 'moderates' of course while those who tried to persuade them not to cross the line were necessarily 'extremists' and even 'criminals'. The fact that they were 'extremists' justified the use of the full coercive powers of the state. 'Violence' was another weasel word. It was employed by the extremists when they intimidated those who simply wanted to do a fair day's work for a fair day's pay. It was not violence when mounted police rode down and seriously injured unarmed miners' wives, for example.

The nadir was reached when Thatcher referred to the miners as 'the enemy within'. They were working men who risked their lives every time they went underground and often contracted debilitating and potentially fatal diseases as a result of their occupation. They did more real work in a single shift than many of those who derided them did in a month or more. What made them so odious to Thatcher and the Tories was that they were prepared to take a stance on behalf of their class. For this they were insulted and ridiculed in the media, many were beaten up or seriously injured by police officers who were sometimes out of control, substantial numbers of them suffered major hardship during the strike and when it was over, lost their jobs when the pits closed and the communities in which they lived lost their reason for existence.

Allusions were made during the dispute to the NUM receiving 'Moscow Gold'; to the work of dedicated 'Communist agitators'; to 'fascists' on the picket lines and that hoary old chestnut which comes out every time there is a serious industrial dispute - 'outside agitators' stirring up trouble. The latter is an indication of just how much contempt the enemies of the labour movement have for striking workers. They clearly think that working men and women are so stupid that they are just like putty in the hands of manipulative outsiders who parachute in with their own sinister agenda to foment discontent in the workplace and to incite strikes. The idea of outside agitators provoking trouble is intended to divert attention from the real and usually justified reasons which led to the industrial action in the first place.

Almost total ignorance of the mining industry, the mining communities and the culture and traditions strongly entrenched around them was no obstacle to people in certain quarters expressing their deep hostility to the strike, to the striking miners and to Scargill as the *bête noire*. At Oxford University, a longstanding bastion of the privileges that come with the accident of birth, formal debates took place around motions calling for Scargill to be charged with treason or for him to be mutilated so that he would carry distinctive stigmata as reminders of his shame for the rest of his life.

It has often been said, not necessarily as a joke, that the Church of England is the Tory Party at prayer. The Church is certainly an extremely hierarchical organisation. Those occupying the upper parts of the hierarchy unquestionably belong to Britain's social and cultural elite and are expected to uphold the values of the ruling class. Bishops, archbishops and other senior clergy have generally done so although the moral values and actions of Britain's ruling class have not necessarily had much in common with what the New Testament tells us were the values of Jesus of Nazareth. It might be thought that compassion would be deemed a virtue in a senior Christian cleric. However when the Archbishop of York quietly suggested that the cause of the miners should not simply be dismissed out of hand, he was howled down by the likes of Enoch Powell and *The Times* newspaper. David Jenkins, the Bishop of Durham, who had earlier opened up a can of worms when he had called into question the idea of the virgin birth, publicly declared that the miners must not be defeated and made uncomplimentary comments about 'an imported elderly American', referring to Ian McGregor. The reverberations from these statements registered high on the Richter Scale as indignant letters poured onto the desks of editors of the national papers, protesting that a senior man of God was voicing heretical – quasi-Communist, political views. Frequently these letters were written by people whose knowledge of the mining industry and the lives of the mining communities could have been written on the back of a very small postage stamp or have been summed up in one short Anglo-Saxon hyphenated indecency. Senior Tories gave us a taste of their Christian compassion when one MP called for a repeat of the thunderbolt that had caused so much destruction at York Minster only this time it was to be aimed at Durham Cathedral. Others called for the Bishop's instant dismissal and one declared that he should be defrocked! After comments by the Archbishop of Canterbury expressing some concern about the way in which the strike was being handled and striking miners were being treated 'as scum', Nicholas Fairbairn, already well-known for his atavistic opinions, declared that the Archbishop should eat coal in public as a penance. Comments of this kind, while not totally unexpected, reveal just how thin is the veneer of respectability and civilised values which covers the inborn savagery of some members of Britain's political elite.

Union Solidarity

The miners' cause was the cause of the whole of the labour movement. Unfortunately, not all the trade unions and their leaders saw it that way. Even if they had reservations about how the NUM was handling the strike or about Scargill personally, these should have been put side in the cause of solidarity. A defeat for the miners was bound to be a defeat for the whole movement and an enormous setback for the entire working class in terms of their wages, conditions of employment and economic prospects. Scargill was right – having won the dispute, Thatcher's and later Major's government then presided over the decimation of the coal industry. Britain in 2012 is living evidence of how the defeat of the miners enabled the employers to gain the upper hand in the workplace. Union-busting, macho management, bullying, harassment, stress, job insecurity, long hours, low pay, intensified work patterns, low motivation – all these are the realities for working-class people in the twenty-first century. For those 'lucky' enough to have jobs, that is.

There were a number of unions whose members were strategically placed to help the NUM. Prominent among them was the National Association of Colliery Overseers and Deputies (NACODS) whose members were responsible for safety in the pits. If they had withdrawn their labour they would have shut down the entire mining industry in minutes because no one was allowed to work underground without deputies being present. They very nearly, but not quite, came out in support of the NUM. Others such as railway workers, lorry drivers and dockworkers could have largely prevented the movement of coal but most of them (there were honourable exceptions) continued to work as normal. Some railway workers took unofficial solidarity action. An informal 'Triple Alliance' existed between miners, railway workers and dock-workers. Had this been activated, the outcome of the strike and therefore the course of subsequent history might have been very different. In particular the railway workers were bribed with a generous pay offer. We should not be surprised that the government obviously found the resources for an expensive settlement with the workers of this particular nationalised industry. Clearly this action contradicted their general attitude to the nationalised industries but they were prepared to make an exception in order to win the war. A war is exactly what it was.

The steelworkers, organised largely in the Iron and Steel Trades Confederation (ISTC) were, like the NUM, an 'old-fashioned' union in the sense that the membership was largely 'blue-collar'. They worked in a primary industry which had once been a staple part of Britain's economic eminence with a long history of union organisation. Its specific weight within the trade union movement was, however, in decline as the industry's own fortunes were in retreat. Where union membership was growing, it was largely among 'white-collar' workers in the public sector. The ISTC was still recovering from the impact of the 1980 steel strike. With so many job losses having taken place and more in the pipeline, the remaining workers who still had jobs in the industry were understandably reluctant to rock the boat by taking industrial action in support of the miners..

Belgian and Australian miners and dockworkers gave support to the NUM but deliveries of coal from the USA, West Germany and, far worse, Poland, escalated and coal flooded into unregistered ports up and down the east and south coasts.

We have already heard how Nicholas Ridley had encouraged haulage firms to recruit lorry drivers who were non-union members and who would not think twice about crossing picket lines. The 'rugged individualism' of some lorry drivers, especially those who owned their own trucks, appealed to the 'each man for himself' ethos of the New Right. They were a vision of how they would like the working class to be – fragmented, only out for themselves, competitive and dismissive of ideas of collective struggle and collective strength. Such workers were, of course, very hard for the unions to organise. Worse than that; they were often extremely hostile to the unions. They had already been used to help to break a number of strikes earlier in the 1980s.

1926 and 1985

The miners had been at the heart of the General Strike of 1926 and as in 1985 received insufficient support from the leaders of the trade unions and the Labour Party. On both occasions they were left to fight on alone and eventually starved back to work. Their fight had been for the whole of the trade union and labour movement and the defeat of the miners in both cases was a destructive defeat for the whole of the movement. After 1926 it took until the Second World War and the urgent demand for skilled workers for trade unionists to start feeling more confident of taking on the bosses. Apart from in a few isolated instances, the setback of 1985 has not yet been followed by any real resurgence of confidence and militancy on the part of the trade union movement.

Even in a superficial comparison, there are some remarkable similarities between 1926 and 1985. In both cases the Labour Party was headed by leaders in Ramsay MacDonald and Neil Kinnock who believed that the state was a neutral arbiter between the classes and that the use of violence when pickets defended themselves against police aggression was just some deplorable aberration that could not be supported. In both cases an informal 'Triple Alliance' of unions for mutual support was in place and in both cases the leaders of their so-called partners allowed the miners to fight on alone. No wonder that the term 'Cripple Alliance' was coined. There was a breakaway union in Nottinghamshire, the 'Spencer Union' in 1926 which bore remarkable similarities to the so-called Union of Democratic Mineworkers in 1984. Both received moral and financial support from the political right for their strike-breaking activities. The General Strike was often disparagingly referred to as 'Cook's Strike' after the then Miners' leader just as the later one was referred to as 'Scargill's Strike' as if the whim or charisma of one man could bring out a whole union. Both men could only have taken the stand they did because of the support they enjoyed from their membership. Just as in 1926 there were trade union leaders like Jimmy Knapp, Ken Gill and others who lent their support to the miners, in both cases there were eminent union leaders who were openly hostile, Bill Sirs, Eric Hammond and Frank Chappell, for example. There were also significant differences between 1926 and 1984. In 1926, for example, there were no fewer than 1 million miners; in 1947 there had been 750,000 miners, by 1984 there were only 180,000 and today there are less than 10,000.

The leaders of the Parliamentary Labour Party in both 1926 and 1984 were anxious to distance themselves from the dispute but the Labour Party NEC in 1984 stood by the miners while the Labour Party in the constituencies raised more money to help the miners than any other organisation, according to Scargill. We can't imagine many of today's Parliamentary Labour Party or the NEC putting themselves out to support any group of striking workers. Neil Kinnock as Labour Party leader thought that the strike was a repeat of 1926 and gloomily prognosticated that it would inevitably end in defeat. He believed that associating himself too closely with supporting it would damage his electoral prospects. In 1983 he had scurrilously remarked that in his opinion Scargill was destroying the coal industry single-handed. Not for nothing was he known in South Wales as 'Ramsay McKinnock'. The strike was an opportunity for the Labour Opposition vigorously to attack the government and support the miners by raising issues about unemployment and energy policy, civil rights, the activities of the police and the workings of the legal system. Kinnock's craven defeatism was totally unforgivable. It alienated many miners from the Labour Party. It was worse because until recently Kinnock had been a standard-bearer for the left in the Labour Party and he was a miner's son from Tredegar in South Wales.

Some Conclusions

So much more could be said about the miner's strike. The wonderful role played by the women in the strike, for example, particularly the Women against Pit Closures. Although the strike was lost, many in the mining communities had been personally enhanced by the comradeship and by the ingenuity and inventiveness shown in organising picketing, raising money, whistling up resources to provide for those in the worst hardship and travelling and speaking to meetings up and down the country. The experience of many people is that when they are at work, they are treated as hands without a brain but during a strike the positive values of comradeship, class solidarity, pooling skills, knowledge and experience and concern for others were emphasised and those taking part felt empowered as a result.

The miners were depicted as Luddites, hopelessly trying to stem the tide of new technology, stuck in a past when coal was king. The miners had nothing against new technology as such and indeed during the dispute several said to the author that they looked forward to the day that men would no longer have to go down into the filthy bowels of the earth, at great risk to life and limb, in order to win coal. In a capitalist society, technology is not introduced to improve the lot of working people but to increase output, productivity and eventually profits. New technology just means job losses and insecurity, de-skilling and de-motivation for those who still have jobs. A rentier, service economy of the sort that Thatcher wanted would have high skills, high wages and high technology for a minority of the workforce and little or nothing to offer villages in Durham or South Yorkshire where the entire economy and community revolved around the pit. In a democratic planned socialist society, new technology would be used to cut the working week and to put an end to the most dangerous, most monotonous and meaningless jobs and, importantly, it would only be introduced as a result of decisions reached democratically by elected representatives of the workers themselves.

At the end of 1984, the cost to the taxpayer of the strike was estimated as running at £85 million per week. A figure of £350 million was given as the cost of the strike by Nigel Lawson who boasted that it represented excellent value for money if it put the miners in their place. Other estimates at the time put the cost immensely higher. One estimate was £6 billion but whatever was the true financial figure, the government threw money at the dispute in its out-and-out determination to win while having to admit that its programme of closures was only going to save £250 million a year.

The longer-term cost of Thatcher's victory over the miners cannot be computed. When the strike was over closures proceeded rapidly, there seeming to be a bottomless pit of often generous severance payments available for miners who chose to leave the industry. In the ten years following on the strike, £26 billion was spent in redundancy and benefit payments, in keeping pits mothballed and in lost revenue from reduced production. Investment and productivity rose and within a few years the British coal industry was the most advanced in the world. Still the Tories, even after Thatcher had been drummed out of the Party leadership, loathed and feared the unbowed Scargill and the potential of the NUM. In a vendetta of sheer spite, they decided virtually to kill off the British mining industry and so the investment in equipment and the skills of the proud workforce were sacrificed just so the rich could sleep peacefully in their beds, no longer fearful that the making of profit would be interrupted by militant trade unionism.

The labour and trade union movement was put onto the back foot, in a defensive, introspective way. Large numbers of labour movement activists found the miners' defeat and the reaction of the following period too much to take and dropped out, in many cases permanently. Substantial numbers of trade unionists became convinced that they no longer had any collective bargaining power. Many began to question the socialist ideas which had been so much a part of their earlier outlook and activity. A deep pessimism permeated much of the left, some of whom began to believe the triumphalist rhetoric poured out by the supporters of capitalism. Pro-capitalist intellectuals were announcing that we had reached 'the End of History' and that the working class had been bourgeoisified out of existence. With so-called Communism having ignominiously collapsed in Eastern Europe and capitalism having solved all its problems, a better future was assured for all mankind, we were confidently informed. This proved too much for so many on the left and it inflicted damage from which the movement has not yet recovered. At the very time when the left needed the leadership to counter and criticise the ideas of Thatcher and the New Right, it proved incapable of doing so effectively.

History is not about 'ifs'. It is about the concrete; about what actually happened. Nevertheless, an understanding of processes can allow the drawing up of hypotheses. If the miners had won, it is safe to say that the subsequent course of history would have been very different. Thatcher and the Tories would have had little option but to go the country. Had they lost and been replaced by a Labour Government under Kinnock, even such a government would have come under great pressure from a resurgent labour movement moving to the left. Repeal of the anti-trade union laws is likely to have followed. Such prospects scared Kinnock witless. Had the miners won, militant expectations would have been raised and he would have been expected to play his part in meeting those expectations.

The defeat of the miners led the economy to a potentially dangerous dependency on imported oil; the defeat of the miners and the disarray of the left encouraged Thatcher to carry on developing the political culture out of which the ideas of 'New Labour' were to develop. Meanwhile once thriving and tightly-knit working-class communities had their guts torn out and were reduced to despair evinced in unemployment, a breakdown in personal relationships, in drugs, crime and vice.

What followed were twenty or more boom years for casino capitalism, heaven on earth for speculators, asset-strippers and the like. In Western Europe we have witnessed 25 years of severe political reaction albeit in a democratic form. This was the period which gave us the premierships of John Major, Tony Blair and Gordon Brown. The last two rode under the banner of 'New Labour'. There was nothing 'new' about New Labour except the depths to which the Labour Party leaders went to maintain and even refine measures brought in by Thatcher intended to boost the profitability of British capitalism. Part of the legacy of Thatcher, therefore, was a further alienation of the Labour Party, particularly at parliamentary level, from its working class base and a discrediting, by association, of the ideas of 'socialism'. The extensive block of anti-trade union legislation was left almost intact by New Labour, to their eternal shame.

The strike confirmed in the minds of many people that the news media is a conservative-dominated oligarchy of dubious integrity which was prepared to produce and to print total lies as part of its efforts to defeat the miners. It would be wrong, however, to credit the media with something more than the admittedly considerable power it does possess to influence opinion by hammering away at the same limited number of themes time and time again. It cannot 'brainwash'. Working people are perfectly capable of taking information in and coming to their own conclusions about it. Cynical perceptions about 'them' and 'us' in society and the news frequently being selective, biased and sometimes simply a pack of lies are very widespread. Recent revelations about the operations of Murdoch's News International empire have shown the depths to which the media will stoop in order to get its stories. Of course people are influenced by the insidious and ubiquitous nature of the mass media but ultimately the information and ideas that the media disseminates have to have some connection with the experience of its readers, listeners or viewers. Clearly it is not misleading or occasional totally mendacious headlines in the *Daily Express* or the *Sun* or the *Daily Mail* that are the major concern. It was how the deliberate and orchestrated campaign to undermine the position of the trade unions before, during and since the miners' strike constantly produces a highly skewed and one-sided version of conflicts between labour and capital. In their reporting, analysis and commentary, the media are able to portray their output not as biased propaganda and sometimes simply as lies but as balanced coverage representing the 'national interest' and free of any ideological content.

During the miners' strike the media systematically portrayed Scargill, the miners and their supporters as the enemies of democracy. It was people with the courage and convictions of Scargill who had challenged the forces of reaction to win democratic and other reforms in the nineteenth century. It was equally courageous people who fought for freedom of the press and likewise risked the wrath of the law as it then stood. The fights they fought were noble ones from which society gained enormous benefits. However as capitalism makes commodities out of anything marketable, so heavily-capitalised businesses have moved in to own and control and make profits out of their selection and interpretation of what they think we need to know about what is going on in the world. The economic underpinning of the news media is advertising and the only organisations that can afford the rates for constant and very expensive advertising in the media have increasingly become the huge companies that dominate the economy. The piper calls the tune. The media dance to the tune. The tune may be called 'the rule of law' or even 'the national interest' but what it actually refers to is the rule of capitalism, of free enterprise. The domination of the media by Big Business means that those media are anything but free or unbiased and they systematically denied Scargill and the miners the opportunity to put forward their side of the argument during the strike of 1984-5. The trade unions which even in 2012 represent the single biggest interest group in the UK have no daily newspaper to fight their corner. A campaigning radical newspaper that told the truth would, of course, get no advertising from Big Business.

A significant feature of the strike was the magnificent support that came from outside the official labour movement. Up and down the country, people with radical inclinations (and others) found in the miners' strike an inspiration for demonstrating solidarity and practical support as well as their hatred of Thatcher and the Tories. Never since the trade mark 'Heinz 57' first hit the advertising billboards, have so many cans of baked beans been stuffed into vans and car boots and transported across the country to the mining districts.

Striking miners who travelled the country raising money commented on how often they found a very generous and friendly response in areas with large ethnic minority populations. Clearly their fight struck a chord and had the labour and trade union movement leadership put itself at the head of the widespread hatred of the Tory government, it is possible that the strike might have been won.

Long-standing traditions, which made many of the mining districts rock-solid for old-fashioned Labour Party activity, were eroding even before the strike. It was only half-jokingly said that in some constituencies in Lowland Scotland, South Yorkshire and South Wales they used not so much to count the ballot papers at election time as weigh them such was the overwhelming class solidarity expressed by voting Labour. Times were changing, however. Overall trade union membership was in decline and particularly in some of its previously strongest redoubts in the heavy industries. Electoral support for and membership of the Labour Party were likewise in decline. Too often had Labour's parliamentary leaders frustrated the hopes of those whose votes had placed them into governmental office. Frequently Labour's councillors in local government had likewise disappointed those who had vested their hopes in them.

Old class loyalties die hard. Illusions in Labour as the party that could bring about reforms beneficial to working people still had some hold and there were many stalwarts who moaned forcefully but still turned out loyally to vote Labour. Without a doubt, some parts of the labour movement had atrophied by the 1980s, not only appearing to be hidebound but also narrowly sectional. But class instincts were still there. In the absence of a lead from most of the prominent figures of the Labour Party and trade unions, miners' support groups sprung up of which a characteristic was that much of their membership may have been radical in a broad sense but it was not necessarily rooted in the traditional organised labour movement. In the big cities, especially, women's groups, gay and lesbian organisations, young semi-anarchic activists, peace groups ('Mines not Missiles'), ethnic community groups, for example, got stuck in raising money and food. Sometimes such support groups were at their most active in areas well-known for deprivation and serious unresolved social problems. Two such were in Toxteth and Kirkby in Liverpool.

Within the labour movement, local trades union councils made herculean efforts in support of the miners as did many trade union branches and ward, constituencies and affiliated organisations within the Labour Party. By no manner of means did all this support come from areas where labour traditions were long-established and strong. Money and letters of support came in from some of the seemingly most unlikely places deep in the Tory heartlands, suggestive that even in these areas there was much disquiet about how the Thatcher government had provoked and was handling the miners' strike. The existence of elements of a diverse but extensive coalition supportive of the miners makes even more deplorable firstly the lack of an unambiguous, bold anti-government lead from the top of the labour movement. Those right-wing leaders of the trade unions who chose to go public in their attacks on Scargill and the NUM helped Thatcher and the Tory government to inflict serious damage not only on the NUM but on the entire trade union movement and therefore ultimately on the working class.

What is clear is that these initiatives which cut across so many traditional procedures and hierarchies showed the dynamism, the ingenuity and unselfishness, the co-operative effort and the rough-and-ready democracy so often seen in strikes and other collective activity involving working people. We should not allow the fact that the strike was lost to be the abiding impression that is taken away from this struggle. What was so inspiring was the selflessness of those who gave so much while often having little enough to spare themselves; the courage; the organisational and other skills and talents that were revealed and the shared sense of comradeship and class. History never repeats itself in the same circumstances. We can never go back to 1984 and 1985. However the lessons of the past need to be absorbed in preparing a programme and leadership for the struggles that lie ahead.

The miner's strike was a riposte to all those who either deny that a class struggle has ever existed or attempt to argue that the working class had been bought off and that it has lost the will and means to fight for its interests. This was tantamount to saying that capitalism had won the ideological struggle. The opposite was true. The right-wing, pro-capitalist elements in society came together as one man to defeat the miners. The rich and powerful and their toadies and stooges have always been exceptionally class-conscious and aware of what has needed to be done to defend or develop their interests. Through their control of the bulk of the media, they were able to 'explain' that it was in the 'national interest' that law and order should be maintained and that the 'violence' of the miners should be defeated. They chose to ignore the brutality and the breaking of the law by the police. The ruling class maintains its power through a mixture of persuasion and implied or actual violence – the carrot and the stick. Never before had the British state employed physical violence and intimidation on the scale seen in the miners' strike nor subjected 'the enemy' in an industrial dispute to such a battering by hostile ideas. All-out war was declared on the strikers and those who supported them. In the absence of a determined and united fight-back by the leaders of labour and trade union movement, defeat can be seen to have been inevitable.

Nothing had changed by then or since in the fundamental clash of interests between labour and capital despite great changes in the nature of the economy and of employment. In spite of the efforts of the trade union leaders to persuade themselves that it was not so, the class war and the need for class solidarity were as crucial in 1985 as they had been in 1926 or back in the nineteenth century. Class collaboration as practised by too many of the workers' leaders proved as disastrous for the workers' interests in 1985 as it has always done throughout the history of the labour movement. Their weakness, pusillanimity and desire to be judged 'moderate' by the hostile media was seen for what it was and the capitalist class took full advantage of that weakness as they always do. A recurring theme in labour history is how the ruling class are consistently one jump ahead of the leadership of the labour movement in their understanding of the nature of power in capitalist society. Another recurrent theme is that of workers' leaders fawning and prostrating themselves at the feet of the ruling class and hastening to do their bidding no matter how much that betrays the interests of working people. A third theme is the willingness of the rank-and-file of the movement to struggle against exploitation and injustice when given a lead. Many miners had mortgages and a high level of monthly outgoings and yet they remained solid in support of the strike right to the end. So much for the working class having been 'bought off'.

Among the losers after the strike were the men who had formed the Union of

Democratic Miners. They had received fulsome plaudits for their 'principles' and their 'courage' from all those who were hostile to the miner's strike (including Thatcher herself) and vague promises that they would be rewarded by being able to enjoy long-term employment prospects in pits with considerable reserves of winnable coal. There was even talk about the opening up of new pits and miners being able to put in bids to buy shares in the pits in which they worked. It was not to be. It was never intended to be and the industry in the East Midlands went on to be decimated in the same ruthless way as it was elsewhere. Had those who joined the UDM remained solid with the NUM, they might possibly, just possibly, have been able to salvage something. In the event, they lost their jobs too. That was their reward for being Tory stooges and pursuing their self-interest at the expense of the principles on which the labour movement was based.

The final word is that superficially the defeat of the miners looked like a huge success for Thatcher and all she stood for. That is certainly how she saw it. However it may also be seen as the factor which sparked off the process of her political decline. Two or more decades of the media consistently attacking and misrepresenting the unions had had its desired effect of apparently rendering them unpopular. It was to this cynically contrived aspect of 'popular opinion' that Thatcher with her belligerent stance owed much of her early electoral success. However by the time that the bogey of the awful miners had been laid to rest, at least temporarily, there is evidence that voters had had enough of Thatcher's role as a swaggering thug and bully. She had won the 'war' and increasingly seemed to have much less to offer in the way of new populist policies. Her hectoring, self-righteous and patronising manner had always rubbed people up the wrong way and the personal unpopularity which had always been there now began to turn people against her style or as they say these days, her 'brand'. This even included some of her supporters who had thought she made a good 'wartime' leader. She may have believed that she would go on for ever but her days in high office were, thankfully, numbered.

Scargill was proved to be right. In 2012 there are just five deep coal pits left in Britain. Between them they employ about 3,000 workers. In 1970 there were 717,900 miners.

1. Reported in *Yorkshire Post,* 20 July 1984.
2. Speech at the Conservative Party Conference, 13 October 1984.
3. Lecture at the Carlton Club, 26 November 1984.
4. Milne, S. (2004), *The Enemy Within. The Secret War against the Miners.* London.
5. Quoted in Young, H. (1991), *One of Us: A Biography of Margaret Thatcher,* London.
6. Interview with Robin Day, *Panorama,* BBC, 9 April 1984.

9. WELFARE AND PRIVATISATION

The Welfare State was predicated on the idea of support of all citizens from the cradle to the grave. Even the Tory Party in the 1950s and early 1960s went along publicly with the consensus on this question, no matter what individual members of the Party may have thought privately. It was only with the onset of the serious recession around 1970 and a growing awareness of Britain's dismal economic performance that the Tories began to hint that the Welfare State was becoming too expensive. Now it was asserted that the continuously growing demand for its benefits was outstripping the fitful growth of the economy and therefore the ability of the state to pay for these benefits. Possible solutions were an increase in taxes (ostensibly anathema to the Tories) or a cutback on provision. Few Tories argued in favour of across the board cuts to welfare and instead talked weasel words about concentrating provision on those for whom it was most needed.

Tories have always emphasised individual self-help and rugged self-reliance, the role of the family and the efforts of voluntary charity as being more beneficial to the wider community than wall-to-wall state provision of welfare support. People are freer, they claim, if they make provision for themselves. Providing resources for the most needy and vulnerable should not be allowed to undermine business enterprise and self-help, they argued. Many Tories believed that the growth of the expensive bureaucracy associated with the Welfare State was pushing up taxes which in turn were a deterrent to enterprise and investment. They saw benefit as a wasteful mechanism which meant that money made by those who worked hard was being recycled and given to the work-shy.

The Tories were in a cleft stick. The New Right economists were urging cuts in public spending as part of the necessary radical redirection of public policy. However, the NHS and much of the provision associated with the Welfare State were popular with the voters and Thatcher as Tory leader and then Prime Minister went to considerable lengths to assure the public that the NHS was safe in the government's hands. From 1978 to 1989 public expenditure as a whole increased in real terms by over 100%. Expenditure on social security rose from 25% of public spending to 31% in the same period partly because of the unexpectedly sharp rise in unemployment and also because of the growing number of people of pensionable age.

In the search for 'easy' cuts, social security benefits were a tempting target. The government needed carefully to avoid the areas most likely to be contentious. The cuts were accompanied by a sustained campaign of hostile propaganda in the media about 'freeloaders' and 'scroungers' living lives of luxury on benefits paid for out of taxes on the earnings of the honest, decent, hard-working citizens of the 'silent majority'. Capitalism has had centuries in which to develop and refine the tactic of divide-and-rule and the isolation and demonisation of many of those on benefits was only the latest example of this very effective tactic. Earnings-related supplements to many benefits were abolished and increases to other benefits were kept below the rate of inflation, thereby effectively being cuts.

The so-called 'benefits culture' was seen as a social problem which needed to be addressed urgently and was approached using bourgeois moral and political preconceptions. These required the indigent and out-of-work to be stigmatised and then bludgeoned into what (bourgeois) public opinion considered was an acceptable set of values and practices. No more dossing around getting up late, watching tele, smoking and drinking and waiting for the giro to arrive. The work ethic had to be inculcated and the obligations of individuals to family and community emphasised. The insidious nineteenth century distinction between the 'deserving' and the 'undeserving' claimants of benefit was revived and the 'undeserving' were now portrayed as nothing better than feckless scroungers. Whereas Thatcher believed that the City of London should be self-regulating and could be trusted to police itself, armies of snoopers were employed to unearth those abusing the social security system and the poor were encouraged to spy and snitch on their neighbours.

In 1984 Norman Fowler, then Social Services Minister, commissioned teams to review pensions, housing benefit, supplementary benefit and child benefit and to advise on how savings could be made. They reported in a Green Paper in 1985. They recommended that housing benefit be cut to effect a saving of £500 million per annum. More controversial was the proposal to phase out State Earnings Related Pensions (SERPS) over the three following years. Mrs Thatcher spoke of pension payments constituting a 'time bomb' for Britain. She did not know how right she would prove to be.

The Green Paper's proposals aroused a storm of controversy across a wide spectrum of society and even among Tory back-benchers and were revised to appear as legislation in 1986, being enacted in 1988. This was one of Mrs Thatcher's many U-turns. (This is 'Mrs the Lady's not for turning Thatcher' we're talking about). Because of the likely political consequences SERPS was not abolished but scaled down. Although various minor measures were introduced, the back-down on SERPS meant that the much-vaunted major economies and radical reform of the system did not happen. Instead of the implacable and principled figure the myths have created, here we saw Thatcher as the typical pragmatic politician abandoning a course of action because of the possible effect it might have on her electoral prospects.

In fact policy on the Welfare State during the Thatcher years tended to consist more of 'salami-slicing' than direct frontal assault. There was a tendency for benefit increases to lag behind inflation thereby widening the gap between recipients and those in work at a time when living standards overall were rising. The cuts that were made were niggling and parsimonious yet not of the sort that singly aroused sufficient opposition to cause serious problems. For example in 1990-1 students lost entitlement to Housing Benefit, Supplementary Benefit and Income Support. The concept of the Welfare State was marginally undermined with, for example, the restoration of pay beds in NHS facilities. Prescription charges increased regularly. Those who were unemployed and receiving benefit were made to provide more evidence that they were actively seeking work. The percentage of people using private medical insurance went up from 4 per cent to 8 per cent in Thatcher's time. The share of public spending allocated to health increased from 14 per cent in 1978 to 16 per cent in 1988-9. However, per capita Government expenditure on health continued to lag behind that of many other European countries. All this did not constitute 'root and branch' change in British welfare provision.

Thatcher was not known for her sensitivity but was well advised by those around her that the electorate was extremely sensitive when it came to issues such as old age pensions and the NHS. Even she dared not orchestrate a media hate campaign against the old and the ill. Benefit claimants provided a softer target.

Despite the number-crunching which 'proved' that expenditure on the NHS was increasing in real terms and that the provision of services was therefore improving, real-life experience meant longer waiting lists to be seen and treated, staff shortages because jobs were cut or posts not filled, closure of wards and growing pressure on staff. With an increasingly aging population, the demands on the NHS were growing with every passing week. Despite the government's rhetoric, spending on health per capita was the lowest in northern Europe for much of the Thatcher Years. The reality was that Thatcher was hostile to the whole idea of the NHS, of tax-funded healthcare. She could not, of course, admit this publicly.

Some of the most controversial 'reforms' were those which went under the general name of 'Care in the Community'. The ideas on which they were based did not actually originate in the Thatcher era nor were they implemented until after she had left office although her name came to be closely associated with them. The concept involved treating and caring for the mentally and physically disabled in their own homes rather than in residential establishments. The idea originated in the 1950s and was characterised as a more cost-effective way of caring for mental and physical disability. During the 1950s and through to the 1980s a number of scare stories had received considerable publicity in the media. They related to shortcomings or actual abuses of care that had allegedly or actually occurred in a number of long-stay establishments. This was against the background of what seemed like an unstoppable increase in the numbers of patients requiring such care and the cost of providing it. As usual, much less media attention had been focussed on those establishments which just got on with providing care that was first class given the available resources. Even though there may have been some problems, many people in the relevant professions were deeply concerned about the risks that might occur if residential care was abolished or severely cut back.

In 1988 the Griffith Report led to the production of a white paper in 1989 called 'Caring for People'. This viewed the issue largely from an actuarial and managerial standpoint looking for enhanced 'value for money' rather than putting the human dimension first. The white paper formed the basis of the National Health and Community Care Act of 1990 which was implemented from 1993. The Act was widely criticised at the time and since but it accorded with Thatcher's thinking because it transferred responsibility for care from the state into that most private part of the community, the family. Some called it 'dumping on the poor' because the burden of change fell heaviest on the less well-off. Those with money who needed to care for a relative could do so by simply throwing cash at the problem but the poor did not have this option. The most immediate visible effects of the Act on the general public were the appearance of substantial numbers of beggars, sometimes acting aggressively, and of homeless people dossing uncomfortably in shop doorways and 'cardboard cities'. Such was progress in the 'Thatcher Age'.

'Care in the Community' proved to be an extremely expensive and complicated system requiring the co-operation of local authorities, doctors, social workers, district nurses and housing officers. Too many people slipped through the net. It was an immensely bureaucratic way of dealing with an intensely human problem.

Thatcher always had a very selective relationship with 'Victorian Values'. The often enormous, mansion-like, largely self-contained asylums she wanted to close down to save money were deeply rooted in the world-picture of the thrusting Victorian bourgeoisie whose values she claimed so much to hold in awe.

The thrust of Thatcherism was not to confront and totally destroy state welfare. It was more ideological and insidious than that because it was an attempt to erode the social assumptions which were at the base of post-war public welfare – the importance accorded to social justice, equality and the social rights of citizenship.

Under Thatcher total public spending as a percentage of GDP remained fairly static but how it was spent changed considerably. Whereas in 1979 spending on public sector housing had amounted to twice what was spent on law and order, by 1985 the situation had reversed and spending on law and order and defence had increased between three and four times more quickly as overall public spending. In other words, Thatcher's preference was for spending money on missiles and anti-riot gear rather than on the NHS and welfare.

'The Welfare State remained remarkably un-rolled back thirteen years after Margaret Thatcher took power… the stark change… was the growth in economic equality.[1]

Privatisation

The process of privatisation had several prongs. One was denationalisation. This involved selling assets and shares owned by the state and opening some of these up to ownership by members of the general public, not normally thought of as having a stake in this aspect of the economy. Another was liberalisation or deregulation where a state monopoly was relaxed or abolished and competitive tendering and 'market forces' introduced. The third was the cherry-picking of those areas of state or local government activity from which entrepreneurs could make profits. It was alleged that the introduction of the market would increase choice and efficiency, provide better value for money and roll back the tide of creeping statism and bureaucracy. Nigel Lawson as Thatcher's economics alienist put it succinctly: *No industry should remain under state ownership unless there is a positive and overwhelming case for it doing so.*[2] This should read: 'Any industry which has at least some money-making operations or potential should be plundered for the benefit of private profit'.

Less clamour was made about the fact that the trade unions were well organised in local government and other parts of the state sector and that a major intention of the drive for privatisation was to weaken the base that they had established. The government would then be able to drive down wage levels and cut jobs. For this purpose a propaganda drive in the media was launched alleging that public sector workers were 'unproductive' and overpaid, had guaranteed, overly generous pensions, did very little work and were a burden on the good old honest tax-payer. This was a crude attempt to open up divisions between workers in the public and the private sectors. The trade union leaders failed to launch an effective campaign to counter these lies at the time and their failure to do so has its legacy in the sustained attack on public sector workers and their pensions under the present Coalition.

Privatisation was one area of policy in which there was a very distinct break with the practices of the previous thirty years. What was done was consistent with Thatcher's belief bordering on an obsession that state intervention in the economy should be reduced and more emphasis be given to the free market. It was her deeply-held conviction that nationalised industries were inherently inefficient and that they were a barrier to the reconstruction of British industry along lines that were more dynamic and responsive. This argument was typical of Thatcher's skewed view of reality. The record of much of British industry under the stewardship of private enterprise was pretty dismal and even massive subsidies and handouts from the state had proved insufficient inducement to produce the large-scale investment in research and development and in new techniques, plant and equipment needed to effect major improvements in productivity, output and international competitiveness.

The industries that had been taken into the state sector in the big swathe of nationalisation after the Second World War were mostly those which provided essential services for capitalism but which in private ownership had become rundown and starved of investment over the previous twenty or so years. The railways and canals, the iron, steel and coal industries and the public utilities were examples. Their previous private owners had been rewarded for their neglect by hugely over-generous compensation for which money had to be borrowed thereby saddling the nationalised businesses with prohibitive interest charges for decades to come. The previous managers were often kept on and they were frequently hostile to nationalisation and less than thrilled that the state had become their master. They mostly tried to carry on much as before and few ever championed or even defended the concept of state-ownership. Over the years the nationalised industries became political footballs. They were kicked from pillar to post and back again entirely at the whim of the government of the time and in keeping with each government's policies and priorities. Their main purpose was to provide cheap goods and services for the dominant private sector of the economy.

Limited amounts of nationalisation had taken place before the Second World War going right back to the Port of London which became nationally owned in 1908. The Central Electricity Board, London Transport and British Overseas Airways followed between the wars. After the initial burst of nationalisation by Labour after 1945, both governments carried out sporadic nationalisations especially of 'lame ducks' such as British Leyland (1974) and various bankrupt shipbuilding firms in 1977. Rolls-Royce and British Aerospace were 'high-tech' industries which came into public ownership in 1977 and 1971 respectively. The National Enterprise Board was established in 1975 to provide equity and loan funding to a range of companies in the private sector. When Thatcher came to office in 1974, the state sector's share of GDP was 11 per cent. Post-Thatcher, in 1993, nationalised industries accounted for just 2.3 per cent of GDP.

The nationalised industries were on a hiding to nothing, being small islands of public ownership in an ocean of private enterprise. Ironically they found themselves being held up as examples of what 'socialism' meant when in practice they had little or nothing to do with socialism. By the 1970s they had few friends. They were, however, substantial players in the national economy. In 1979 they still accounted for 10 per cent of GDP, 15 per cent of national investment and 8 per cent of employment. The public sector as a whole accounted for around 30 per cent of employment. Rolling that lot back was going to be a major task!

Of major concern to Thatcher and co was the fact that trade unions had built up a very powerful position in parts of the public sector such as the coal, railway and power industries. The Tories were still smarting from the hiding that the miners in particular had handed out to the Heath government of 1970-4. They had also witnessed how failure to control the public sector unions had brought down the Callaghan government in the so-called 'Winter of Discontent'. Something had to be done and done it was.

Many Tories contrasted the private and the public sectors. Thatcher and Company liked to think of the private sector as wealth-creating, vigorous, innovative and responsive. The public sector was perceived as a lumbering behemoth, prodigal of tax payers' money, monopolistic, lacking enterprise, feather-bedded and a watchword for poor industrial relations. This point of view was taken up and systematically disseminated by large sections of the media but was not necessarily true. The telecommunications side of what was then the General Post Office, British Gas and British Oil, for example, were all making handsome profits when they were nationalised. Fashionable Tory views of private enterprise omitted to mention that so-called 'private enterprise' received all manner of subsidies from the public purse courtesy of the taxpayer, to the extent that to call it private enterprise almost amounted to a travesty.

As far as New Right thinking was concerned, private ownership would transform unprofitable public businesses into profitable and efficient ones. A healthy spirit of competition would encourage enterprise and provide choice and cheaper prices for consumers. Popular share ownership would provide ordinary citizens with tangible evidence of the benefits of capitalism as well as a financial stake in its success.

Thatcher's views on privatisation were partly ideological and partly pragmatic but the manifesto with which she and her party won the 1979 election made scarcely any mention of denationalisation. Earlier governments had tinkered about with the nationalised industries but to little effect. They could be allowed to stay much as they were in which case they would almost certainly continue to be a source of constant problems. They could be taken into the private sector lock, stock and barrel but did the private sector really want to be lumbered with taking on businesses which had been starved of investment and which by their very nature had a responsibility to provide services rather than necessarily having the ability to deliver profits? The railways, for example, had many operations which could never hope to be profitable. There was another possibility. Might the private sector be persuaded to cherry-pick and obtain profitable operations at bargain-basement prices with or without taking on those that were inherently loss-making?

We must never lose sight of the fact that Thatcher and those who gave her advice were pro-capitalist to the core. Just as socialists approach economic, social and political issues from the standpoint of the interests of the working class, so Thatcher and her ilk applied a very different litmus test to these same issues. Were there profits to be made, preferably quickly and easily? The search for ever-increasing profit is the constant driving force of capitalism. Privatisation had great appeal at this time for Thatcher and the Tories. On the one hand it provided an opportunity for capitalists to obtain cheaply some financial operations that were already profitable. On the other hand, in conjunction with and as part of the strategy of reducing trade union power, it offered the possibility of future profit-making by fragmenting the powerful public sector unions and driving down the terms and conditions of their workforces. Competitive tendering in the NHS did not necessarily lead to the provision of better or more efficient services but it did weaken the unions. For Thatcherites, no wonder it was 'private good, public bad'.

For many on the left, Thatcher was and remains a hate figure. This was very understandable because on a political and personal basis many found her repugnant. However, to allow criticisms of her politics to become influenced by the nature of her personality obstructs any attempt to understand what she stood for and her role in history. Thatcher did not carry out the policies she favoured simply because she lacked compassion, was ruthless, calculating and totally convinced of the rightness of her 'mission'. Long ago Karl Marx said that men (people) create their own history but not in circumstances of their own making. The material realities underpinning Thatcher's policies and those close to her were the serious structural and long-term weaknesses of British capitalism which had been developing over decades, had been at least partially disguised during the post-war economic boom and were being painfully revealed with the onset of worldwide recession from around 1970.

Thatcher was incapable of considering that there could be any alternative to the continuance of the capitalist economic system. She was perhaps rather more dogmatic and inflexible than many of her economic and political associates but this overall mind-set was one that they all basically shared. All of them were prepared to do whatever was necessary to maintain and boost the economic system in which many of them had large and lucrative stakes. Capitalism is about making profits. Profit-making does not concern itself with scruples about who gets hurt, pushed aside or beaten down in the pursuit of those profits. Critics of Thatcher often fail to grasp the fact that her policies were not the mere personal whims of a heartless, dysfunctional woman but policies which made sense when viewed as component parts of an overall strategy to reinvigorate British capitalism even though it was a project doomed to failure.

The various policies and attitudes collectively known as 'Thatcherism' keyed into each other like the pieces of a jigsaw, interacting with and dependent on each other and contributing to the whole. Privatisation and the reduction of the power of the unions were integral pieces of the jigsaw. An early tactic was the appointment of tough street-fighters as heads of certain nationalised industries with a remit to cut costs and take on the unions. Hence Ian McGregor was appointed to chair British Steel in 1980 and then British Coal in 1983 while John King was appointed to head up British Airways and Michael Edwardes went to British Leyland. King and Edwardes were instructed to start processes leading to the return of their businesses to the private sector.

The government seemed to think that it was on to a good thing with privatisation and consequently it got rather carried away. The manifesto on which Thatcher swept to power in 1979 had promised fairly modestly to put back into the private sector the recently nationalised aerospace and shipbuilding industries and sell off the shares in the National Enterprise Board and National Freight Corporation. By 1983 sales of these and other nationalised assets had fetched nearly £1.8 billion. During the 1983 Parliament, Sealink, Jaguar, British Telecom, British Gas and British Airways were all sold off and British Telecom alone raised £3.9 million. In 1985-6 alone, the sale of nationalised assets raised over £2.5 billion. By 1988 600,000 jobs had been shifted from the public to the private sector and the nationalised industries' share of GDP was down to 6.5 per cent. The denationalisation bandwagon rolled on, even after Thatcher was dethroned and it was eventually to include the railways, the most contentious of all the assets to be privatised and a mistake of monster proportions.

Thatcher certainly did what she said on her tin as far as privatisation was concerned. Even by the end of 1988 £24 billion had been raised by selling off state assets and some of this money went to help the government reduce the public sector borrowing requirement. Privatisation certainly made great sense politically, at least from Thatcher's point of view. Share ownership had been considerably widened and it gave a substantial number of people who owned shares for the first time a good reason for voting Conservative given that there was threat that an incoming Labour Government might embark on a renationalisation programme. With share-ownership in privatised industries being widely-diffused, it would be hard for a future Labour government to take them back into the public sector.

Privatisation became the leitmotif of Thatcherism and was seen as bringing capitalism to the people. In fact it was a cheap political gimmick. It helped further to weaken the power of the trade unions in what had previously been some of their most entrenched bastions. State assets were sold off, frequently way below their real value, referred to disparagingly by no less a Conservative grandee than Harold Macmillian as 'selling off the family silver'. Although some of the industries concerned such as steel-making showed considerable improvements in productivity and profits, privatisation was no magic bullet and industries did not necessarily become more efficient under private enterprise, greater competition did not necessarily follow nor did the goods and services they provided necessarily become better or cheaper. Rail fares and water bills, for example, have increased way beyond inflation since privatisation. John Major as Thatcher's successor was so carried away with the idea of privatisation that against advice from across the political spectrum he applied the principle to the railway industry. Even Thatcher was not convinced that privatisation was appropriate in the case of this industry and it turned an industry with problems into something far worse, rightly mocked throughout Europe. Britain's railways ceased to be a system and became a confusing potmess. The franchises were handed out to train operating companies more concerned about their liveries, logos and mission statements than providing punctual, clean and cheap services. Pricing became a nightmare of confusion and fares rose way beyond the level of inflation. Trains from different companies no longer made time-honoured connections for the convenience of passengers. We could go on.

The idea of widespread share ownership proved to be somewhat illusory. Those who had the money to spare snapped up some shares at bargain-basement prices, scarcely able to believe their luck. As the price of these shares rose rapidly, they then sold them and made a handsome paper profit while the shares then frequently fell into the hands of wealthy individuals and corporate shareholders precisely as opponents of the concept had always argued would happen.

Privatisation was pursued with almost fanatical zeal as money was thrown into some of the flotations. The Government seemed almost desperate to sell off BT. An extremely expensive mailshot was organised and special call centres were at one stage handling over 36,000 enquiries per day. Absurd but expensive advertising campaigns were launched in the media in 1976. 'Buzby' was a ridiculous yellow and later orange talking cartoon bird devised to persuade people to buy shares in the privatised BT. 'Tell Sid' was an equally banal campaign in 1986 used to encourage the buying of privatisation shares in British Gas, suggesting that 'Sid' was an ordinary working bloke who was on his way to becoming rich having bought a handful of British Gas shares. The price of the latter in particular soared but few of the shares remained for long in the hands of the people who originally bought them. By 1991 over 80 per cent of the shares sold in privatisation projects were held by big institutional investors. Privatisation created a mass of lucrative work for the City of London but it was paper wealth, a small-scale speculative bubble doing nothing to address the continuing deep-rooted problems of the British economy. A Labour Party leader described the gross under-pricing of precious national assets as 'bribing people with their own money'. It was one aspect of the degeneration of once-proud British capitalism into 'casino capitalism'.

The long-term fall-out from Thatcherite policies on privatisation was evident in 2002 under 'New Labour' when the privatised company British Energy announced an annual loss of £493 million and was promptly and unblushingly bailed out by the government with tax-payers' money to the tune of £650 million. This was at the same time that the company's executive chairman who should have carried the can for gross incompetence, walked off with a salary of almost £480,000 plus a bonus of £185,000. The subject of grotesquely generous salaries and obscene bonuses for senior executives in the finance sector just for doing their job and even for those who totally foul things up is at the forefront of current debate. Those who ask how such legal theft could have been allowed to occur need look no further than the philosophy of Thatcher and her admirer Tony Blair.

Even in the mid-1990s, opinion polls indicated that less than a quarter of those questioned considered privatisation to be a good thing. According to *The Observer,* most people did not think the utilities should be privatised. 79 per cent were opposed to water privatisation while 84 per cent made it clear that they had no intention of buying shares.[3] Although some businesses such as British Aerospace and British Airways enjoyed improved profitability after they were privatised, they had benefitted by having substantial debts written off before the privatisation took place (another flouting of the free market principle). The road to profitability for many previously nationalised concerns also involved large-scale redundancies, increasing the intensity of labour of the remaining workforce and raising prices and charges.

Economic deregulation was manna from Heaven for every kind of speculator and shady shyster. Thatcher frequently returned to the theme that her task was not just about reinvigorating the economy but also about restoring a sense of morality, of higher purpose to a society in which too many people had been allowed to become freeloaders. Yet where was the morality in encouraging small-time chancers to buy undervalued shares in British Telecom or British Gas one week only to sell them at inflated prices a month or two later? Certainly some people enjoyed a bonanza of unearned income from having a flutter from which they could scarcely lose. However such 'enterprise' had very little to do with the so-called Victorian virtues of hard work, thrift and diligence which Thatcher claimed she wanted the nation to embrace. As so often with Thatcher, the reality of what actually happened was very different from what she proclaimed as being her aim. One estimate was that the public purse lost £1 billion through the sale of undervalued shares.[4]

The number of individual shareholders rocketed briefly. Despite the Government encouraging the growth of shareholding through tax concessions created specifically for shareholders while also raising the thresholds on capital gains tax and capital transfer tax, by the time Thatcher was pushed out of office, the overall proportion of shares held by individual shareholders was continuing to decline. Whereas the proportion of the British population which held shares rose from 7 per cent to 29 per cent during the 1980s, this was actually a smaller proportion than in 1950. The boasts of popular share-ownership remained just boasts because the purchase of shares was not spread equally across the different socio-economic groups or even geographically. Most new owners of shares were, predictably, white, middle class, middle-aged, already at least moderately well-off and likely to live in the Home Counties.

A scion of the Adam Smith Institute went so far as to say that privatisation 'achieved the largest transfer of property since the dissolution of the monasteries under Henry VIII'. Perhaps he was into irony. The dissolution took place after Henry VIII had greedily seized the property of the monasteries. It then involved the state selling off valuable assets way below their market value to make some quick money and various opportunists on the make and selected sycophantic favourites made a killing. Some of the aristocratic dynasties which feature so prominently in Debrett's 'Peerage and Baronetage' got the leg-up they needed to start climbing up the greasy pole of accumulation and social privilege by being around at just the right time and jumping on the dissolution bandwagon.

Deregulation in the City is dealt with elsewhere but another deregulation was that of the bus industry and this was an absolute fiasco. Most people were surprised when the deregulation of buses was first mentioned since it was hard to believe that Thatcher and Ridley even knew what buses were, never mind actually ever having ridden to work on them or having had to wait around at a shelterless, windy stop for a bus to arrive. As a result of the Transport Act of 1985, deregulation of buses took place in October 1986. We were told that the great advantage of deregulation would be that the bus industry would now be freed from the 'shackles' of 50 years of closely regulated bus services and licensing and fare structures. Now there would be healthy competition, new routes, cheaper fares, more and newer buses – it sounded too good to be true and, typically of Thatcher's promises, it was. Overnight it seemed, the streets of certain towns and cities, and Glasgow was probably the most notorious of them, became gridlocked as buses of every colour and vintage appeared, seemingly in hundreds, touting for the travellers' business. It was possible to find, say, three buses of three rival operators, attempting to leave the same bus stop at the same time on the same route for the same destination. If they ever managed to extricate themselves from the resulting vehicular melee, they would then attempt to race each other to the next stop down the road. In places fares did tumble temporarily and some operators even offered free rides so as to push out the competition. Some of the vehicles looked as if they had been rescued from the scrap yard, had no blinds indicating the route number or destination and had drivers recruited and sent out on the road so quickly that they had to ask the passengers which way the route went and where to stop. It was not unknown for buses whose drivers were lost to find themselves stuck down dead end roads where it was impossible to turn round. They had to suffer the ignominy of being tugged out backwards.

Where there were several stops in close proximity, the atmosphere became semi-opaque, a choking toxic smog with dozens of bus engines idling as their drivers, seething with impotent rage, sat in the logjam until something eventually moved. It was not unknown for drivers from rival companies to get into fights. Hundreds of fly-by-night operators with clapped-out vehicles parachuted into places where they thought there would be rich pickings only to disappear overnight when they were disabused by harsh reality. Well-known and respected companies with an established operating base in town X got caught up in the mania and suddenly started running additional services in town Y, 50 or more miles away only for these to collapse quickly. Timetables changed frequently and seemingly on an entirely random basis. Passengers were totally bemused and some, if they could, made alternative travel arrangements. Despite there being a vast increase in the quantity of buses on the streets, large numbers of them ran virtually empty as passenger usage fell away. Few operators could afford new vehicles and the quality of the service available deteriorated as badly-maintained ancient vehicles, perhaps with their fourth or fifth owners, chugged fitfully through the streets, belching out foul fumes as they went.

In spite of what its supporters will tell you, the tendency of capitalism is not towards competition but monopoly or, rather, oligopoly. Looking back, most of the worst fly-by-night operators left the bus scene pretty quickly and the industry predictably came to be dominated by a small number of very large national companies with fingers in many other pies and the result was little or nothing in the way of increased consumer choice. Fares continued their inexorable rise. It had all been exceptionally disruptive and pointless and the claims of the Tory government that they wanted to improve bus services had rung extremely hollow when they were made and were proved completely false by events. Bus travel has improved since the 1990s with brighter, more user-friendly vehicles and in some places more convenient services but the credit for this lies elsewhere than with Thatcher and Ridley, her chain-smoking gofer.

Brian Souter and his sister Ann Gloag were Thatcher's kind of people. They were God-fearing born-again Christians who built up a huge portfolio of bus companies under the Stagecoach name across Britain having started with nothing but a couple of clapped-out double-deckers in Scotland. Like her, they passionately believed that free enterprise was to everyone's advantage, encouraging competition and leading to lower prices and better services. Except that they didn't really believe in competition.

Darlington had a municipally-owned bus operation which the local council decided to pull out of and it invited tenders from operators who wished to take over. The contract went to the cheapest bidder who had no sooner started services than Stagecoach appeared in the town with vast numbers of buses, completely outnumbering the new operator and competing with it on all the routes and providing its services free of charge. It took just five chaotic weeks for Stagecoach to see off its competitor whereupon it was awarded the exclusive contract to run the services. Many of Stagecoach's vehicles were sent back whence they came. Those that remained were no longer free and before long the bus-users of the town were realising just what a Stagecoach monopoly really meant as fares took off and services deteriorated. Even the Monopolies and Mergers Commission, not normally particularly critical of the more extreme activities of private enterprise, was forced to describe Stagecoach's actions as 'Predatory, deplorable and against the public interest'.

Late in Thatcher's term of office was the creation of the Urban Development Corporations or 'Enterprise Zones'. These were intended to reinvigorate areas of serious industrial and social decline and decay. They provided a generous package of financial measures (bribes) and exemptions from various normal planning, fiscal and legal requirements as a way of encouraging businesses to move in and create jobs. These UDCs were dominated by appointees from business and finance. The best-known of them was the London Docklands Development Corporation which even built a light railway, an extraordinarily expensive tube railway and an airport to serve this statement of 'free enterprise' and Britain's reinvention of itself as a world centre of finance. A needlessly tall totemic tower reared up over Dockland at Canary Wharf as the centrepiece of this temple to Mammon. The astral cost of the scheme was personally authorised by Thatcher but could only be met by quietly putting other projects elsewhere on hold. The bill came largely out of the pockets of the taxpayers who found themselves, as has so often happened, effectively subsidising 'free enterprise'.

For a government supposedly committed to rolling back the frontiers of the state and claiming to be the enemy of quangos, the powers and lack of democratic accountability of the UDCs were quite breathtaking. In Docklands the needs of the local, predominantly working-class population were callously and ruthlessly thrust aside as the area became a paradise for 'yuppees' or young affluent so-called professionals and Porsches replaced push-bikes and street-corner boozers became expensive café-bars or trattorias.

The sale of council houses to their sitting tenants was a policy initiated under Edward Heath but it only made faltering progress at that time. Under the subsequent Labour government, between 1976 and 1979 a total of 92, 520 council homes were sold so this was not one of Thatcher's innovations although it was something she thoroughly approved of. In 1979 about one-third of all housing in the UK was owned by local authorities, a far higher proportion than any found elsewhere in Western Europe.

Council-housing had got itself something of a bad name. The demanding (and expensive) building standards which had generally been adhered to by local authorities from the 1920s through to the 1950s to create a quality council housing stock were lost sight of particularly in the 1950s to 1970s with a panic rush to replace Victorian 'slum' housing with new stock, significant amounts of which consisted of high-rise or deck access walk-up flats. Some of these buildings could be erected from prefabricated parts using semi-skilled or unskilled and therefore cheaper labour. While these dwellings may have had bathrooms and internal toilets and even central heating, they were often built on the cheap and tended also to have structural problems, damp, noise, faulty lifts and refuse disposal facilities and a host of other drawbacks. One even blew up and partially collapsed. The estates and housing schemes involved frequently lacked much in the way of social facilities – one large scheme built on the outskirts of Liverpool was even laid out without pavements! Those tenants who could do so rented elsewhere and some councils used these estates as dumping grounds for their 'difficult' tenants. They became, rightly or wrongly, associated with drugs, crime, deprivation and despair.

Thatcher latched on to council-housing seeing it as a vehicle which she could use to achieve the Tory ideal of the 'property-owning democracy'. Her intentions were outlined in the Housing Act of 1980. This gave council tenants with three years' residence the right to buy their properties at a substantial discount. By December 1988 over a million properties had been taken from the local authority and transferred to private hands. In late 1986 UK owner-occupied dwellings constituted 67 per cent of the total housing stock which was the highest proportion in Europe.

With Thatcher there was, as ever, a crude political point when it came to the sale of public sector housing. Council tenants, if they voted, were known to be likely to support Labour while home owners tended to favour the Tories. If Labour voters had bought their houses cheaply under a Tory government, they might be so grateful that they would vote Tory by way of thanks. It was also argued that council housing had some effect in preventing the development of the flexible labour market which the Tories craved. This was because council tenants cherished their cheap subsidised housing and were unwilling to up sticks and move to where jobs might be available, unsure that they could find something similar in the places to which they moved. From 1979 to 1989 the sale of council houses had raised an enormous £17,580 million and was, of course, proving highly popular except with Labour-held local authorities who were forced to sell but managed to look like Scrooge when they grumbled about having to let their housing stock go.

The Tories cared little for those who could not afford to buy or simply did not want to do so. Speaking in generalisations, it was obviously the more desirable council residences that their tenants wanted to buy and those who bought were predominantly skilled or semi-skilled workers, likely to be middle-aged and in regular work. A consequence of council house sales was the intensification of a trend towards ghettoisation. What were already seen as 'problem' estates became more so because those living on them, many on low wages or on benefit, were unable to buy even if they wanted to. Perceptions of individual citizens were influenced by the post codes of where they lived and tenants or owner-occupiers on certain housing schemes might find it hard and expensive to get favourable hire-purchase terms or insurance, for example. Thatcher spoke in glowing terms about how ownership of their homes gave people a stake in society but as usual, the effects of her policies were to prove divisive. Local authorities were prevented from using revenue generated from council house sales to build new homes. Very little new public sector housing stock was built during this period and Britain's ever-present housing crisis intensified. 'Cardboard cities' appeared in parks, underpasses and other locations in towns and cities across Britain.

Between 1981 and 1995 about 1.8 million council-owned homes were sold to their tenants. Whereas in 1978 32 per cent of all housing was owned by local authorities, by 1995 councils owned a mere 19 per cent. 'Social housing' increasingly came to be identified as the places where the poorest members of society lived and were stigmatised for doing so. It made ghettos of many of the estates and housing schemes that remained and was extremely divisive in emphasising the contrast between 'haves' and 'have-nots'. The insidious concept of an 'underclass' made its appearance, the kind of threatening people who were going to swamp 'middle England'.

Generous tax relief (yet another intervention in the market) was available to mortgage holders and rose from a total of £1,639 million in 1979 to £5,500 million in 1989 while subsidies to local authority housing fell from £1,258 million to £320 million. As a warning of what lay ahead, house prices started rising far more rapidly than general prices especially in London and the south-east and also in a few favoured spots in the provinces. Here was the beginning of a financial bubble which was later to leave many owner-occupiers being grossly overstretched and wishing they had never taken the bait. Between 1978 and 1988 loans for housing purposes increased from £6 billion to a staggering £63 billion. This orgy of borrowing and of irresponsible lending contrasted sharply with Thatcher's sanctimonious utterances about thrift and the moral responsibility of people to live within their means. A 'property-owning debtor economy' was created. Thatcher's policies had the intention of creating upwardly-aspirant families in effect competing with each other in pursuing their own narrow interests. Once more there was a marked difference between what Thatcher said and what actually happened.

The private sector was encouraged to become more involved in pensions provision, this being identified by ardent Thatcherites in the Centre for Policy Studies as a new area where quick and easy profits could be made. The phrase 'portable pensions' was bandied about as being a path to freedom and an escape from the trammels both of state pensions and the increasing number of occupational pension schemes which, by the bizarre logic of right-wing thinking, were characterised as 'collective' and even 'crypto-socialist'. The banks, building societies and insurance companies licked their lips in greedy anticipation of enrichment. Despite warnings from various quarters that the financial institutions were likely to be greater beneficiaries from this new found 'freedom' than those who bought private pensions, Thatcher enthusiastically instructed Norman Fowler to draw up legislation which became the 1986 Social Security Act. Like half-starved vultures, armies of hastily-trained agents mostly working on commission tried to persuade anyone who would listen that by opting out of their workplace pension schemes not only would they pay less in but they would in some mysterious way get more out.

It sounded too good to be true and of course it was. It was basically a scam with government backing and the added bonus that it was making some reduction in the provision of pensions by the public sector. It was important enough to the Tories for them to give tax and national insurance concessions to those who opted for the 'portable pensions'. Between 1989 and 1992 around half a million people did as the government wanted them to do. Billions of pounds of pension money went from relatively safe schemes to much riskier ones. The balloon went up after Thatcher left office which does not mean that she should not take some of the blame. In 1993 a detailed report on the selling of these pensions claimed that only 9 per cent seemed to comply with the ethical requirements of business. The bulk of the other pensions sold were evaluated as 'unsatisfactory' while 8 per cent were identified as neither more nor less than a rip-off. What had this got to do with the morality which Thatcher claimed to be a vital ingredient of her economic revival? It was also evidence of just how degenerate British capitalism had become. It was now far from the progressive force of Victorian times that Thatcher seemingly admired so much. It was reduced to making quick profits by conning the very people she claimed to champion out of their hard-earned financial provision for old age.

1. Timmins, N. (1995), *The Five Giants: A Biography of the Welfare State*, p.508.
2. Lawson, N. (1992), *The view from no 11: Memoirs of a Tory Radical*, p.111.
3. *The Observer*, 'Water Privatisation, 2 July 1989.
4. Brown, G. (1989), *Where there is greed...* p.98.

10. THATCHER'S ECONOMICS IN PRACTICE

The Right Approach to the Economy

The concept that was central to the 'Thatcher Mission' was to arrest and reverse the relative economic decline of the UK. In 1976 Conservative Central Office had published *The Right Approach to the Economy* which laid out the economic policies that a future Conservative government would implement. This document was not written by Thatcher but there was little in it with which she would not have agreed. Earlier Tory and Labour 'consensus' governments had used macroeconomic policy as a way of regulating aggregate demand and maintaining employment, When unemployment looked to be rising uncomfortably, they had used Keynesian economic policies, employing lower interest rates and taxes with increased government expenditure to stimulate demand and employment. The new Tory approach would be to tackle inflationary tendencies by using Keynesian macroeconomic policies in reverse. Interest rates and taxes would be raised and government expenditure lowered to take demand out of the economy and hold down inflation. The money supply would be strictly controlled. Future Chancellor Nigel Lawson explained: "It is the conquest of inflation and not the pursuit of growth and employment, which is…the objective of macroeconomic policy." Sadly from the point of view of Lawson, Thatcher and Co and other like-minded supporters of capitalism before and since, the total eradication of inflation has proved as chimerical a project as was the search for the philosopher's stone.

Underpinning the grand plan was the claim that by reducing the growth of public spending a margin would be created for tax reductions to create incentives that would encourage and liberate the seemingly latent entrepreneurial talents of the British people. The government would ensure 'sensible' wage settlements in the public sector partly by strictly controlling the money available and it was intended to provide an example for similarly 'responsible' wage settlements in the private sector. Employers would be encouraged to shed jobs in the drive for greater efficiency and productivity and this would mean a temporary increase in unemployment until such time as the new spirit of liberated enterprise saw economic expansion and the large-scale creation of new jobs. A reduction of what was seen as the parasitic public sector and of various 'unhelpful' regulations on business activity would create the conditions for a revitalised and far more market-orientated economy. A reduction of the budget deficit and of government borrowing would help to bring interest rates down. These measures were to be viewed in conjunction with reforms of trade union procedures and legal changes to their status which would compel them to act more 'responsibly' and stop pursuing 'unrealistic' improvements in pay and conditions unmatched by increased productivity.

It is easy of course to point out that the purpose of this package of measures was little different in intention from that of previous post-war governments. After all, these earlier governments had tried with varying degrees of success to strike a balance between the economic aims of low inflation, significant economic growth, a favourable balance of trade and the achievement of full employment. However the crisis facing the British economy was becoming more serious with every passing year and Thatcher's was a more thoroughgoing and cohesive strategy which broke with some of the previous orthodoxies such as the perceived need for full employment. Thatcher was convinced that consensus politics had meant that political leaders of both main parties had shied away from taking the drastic and controversial measures needed to tackle Britain's relative decline. She now put herself forward as being ready, willing and more than able, at least in her own opinion, to implement the drastic and sometimes unpopular measures needed to get Britain plc back on track.

It has already pointed out that her predecessors as Prime Minister in Edward Heath, Harold Wilson and Jim Callaghan had rather more tentatively started down the road of attacking the post-war consensus and had come unstuck. Mrs Thatcher was not prepared to give them any credit for paving the way, as it were, and she was determined to succeed where they had palpably failed. Did Thatcher preside over a painful but marked renaissance of Britain's earlier economic virility? Did she set in train processes that put the British economy back on a sound long-term footing or could some of the subsequent problems experienced by the economy be ascribed to the policies, ideas and attitudes associated with Thatcherism?

The rhetoric of Thatcher and the Tories was that their policies had transformed the British economy between 1979 and 1990 and had beneficial effects on British society and general culture. They pointed to inflation having fallen from a peak of 20 per cent in 1980 to single figures after 1983. Many previously nationalised companies had been sold off allowing an expansion of public share ownership from 7 to 14 per cent. The privatised companies were enjoying rates of return on capital up from 3 per cent in 1981 to 13 per cent in 1988. Substantial reductions had been made in income tax with the top rate reduced from 86 per cent in 1979 to 40 per cent in 1988 and this acted as an incentive to business enterprise and industrial investment which had increased markedly by the end of the decade. Manufacturing output was running at record levels and productivity had increased faster in the UK than in any other major industrial economy. A new mood was evident, they exclaimed triumphantly, and it was evinced in improved industrial relations and in a spirit of healthy enterprise.

Inflation

Inflation seemed to be not a British monopoly but definitely something of a 'British disease'. A certain level of Inflation tends to be tolerated as being inextricable from capitalism and it is only when the rate reaches a critical figure that alarm bells start clanging in government circles. This is what happened in Britain in the mid-1970s. The simultaneous appearance of unacceptable levels of inflation in the USA had been a major factor in provoking the appearance of the 'New Right' economic and political ideas on which Thatcher drew selectively.

Between 1961 and 1970 the average annual rate of inflation in the UK was 4.1 per cent, markedly higher than that in the OECD countries where it stood at 3.3 per cent. In the 1970s the gap widened to an annual average of 13.7 per cent in the UK and 9.0 per cent in the OECD.

Orthodox thinking in macro-economic policy-making is that low inflation (aka monetary stability) is necessary for sustained economic expansion. Inflation is evidence of volatility in the economy and means that as the general price level rises, each unit of currency buys fewer goods and services. Inflation obviously hits consumers who find they can buy less with their existing wages and this is then reflected in higher wage demands as workers try to maintain their living standards. Inflation in the price of staple food items and other necessities can seriously destabilise society because it hits poorer people hardest. Uncertainty about the future purchasing power of money discourages investments and savings. It also makes short and long-term economic planning difficult although the latter in particular is difficult enough under capitalism at the best of times. If inflation is persistently higher in Britain than in its major international trading partners, UK exporters are likely to lose international competitiveness because of their inflated prices and may well experience increased import penetration.

For much of Thatcher's time in Downing Street, the government was able to claim that its policies to combat inflation were proving successful. In May 1980 inflation stood at 21 per cent and then fell to 2.5 per cent in July 1986, this being the lowest figure since 1967. The achievement of such a low figure was partly because the strength of sterling made it sought-after as an oil-backed currency. The down side was that exporters complained that this made their goods less competitive abroad. At the same time imports came down in price which pleased consumers. In their 1987 election manifesto the Conservatives boasted that their record on inflation was the best possible indication of their fitness to govern whereas, we were told, Labour government were profligate spenders. In April 1989, however, the UK had one of the highest inflation rates in the European Community at 8 per cent. In 1990 it reached 10.6 per cent.

Thatcher was by no means the first capitalist politician to make some initial headway against inflation only to find out that it had the last laugh. Like all the others she treated inflation as though it was the disease whereas it was only a symptom of the various malfunctions inextricably linked with the capitalist economic system. Thatcher was only too happy to trumpet aloud what she regarded as her successes. She was far more reticent when it came to her failures, which were many.

Public Spending

Central to Thatcher's self-proclaimed mission to restore Britain's greatness was the task of reducing public spending. This was partly ideological, being central to her illusory process of 'rolling back of the boundaries of the state'. It was also seen as a necessity to reduce government borrowing and offer tax cuts. Most previous Chancellors and Prime Ministers had found that public spending was like a Frankenstein's Monster – it simply could not be kept under control. The only administrations since the war to have reduced public spending as a proportion of the Gross Domestic Product were Labour in 1975-6 and 1977-8.

Chancellor Sir Geoffrey Howe in 1980 planned for a cut of 5 per cent in public spending over the following four years only to find that instead it grew by 8 per cent in that time. The government was committed to increased expenditure on pensions, defence and law and order, for example but did make cuts in some areas such as housing. The costs of social security soared not least because of rising unemployment. A commitment to make a greater contribution to NATO finances creamed off a substantial additional sum. Instead of giving the usual purring approval for Thatcher's every word and action, a leader-writer in *The Times* took her to task on 16 January 1984 for the failure to curtail public spending and virtually accused her of reneging on her promises. It was not until late on in her premiership in 1988-9 when unemployment was falling and there was marked economic growth that Thatcher was able to deliver, albeit modestly, on her promises about public spending. By the time she left office however, public spending was creeping upwards once more.

Even before the time that Thatcher was ousted, the word 'monetarism' had been quietly buried. This was as a tacit acknowledgement that her governments had acted pragmatically rather than according to doctrine or dogma. The money supply had been allowed to grow, although erratically. The Public Sector Borrowing Requirement (PSBR) had been 'adjusted' by the trick of subtracting the proceeds of privatisation from government expenditure.

In 1977 total public spending in the UK was £55 billion. By 1987-8 it was £177 billion, a huge increase even allowing for inflation. Even by New Right thinking, Thatcher's policies on public spending were unsuccessful. Despite the fortuitous revenue provided by North Sea Oil, it could well have been argued that it was income simply squandered on unemployment benefit and other costs related to social security.

It might be appropriate to consider the record of Thatcher's governments on health provision at this point. They argued strenuously that they were spending more on health than any previous governments but these claims have been contested.[1] It may have been more in hard cash terms but it was not keeping up with the increase in demand for the services of the NHS. As a proportion of GDP, government spending on health fell by over 7 per cent between 1981 and 1990 and this was a much lower percentage than that which obtained in her close neighbours on the European continent. It was a question of priorities. Thatcher's governments chose to spend what many would regard as disproportionate amounts on defence while arguing that the tax cuts that they were carrying out enabled people to make their own provisions for health care. For those on medium and low pay, this was rarely an option. The cost of prescription charges rose by 1000 per cent by 1987. Time and time again polls showed that the public did not think that the NHS was safe in Tory hands and they wanted more money spent on it.

Taxation and Incomes

Before she came into office, Thatcher had made much of the need for income tax cuts. Just as would be expected from such a class-conscious government, the tax cuts when they came in the 1979 budget were highly regressive as Thatcher rewarded the rich for being rich by helping them to become even richer. Those in the top bracket enjoyed a bonanza when their rate was cut from 83 to 60 per cent. Those who paid tax at the standard rate had to make do with a niggardly reduction from 33 to 30 per cent. Not content with this redistribution of wealth in favour of the wealthy, in 1988 the top rate of tax was cut to 40 per cent. The rich always squeal about how they are bled white by income tax. While substantial numbers of them find ways of paying little or no income tax, they love nothing better than a good rant about 'benefit scroungers and cheats'. As an example of cant, some Tories welcomed the cut to 40 per cent as being likely to promote 'honesty'. By this they meant reducing the incentive to tax avoidance and tax evasion.

Tories do not like direct taxes so it was only to be expected that they would raise indirect taxes. These taxes hit the less well-off hardest although Thatcher did not think to share this information with the poor. VAT virtually doubled from 8 per cent to 15 per cent and increased employers' national insurance contributions offset their well-publicised cuts in income tax. In 1979 30 per cent of tax revenue was raised from income tax. By 1989 this figure had come down to 24 per cent. Overall, from 1979 to 1988-9, total taxation rose from 33.1 per cent of GDP to 37.6 per cent.

The Tories have always looked after their own class, a trait they do not share with Labour governments who have consistently put the needs of capitalism before those of the working people who elect them to office. True to form, statistics produced by the Inland Revenue showed that between 1979 and 1983, the wealthiest 50 per cent of the population increased its share of total marketable wealth from 79-83 per cent to 80-84 per cent. From 1979-87 the bottom 10 per cent of wage earners gained a 5 per cent increase in their share of wealth whereas the top 10 per cent walked off with 28 per cent. As Gordon Brown pointed out, no other advanced economy had seen such a growth of inequality of incomes as did the UK under Thatcher.[2] Only the UK at that time introduced regressive taxation while simultaneously removing minimum-wage legislation and cutting social security benefits.

The existence of the class system tends to be denied most of all by those who are the greatest beneficiaries of its existence. The wealth of the top 1 per cent more than doubled to 17 per cent of total wealth from 1979 to 1989. The glaring inequalities contained in this figure meant enormous disparities in access to life opportunities and as regards health and mortality, education, employment, welfare and even access to equity under the law.

The honours system is deeply-flawed. It provides rewards to those who the Establishment feels uphold the values of and contribute to the continuance of the status quo. Thatcher during her early years in office made uncomplimentary references to bastions of snobbery and privilege and compared them unfavourably to her aim of developing a meritocratic British society. She then revived hereditary peerages by conferring one on her puppy-dog William Whitelaw. In her retirement honours list, she ennobled her long-suffering husband with a hereditary title. This title on his demise was of course passed on to her wastrel of a son, Mark, thereby further debasing the whole concept of honours within a class society.

The New Right would have us believe that the pay of top earners is a reflection of their performance. It was in the 1980s that pay awards and bonuses to top executives began their astronomical rise, a trend which has continued to this day and which is attracting mounting criticism. Even then the amounts involved and the people to whom they were given was not necessarily a reflection of their performance. In 1989, for example, Bob Bowman of Beecham had a salary increase of 88 per cent when the company's profitability had risen by just 15 per cent. One director of Morgan Grenfell received a 71 per cent rise despite a fall in profits of 44 per cent. When the Midland Bank reported a loss of £261 million in 1989-90 and promptly awarded its chairman an increase in salary of 25 per cent which amounted to a cool £329,616, a spokesperson for the bank airily admitted what everybody else already knew - that senior boardroom salaries were not necessarily performance-related.

This was the kind of greedy cronyism of the rich and powerful encouraged by the culture of the Thatcher years and we are living with its legacy in the second decade of the new century. It would have taken an ordinary employee of the Midland Bank on a salary of, let's say £15,000 at that time, more than twenty years just to earn the boss's bonus and it was unlikely that any considerations of performance would have been allowed to influence what he or she was paid although any perceived incompetence might well have lead to dismissal. This kind of practice was light years away from the ethos of hard-working and hard-pressed Alderman Roberts running his grocery business in Grantham. Always happy to refer to her father's struggle for economic security and status in the community, the strak contrast between how the rich looked after each other and how the world of private enterprise put her father and tens of thousands of other small businessmen like him through the hoops in their attempts to establish themselves, stared Thatcher in the face. She either could not see it or, more likely, chose to ignore it.

When Tory ministers back in the 1980's, and Coalition ministers now, tell us that we must make necessary sacrifices in the 'national interest', they have no intention of requiring these financial nabobs and other 'wealth creators' to show the way by coughing up an increase in their taxes proportionate to their grossly inflated incomes. Instead they express their concern that if the tax regime is not further relaxed, these mandarins of the financial world may take their talents elsewhere and Britain plc will be the loser. Substantial numbers of people are not convinced by this 'argument'.

Integral to the thinking of Thatcher's governments was cutting taxation and they liked to boast of their success in doing so. In fact this was sleight of hand. They knew that most people equate tax first and foremost with income tax. They drew a veil over the fact that indirect taxes impose a burden often greater than that of income tax. Under the Tories, income tax as a percentage of revenue was reduced from 34.6 per cent in 1978-9 to 28.1 per cent in 1988-9. However, increases in VAT and national insurance meant that most people were more heavily taxed in 1988-9 than they had been in 1978-9 and this hit average and lower earners hardest.

Unemployment

Unemployment was an everyday experience for millions in the 1980s and put down deep roots in the popular culture of the time as manifested, for example, in Alan Bleasdale's pessimistic but pithy television play *Boys from the Blackstuff* and its tragic-comic central character 'Yosser' Hughes with his pet phrase, "Gi'e us a job." A leading band had the ironic name 'UB40'. 'The Angelic Upstarts' called one of their albums *Three Million Voices*. The film *The Full Monty* (1997) involved a group of ex-steel workers from Sheffield who were driven to stripping as a result of their desperation on not being able to find proper jobs. The film was bittersweet and showed that the 'feel-good factor' had bypassed substantial sections of the population.

When Thatcher took office in 1979 unemployment was running at 5.4 per cent or 1.2 million and this rose rapidly to a figure of 12.7 per cent or 3 million in November 1983. Given that industrial output fell by over 11 per cent in the same period and that the rising cost of providing benefit was frustrating the government's spending plans, Thatcher's claims that her economic policies were working tended to elicit the question, "And when will that be, before or after Nelson gets his eye back?" Her attempt to blame it on the international capitalist recession fell flat because Britain's performance was markedly worse than that of other western countries who were also affected by the recession.

It was during her first and second term of office that Thatcher's record on unemployment was at its most dismal. At this time, Thatcher and the Tories were still espousing their own version of Friedmanite monetarism which said that governments could not influence the level of unemployment. This peaked at 3.2 million in June 1985 after which it fell, declining to less than two million in January 1989. A high percentage of the new jobs that people found had low pay, poor terms and conditions of employment and trade union membership was 'discouraged'. Many of the recipients of these jobs were just glad to be working again and would take anything they could get. Thatcher spoke like a latter-day Gradgrind when she criticised the minimum wage claiming that it would ruin industry. Such myopic heartlessness was not surprising because despite the supposedly humble background that she had come from, which had actually not quite as desperate as she pretended, she herself was well insulated from worries about how she was going to pay all the bills.

Official statistics on unemployment became an object of derision as new ways were constantly being found of readjusting the figures (cooking the books) to exclude various categories of people who most certainly did not have jobs but were no longer officially in the statistics of the unemployed. No less than 29 changes were made to the way in which unemployment figures were compiled during Thatcher's premiership. The existence of unemployment on such a massive scale added considerably to public spending because the Tories could not, although some might have liked to, abolish benefit for those out of work. Capitalism is an economic system which wilfully wastes resources. Large-scale unemployment means lost tax revenue, lost potential production of wealth in terms of goods and services and the squandering of the opportunity of vast numbers of people to make a useful contribution to society and the economy. Unemployment seriously damages self-esteem. Numbers of those who could not find work committed suicide.

While fear of unemployment was used as a deliberate tool of economic policy to cow workers into submission in the workplace, a cynical propaganda campagin was launched against the unemployed. They were lazy, they were freeloaders and they were scroungers. Benefit claimants as a whole were now depicted as idle parasites, happy to live off the efforts of others. The number of tax inspectors was slashed while extra snoopers were taken on to ensure that no one was receiving a penny more benefit than that to which they were entitled. Citizens were encouraged to snitch on anyone they thought was abusing the system. At the same time the real value of benefits fell in relation to the earnings of those in employment despite the onset of a low wage economy.

The massive rise of unemployment saw the exponential growth of the Manpower Services Commission. The MSC's main achievement was probably to create jobs for well-paid bureaucrats who then developed a vested interest in the continuance of unemployment on a mass scale so that their monolithic, largely unaccountable quango could continue to flourish and expand. The MSC will be remembered for numerous half-baked training initiatives whose effects on unemployment were, at best, cosmetic. The author remembers one project which involved building a dry stone wall probably a couple of miles in length. It took a group of unemployed workers several months to complete the job while keeping them out of the official unemployed statistics. The skills gained must have been particularly satisfying. Unfortunately even in the event of a massive turn round in the economy, demand for such walls was bound to be a limited one. If unemployment fell it was due to wider economic factors over which the MSC had no influence. The MSC was rather like a doctor treating a patient by dealing with the symptoms of the illness rather than diagnosing and treating its underlying causes. Creating a few dozen jobs here and a few dozen somewhere else did not, could not, attack the malaise of the economic chaos and waste built into the capitalist system.

By 1989 11 per cent of the workforce was self-employed. While Thatcher welcomed this as evidence of the encouragement of business enterprise, this sector was particularly vulnerable to the vagaries of economic forces over which those involved had no control. Spreading the idea that everyone could be an entrepreneur was cruelly misleading. Large numbers of the new self-employed had their fingers badly burned and bankruptcies boomed. Her father had worked hard to gain some degree of economic status but he and others like him lived under constant threat from economic forces far more powerful than anything they themselves could muster. They could not stand up to the power of monopoly capitalism.

We have noted that Mrs Thatcher had a passionate dislike of the Civil Service as obstructive, inefficient and wasteful. She boasted proudly that between 1979 and 1986 the number of civil servants was reduced from 732,000 to 600,000 at a saving of £1 billion. This meant fewer civil servants to process the needs of the increased number of unemployed brought about at least partly by the her governments' own policies. Tax evasion lost the Exchequer far more than social security fraud and yet there was a 22 per cent reduction in the staff of the Inland Revenue.

Economic growth

British GDP grew by an annual average of 1.3 per cent between 1973 and 1979. From 1979 to 1988 the annual average growth rate was 2.2 per cent. In the same period growth of output per employee in manufacturing rose from 0.75 per cent to 4.2 per cent. From 1986 to 1988 the growth in Britain's GDP was higher than nearly all the other OECD countries. These figures, drawn from OECD *Main Economic Indicators,* might suggest that the policies of the Tory governments during this period were an unalloyed success. However, these growth rates have to be measured against the disastrous collapse of the industrial economy between 1979 and 1981 when 20 per cent of UK manufacturing capacity was destroyed. The level of industrial production in early 1974 was not reached until 1988. The Tories were not fixated by the need to maintain full employment and unashamedly used the threat of job losses to 'persuade' workers to raise productivity. While output and productivity gradually increased between 1979 and 1988, it was from a very low base and on the back of an army of the unemployed. On the criterion of GDP per capita of population, OECD figures for 1990 relating to a sample of western capitalist countries showed that in that year only Greece and Italy had lower GDP per capita growth than the UK. On the basis of productivity per person employed as opposed to productivity per hours worked, Japan was performing about 50 per cent better than the UK. Just as telling are figures on the rise of manufacturing output in a number of leading European economies between 1973 and 1988. In those years manufacturing output in Italy increased by 33.53 per cent, in West Germany by 17.75 per cent, in France by 13.26 per cent and in the UK by a paltry 3.26 per cent. This was not much of a miracle.

The pound sterling was attractive on international money markets in the period we are considering at least partly because the UK found itself in possession of the free gift of North Sea Oil. The government utilised the strong pound as part of its anti-inflation policy. In spite of her famous speech about not being for turning, Thatcher made as many u-turns as someone trying to negotiate the Hampton Court maze. Her government had made it clear that it would leave the fate of the pound to the international money markets but twice they intervened to reverse a fall in the exchange rate. In late 1981 the base rate was raised to 16 per cent and raised again in January 1985, this time by 1.5 per cent.

The very high interest rates were a boon for holders of sterling but had a harmful effect on manufacturing industry. The fall in industrial output between 1979 and 1983 has already been mentioned. Between 1979 and 1985 1.5 million jobs were shed by industry. In 1979 there had been a £2.75 billion surplus balance of trade in manufacturing. This had become a deficit in 1984 of £3.75 billion. In 1983 and 1984 the once-proud former 'Workshop of the World' was in deficit on its international dealings in manufactured goods. No other economy in the western world lost competitiveness on international markets as rapidly as Britain. During the period that Thatcher was Prime Minister the productivity of British manufacturing industry rose by 4.2 per cent, a figure above that of the 1960s. Over the whole of industry the increase was only 1.9 per cent which meant that Britain was lagging far behind her major competitors on international markets. Thatcher, despite her rhetoric, had no magical panacea for raising poor productivity and the sluggish growth characteristic of the British economy.

It has been said that Thatcher's governments presided over the destruction of more manufacturing than that which had been flattened by the activities of the German Luftwaffe in the Second World War. With legalised vandalism on this scale, some of Britain's proudest cradles of early industrialisation were laid waste and ceased to have any real purpose. The destruction of manufacturing industry was not just the eradication of 'lame ducks'; it was deliberate economic policy and not simply the continuation of a historical trend. No other European country attacked manufacturing industry with the zeal that Thatcher displayed for this particular task. Between them, the high pound and high interest rates militated against the interests of much of manufacturing industry but Thatcher had brought into the received wisdom of the time that manufacturing was old-fashioned and that the future lay with growth in the service sector.

The 'Lawson Boom' of 1983-7 was based on reckless consumer spending assisted by all-too-easy credit and tax cuts paid for out of revenue from the finite resources of North Sea oil and from privatisation. The growth was partial, unbalanced and unsustainable and the very opposite of what was actually needed which was investment in the means of producing competitive goods and services on a long-term base. Average incomes rose by 35 per cent between 1983 and 1987 but personal debt rose four times as fast in the same period. In 1986-7 alone, the number of homeowners with mortgages doubled. For the first time ever, the average British household was spending more than it was earning. People were living beyond their means and all this was being presided over by the daughter of the frugal grocer of Grantham!

With so much credit available, there was a huge growth in the fashion of eating out, in fitting homes with new windows and conservatories, in foreign holidays, in electrical gadgetry and consumerism in general. New businesses sprang up eager to service the boom in consumer credit and the spending power it superficially injected into the economy. These businesses were to prove very vulnerable to the vagaries of the economy. All this was like building a house with its foundations in shifting sand and was a long-term contributory factor to the credit bubble which collapsed with such devastating effect in 2007.

'Greed was good', Thatcher assured us. Twenty years later the chickens came home to roost. Taxpayers are stumping up billions of pounds to pay for the foul-up caused by the greed and incompetence of the bankers whose actions were the logical outcome of the economic behaviour that Thatcher so zealously encouraged.

Thatcher was under Lawson's thrall. At this time, as far as she was concerned, he could no wrong. The illusion of an economic miracle was created. The reality was very different. In 1987 Britain's GNP fell below that of Italy. Revenue from North Sea oil was a bonus which served to disguise the continuing seriousness of the situation. Headlong spending using credit was sucking in imports, especially of consumer goods, while at the same time British manufacturing capacity had been devastated. In 1978 the UK had a trade surplus in manufactured goods of £5 billion. In 1989 this had turned into a deficit of £20 billion. Even the Adam Smith Institute with its staunch right-wing credentials had to comment: 'It cannot be a source of pleasure to note that Britain is now incapable of making its own machine tools and has to allow all of the activity to the Germans'.

In 1989 the government jubilantly announced that profits had reached a 20-year high. Did this encourage business investment? Rather the opposite because profits tended to be dispersed as higher dividends rather than being reinvested as a means of creating further wealth. Between 1979 and 1988, total investment in the UK was 17.3 per cent of GDP compared to 20.5 per cent in Germany and 29.5 in Japan. Evidence of the government's priorities was that between 1979 and 1988 there was an increase of 300 per cent in new plant and equipment for the financial services industry while manufacturing industry had to make do with just 8 per cent.

With equal exuberance in 1988 and a similar lack of concern for verity, the government had crowed that on any measure of performance British industry was in better shape than it had been for years. It has already been pointed out that the record of investment in manufacturing business was abysmal and where increased productivity and profitability had been achieved, it was the consequence of intensifying the rate of exploitation of the labour of the fewer people in work rather than investing in new plant and machinery to increase productive capacity and productivity. The profitability of British industry was becoming increasingly predicated on the existence of a low-waged and low-skilled economy. Such an economy was severely disadvantaged when competing with more highly skilled and capitalised workforces elsewhere.

In the areas of management, research and development and education and training the Tory governments between 1979 and 1992 presided over a continuingly dismal record. Through the 1980s and ever since there has been a strong tendency for management styles to become increasingly authoritarian and adversarial with a markedly harmful effect on morale and motivation among the workforce. Throughout the period British companies consistently spent less on research and development as a proportion of GDP than did competitors in Europe and elsewhere. Tom Wilkie ruminated gloomily: 'There is no plan, no overall scheme: above all no confidence in the future. And all the while our major economic competitors are investing a greater proportion of their national wealth in support of civil research and development'.[3]

A measure of the low regard in which leading scientists felt they were held in the UK was when a petition signed by no fewer than 1,600 scientists British working abroad was presented to Mrs Thatcher in February 1990. Among their numbers were 200 professors and 24 members of the Royal Society but they were unable to elicit an acknowledgement from the Tory government that the culture they were creating was encouraging leading researchers to emigrate and badly affecting the morale of those who remained. In 1987 the UK produced fewer patents per capita than Finland, Greece or Austria. New Right thinking was preoccupied with short-term profitability at the expense of the creation of wealth and utilisation of native skills and talents for longer-term gain. Although a disparagement of science and technology was not exactly a new feature of British culture, the New Right by its actions encouraged this insidious tendency.

Selling the Family Silver

Home ownership was almost an obsession with Thatcher. Politically, it was intended to wean people away from loyalty to Labour. With mortgage payments to meet, it was argued, homeowners were likely to think twice before becoming involved in industrial action. For all that Thatcher worshipped the 'market' and talked about encouraging its freedom of operation, she actually distorted it by her policy of subsidising mortgages through tax relief. The ready availability of mortgages encouraged reckless borrowing and by sending land and home prices rocketing, encouraged inflation which hit the very people she ostensibly set out to assist. Mortgage-interest tax relief was a subsidy to 'her people', those for whom she saw herself as the champion and for those she was trying to lure on board. However by putting political consideration before economic ones, she was effectively intervening in the workings of the market. The money lost to the Treasury through tax relief was a diversion from investment in the means of producing real as opposed to paper wealth. In her anxiety to subsidise (bribe) 'her people', during the 11 years that she was Prime Minister, the amount of public money spent on subsidising mortgages doubled. Owner-occupancy rose from 55 per cent in 1980 to 64 per cent in 1987 and 67 per cent in 1990. Only 22 per cent of occupiers then lived in council housing and Thatcher, in her typically thoughtful, open-minded way often referred to them as no-hopers living on welfare benefits.

Many of those new owner-occupiers who had obtained mortgages that seemed too good to be true, soon found that that was exactly what they were. When the next recession arrived in the early 1990s, inflation meant that they could not maintain their payments. Later on when prices fell to more realistic levels, they might find that they were victims of the new phenomenon of 'negative equity' where their homes were worth less than their mortgages. The number of homeless in Britain increased by 38 per cent between 1984 and 1989.

The sale of shares is dealt with elsewhere but the 'enterprise economy' was intended to fill the gap left by the decline of Britain's old manufacturing base. It involved investment in a host of 'sunrise' business ventures around communications technology, for example. The result was the appearance of a large number of small-scale, consumer-driven service industries. All manner of so-called 'consultancies' started trading as well as advertising agencies, public relations companies, training consortia, ambulance-chasing legal practices, financial advisors and the like. It might be unfair to describe all of them as 'parasitic' but these kinds of enterprise contrasted unfavourably with the long-term heavy investment in primary industry and the massive creation of real wealth associated with the Victorian period with which Thatcher claimed to be so enamoured. It was symbolic of how the progressive role of capitalism during its rise to domination had become played out and its constant attempts to find new sources of profit had degenerated into the type of activities which Thatcher thought pointed the way back to economic greatness. She could not have been more wrong.

Another bright idea that the Tories came up with was to demutualise the building societies. These were not-for profit businesses or 'mutual societies' which handled vast amounts of money for those wanting to become owner-occupiers but on a not-for-profit basis. The government's friends in the world of finance positively salivated at the prospect of getting their hands on this money but a few old-fashioned legal restrictions stood in their way. Once these regulations had been seen off, they embarked on a high profile propaganda campaign to persuade investors in the building societies to vote in favour of them converting to banks. A majority of shareholders was needed in order to achieve this conversion whereupon all the tedious old regulations could be thrown into the garbage can. This was a green light for profit-making! Oh what a wonderful place is the free market!

Unashamedly appealing to individual greed, the members were bribed to reach the right decision by offers they could scarcely refuse. The investors in the Abbey National, for example, were offered £100 in free shares which they were told would be worth £116 if they sold them on the first day. The media of the day trumpeted about this wonderful new 'freedom' and how only a nincompoop would vote against demutualisation. Absolutely no real wealth was created as a result of these shenanigans nor was there some bottomless money-pit to draw from to finance these freebies. Some people made a quick killing. The terms and conditions of employment of the workers in the industry took a nose-dive, the unions were put on the back foot and under the guise of the weasel words 'customer care' the service for investors generally deteriorated.

All these economic initiatives kick-started by Thatcher's governments resembled the economic activities of a dodgy casino. So much for Thatcher and the moral revival that would accompany the economic miracle she claimed to be bringing about.

Reforming the Public Sector

Thatcher did not know the meaning of the words 'leave well alone'. She was always angry. She always had to have something in her sights that she disliked and wanted to change or abolish. Having privatised a significant number of areas of former state activity, she turned her reforming or destructive zeal on other areas of the public sector which, while not being threatened with privatisation, she thought required powerful doses of the enterprise culture in order for them to be more efficient and to provide better value for money. Thatcher talked fulsomely about 'freedom' but this was only for public statements. She was a total control freak and in her usual contrary way set about reforming the public services in the name of freedom only to achieve the result that they became more subservient to a greatly extended and more powerful state. She set in motion a process continued by her successors down to the present day where 'reform', 'change' and 'modernising' are the buzz-words. Now in 2013 the Coalition Government is intending to embark on an extensive reform of the NHS which may come as something of a surprise to many of those who pay for it, work in it or use its services because the impression they get is that it's been in a continuous state of 'reform', of turmoil and flux for the best part of thirty years – and it hasn't got any better.

In local government there was compulsory private tendering of many authority services. Refuse disposal and street-cleaning, for example, have been among the kinds of service which have often been taken over by outside contractors. The new arrangements may or may not have resulted in more efficient and cost-effective services but the workers involved have frequently experienced a serious reduction in their terms and conditions of employment in the longer term. More seriously from the point of view of the trade unions, the process of tendering has weakened their bargaining power because it has atomised what were frequently large and well-organised workforces and broken them down into smaller units with much less potential bargaining clout. This has been intentional but it was a disgrace that so-called Labour governments also actively promoted this back-door privatisation and attack on the unions.

Thatcher and her successors have subjected public services to a continuous and continuing process of upheaval and autocratic top-down reorganisation from which the major beneficiaries have probably been not so much the general public nor the employees as the armies of consultants whose so-called expertise has been drawn on to assist with the changes and whose services come with a very hefty price tag. Thatcher saw the health service, schools and universities and local government, for example, as centres of insidious socialism, dominated by left-wing dogmatists and where trade unions had been allowed to get away with murder for far too long and therefore needed to be cut down to size.

It is not intended to trace the process of reform in the NHS in detail but to say that Thatcher at first fought shy of tackling such a hot potato and it was not until 1987 that she became won to the idea. Like others before and since she proved incapable of reining back expenditure but she initiated a process of change which has continued to batter those who work in the service and use it and the lack of success of this reforming zeal can be measured by Gordon Brown, upon becoming Prime Minister in 2007, declaring that a fundamental review of the NHS was needed. This was the fourth such initiative since 1997.

Thatcher's great education commissar was Kenneth Baker. He swept through the world of education like an avenging angel and his Education Reform Bill was so bafflingly complex that 800 new staff had to be taken on just to try to make sense of the Bill's proposals on assessment methods. As the Bill made its ponderous way through Parliament, it underwent 570 amendments in the House of Lords alone. Far from inaugurating a new era in freedom, it placed the entire school curriculum within the purview of central government giving it an uncanny resemblance to the prescriptive hold which the government in Russia had over its education system at that time. Not content with creating confusion in the nation's state schools, Baker *qua* Thatcher went on to wreak havoc in the universities which came under much closer government control. They too were in the hungry maw of socialism so far as she was concerned so the 1988 Education Reform Act set up a new state funding council to replace the old University Grants Committee. Academics were in a minority on the new Higher Education Funding Council and tame scions from the world of business and enterprise would scrutinise the activities of the universities to ensure that what they were doing was in line with what they perceived to be the nation's needs. Thatcher famously told an undergraduate at Oxford that the History course he was studying was a 'luxury'. Not content with bringing the old-established universities closely under the state's thrall, Baker went on to do the same for the polytechnics. These were colleges funded by local authorities that contained substantial numbers of higher education courses of a vocational nature reflecting the needs of local industry. Both Thatcher and Baker were sceptical about local authorities and since the polytechnics were under local government control they could not be left to get on with their job. Between them, Thatcher and Baker was as interventionist as any so-called socialist planning commissar.

The 'Enterprise Culture'.

Fundamental to Thatcher's microeconomic policy was the development of an 'enterprise culture', making it both fashionable and rewarding for entrepreneurs 'to chance their arm'. Nigel Lawson stated it unambiguously: "It is the creation of conditions conducive to growth and employment…which is…the objective of microeconomic policy." The creation of this favourable climate for business innovation involved removing what were seen as obstacles. Hence pay, price, dividend, foreign exchange and bank lending controls all came under close scrutiny. Other parts of the package included tax reductions, privatisation and the elimination of monopolies and restrictive practices (meaning mainly but not exclusively the trade unions). The argument was that enterprise was strangled by a mass of unnecessary and ill thought-out practices which had been allowed to develop over time and had been tolerated only because no one before Thatcher had had the bottle to challenge them. It was argued that with these artificial barriers removed, a new economic climate or culture would provide the freedom in which 'wealth-creators', both large and small, would know that their efforts would be recognised and rewarded. The surge of economic activity that would follow would create jobs and introduce a kind of vitality in the business world the likes of which had not been seen since the great days of Victorian Britain. The British people would find a new purpose, according to Thatcher a morally higher one, and UK plc would be on its way to greatness once again.

In 1951 Britain's share of world exports of manufactures was 22 per cent. In 1985 it was 7.8 per cent. The causes of this decline in competitiveness were not simply macroeconomic ones. Factors such as poor management, low levels of education and training and poor industrial relations made their contribution. Thatcher had a mountain to climb if her policies were to rejuvenate the tired, creaky old animal which was British capitalism.

Did she manage it? As is only to be expected, economists and others have gathered vast amounts of quantitative evidence to back up their beliefs that she did or did not. A few figures suggest that she masterminded no great economic miracle. If we look at the period 1979 to 1985 when Thatcher came nearest to implementing monetarist policies before any intentions to do so were quietly buried, GDP grew by a dismal 1 per cent while unemployment rose by 2 million. Inflation which was a major target of her policies fell a significant 8 per cent. However, by the end of her period in office, the UK was once more high up in the league table of countries whose economies were blighted by inflation.

Even with the windfall of North Sea oil, GDP from 1979 grew by only 1 per cent per annum which contrasts unfavourably with the 3.1 per cent achieved during the period 1960-73 when the now-derided Keynesian ideas were being applied. Truth is always concrete. Despite superficial signs of improvement, the deep-rooted structural problems of the British economy remained. Counter-factually, without North Sea oil, these problems would have been far worse.

If Thatcher's economic miracle was going to work, British goods and services had to be far more competitive overseas. This was by no means just a question of price. Companies need constantly to develop new and improved products and this requires resources being devoted to research and development, new capital equipment and the training of skilled engineers, technicians and operatives. The record of the Thatcher governments in this respect was a poor one. The 'fresh wind of change' which Thatcher wanted to whistle up did not fill the sails of British industry. Specialised workers can command higher wages and their training has to be paid for before the company concerned can gain any benefit. This was precisely the kind of investment that was desperately needed but which British industry had for long fought shy of putting in place. The City often looked askance at lending to companies to finance research and development, regarding some of them as too far gone to be good prospects. In the event many British companies that found themselves falling behind in the competitive race simply cut production, clung to market niches where international competition was weak or exploited the minimal costs associated with the use of written-down plant or low wages. This was tantamount to closing their eyes and hoping for the best, for some miracle to happen. It was evidence of just how decadent much of British industry, especially manufacturing, had become.

The Tories seemed indifferent to the fate of manufacturing industry and applied just one yardstick to any company. If it was profitable all well and good. If not, let it go to the wall. The expansion of the financial and service industries was seen as the replacement for manufacturing. The result is that huge numbers of proud, skilled, time-served workers lost their jobs and were told that those skills were now of no more value than those of chariot-makers. They saw the factories where they had worked pulled down in what became a boom time for the demolition men. Where new employment was created, the jobs were largely semi or unskilled and accompanied by poor wages and conditions. They had to stand by and watch the heart being torn out of what had been vibrant industrial communities. Where once commodities had been created which had sold in the four quarters of the globe, now there stood retail parks, shrines to the new religion of consumerism. Other former industrial sites now became museums or multi-media 'experiences' as much of Britain was turned into a vast theme park indicative of past industrial glories. Between 1979 and 1983 alone around a quarter of British manufacturing capacity closed down for ever.

The Tories talked in glowing terms of how they were encouraging new businesses to get started but the failure rate of such enterprises was extremely high and there was not an unlimited number of one-person and small businesses that could be supported, in the manufacturing sector or indeed even in those tertiary or service industries which were clearly so much more attractive to the Tories. Thatcher's governments were singularly inept at understanding the needs of industry and providing the necessary support. It has to be said that manufacturing declined in importance in most advanced economies in the 1980s and 1990s but because so much British plant and machinery was hopelessly out-of-date through lack of investment, the process seemed to hit harder in the UK than in France, Germany or Italy, for example.

Thatcher's governments used figures about the increasing number of self-employed people and new small businesses starting up as evidence that their policies were leading to a renewed sense of enterprise and aspiration. Lots of those who registered as self-employed did so because many companies cut down on the numbers they directly employed and made much more use of self-employed, contract labour. Grants and loans were available to help people set up businesses but relatively few of these were going to grow and thrive and themselves provide significant numbers of jobs in the future. In 1990, the Confederation of British Industry reported bankruptcies running at their highest level for fifty years with no fewer than 15,000 businesses failing annually.

The Tory's proclaimed free market economic philosophy was not carried out in a fully consistent way. Defence, agriculture and parts of the nuclear industry, for example, were not opened up to the competitive pressures wreaking havoc elsewhere in the private sector. This was because they benefited from being the recipients of large-scale government contracts. The so-called defence industries were on the receiving end of over 50 per cent of all government-supported research and development in 1986. These industries were great little earners on international markets. All sorts of death-dealing hardware and the systems to support it were sold to regimes across the world, some of which systematically imprisoned, tortured and murdered dissidents but this was of no concern to the lady at the helm. She may not have been involved in the transactions themselves but she knew exactly what was going on, and approved of it.

In 1988-90 about £2 billion worth of weaponry was sold to Saddam Hussein, at that time still a good guy. It was never paid for. After the invasion of Kuwait the government which had underwritten the contracts, had to pay the British firms concerned. The Labour Opposition failed to capitalise on this scandalous situation.

Deregulating the City

The City of London was wracked in the 1980s by revelations of malpractice and fraud. Such allegations were by no means novel in relation to various activities taking place in what had once been 'The Square Mile', but this decade witnessed a sustained series of scandals highlighting the glaring scams, illegal practices and simple greedy incompetence that seemed almost to be everyday occurrences. Johnson Matthey Bank comes to mind as an example. This had to be rescued by the Bank of England at vast expense when it was revealed that it had lost hundreds of millions through seriously misguided decisions on lending. It was revealed that the Guinness Company had engaged in a score of illegal or unethical activities while Barlow Clowes managed to defraud investors of £190 million. This is by no means an exhaustive list of misdoings in the City but Nicholas Ridley as Minister for Trade and Industry was very protective towards the City and resisted demands for those guilty of illegal or simply incompetent practices to be called to account because he claimed it was not in the public interest. Was it in the public interest for taxpayers' money to be used to bail some of them out?

In 1979 the Office of Fair Trading started to scrutinise the Stock Exchange. It intended to bring the activities of the oligopolistic City within the jurisdiction of the Restrictive Practices Court and open up competition. The City pleaded with Thatcher personally saying that it could regulate itself, i.e. get on with what it was doing without outside interference. Surprise, surprise, the Tory government conceded and during the 1980s relaxed bank deposit requirements and allowed building societies to demutualise and become retail banks. It also introduced competition into the market for stocks and shares. The City had been too cosy for too long and international high speed electronic communication and other factors were threatening its continuing prominent position. The Financial Services Act of 1986 transformed London's money market along the lines of those on New York's Wall Street.

27 October 1986 was the day marked down for the 'Big Bang', the day on which age-old ways of doing things in the City would be altered for ever. This was an iconoclastic smashing of old City institutions and practices. Free-market principles would be applied and the result would be the generation of massive amounts of new business. The functions of brokers and jobbers were to be brought together. Fixed commissions were to be abolished. Corporate membership of the Stock Exchange was now to be allowed and trading in gilts made open to anyone who had a licence.

The prospects of reform only accelerated the existing trend whereby banks and brokers became bigger. Firms merged partly to be able to diversify their operations. Foreign banks arrived in the City in substantial numbers. Brokers and jobbers were bought out by banks such as Barclay's. The desire to buy in 'expertise' by which was meant the most ruthless and rapacious finance capitalists, led to an explosion of salaries as recruitment agencies went on an orgy of headhunting. We were told that these 'wealth creators' were doing such a vital job that they had to be paid the going rate or they would take their talents elsewhere. The result was the rapid enlargement of the gap in pay between those in the top jobs in the world of finance and those whose jobs, while probably more crucial to the general welfare and functioning of society, were remunerated at much lower rates. If the water-workers, power station engineers, nurses, air traffic control staff, railway and transport workers, prison officers, street cleaners, teachers, etc, etc went on strike, even if only for a couple of days, their action would have a far greater and more harmful impact than a withdrawal of labour by the City of London fat cats.

Takeovers, mergers and acquisitions burgeoned on a scale never previously seen. Whereas in 1985 Burton had bought Debenham's for £579 million in what was then the largest takeover in the history of the City, by the end of 1989, twenty other acquisitions of £500 million or more had been made. The deals may have been done in glitzy glass and steel offices but this was nothing more than institutionalised smash and grab, particularly where takeovers involved what were known as 'hostile bids' – those against the wishes of the managers or shareholders of the targeted companies.

A new breed of brash, arrogant young men (it was predominantly men) appeared on the City scene. The City of London had once prided itself on the bowler-hatted, pin-striped City gent who, at least superficially, was the epitome of respectability and rectitude. He worked for an old-established and understated firm where discretion, knowledge of the customers and proven financial probity were the watchwords. Wealth was not something to be flaunted. To do so was vulgar. No such qualms pricked the consciences (if any) of the children of Thatcher who now thrust themselves to the forefront of the increasingly frenzied City scene in their rush to get rich quick. They were investment bankers, they were stock and commodity brokers and they were loud, loutish and brazenly contemptuous of those lesser souls whose salaries only just crept into five figures. The unashamed worship of money was satirised on television by Harry Enfield's character whose catchphrase was 'Loadsamoney'. It was also the subject of plays like David Hare's *Secret Rapture* and Caryl Churchill's *Serious Money*.

These people were widely but fairly likened to cockney barrow-boys but the latter were infinitely preferable if for no other reason than because they sold useful goods that were within the reach of ordinary peoples' pockets and they were not nearly as arrogant. Talk of a more demotic City where glittering millions awaited those with the right predatory talents irrespective of their social origins was only true up to a point. The City in fact still absorbed a large number of the products of the elite public schools, not that having had such an education prevented them from being yobbish. It also gave them the brass neck not to care two hoots about what the 'unwashed masses' thought of them.

Not only did ex-politicians end up with second careers in the City but some of these wide boys later popped up in the guise of Tory MPs. Two such City 'old boys', and they were among the most obnoxious of Tory right-wingers, were John Redwood and Peter Lilley.

The success of the liberated City raised questions about the essential nature of Thatcherism. The long-term decline of the British economy which had once based itself on iron, steel, coal, textiles, ship-building and heavy industry, the technical and engineering expertise these involved, the respect extended to men of the stature of Maudslay, Whitworth and Brunel, for example, was contrasted to the fly-by-night, essentially parasitical activities of the City slickers who made themselves exceptionally wealthy but actually produced no real wealth themselves. For all the talk of returning to Victorian values, bright, ambitious young people were now looking to use their talents in what, when all was said and done, was nothing better than a glorified casino where the gambling took place with fabulous amounts of fictitious capital. Nothing could be more symptomatic of economic and moral decay and yet here it was being touted by Thatcher as a vital part of the road to Britain's long-term and firm recovery in complete contradiction to her pronouncement on the patience and diligence of her father (never her mother – was she ever mentioned?) Even many Tories were unhappy about the anti-manufacturing industry culture that Thatcher was so keen to promote.

On a short-term basis, the deregulation of the City was a howling success and the envy of money-fixated fanatics throughout the western world and wider. The apparent runaway success of the 'Big Bang' led Thatcher and others to think that at last they had found the answer to Britain's economic problems. Who needed old-fashioned ponderous manufacturing when £100,000s of pounds could be made in seconds by pressing a few buttons on a computer keyboard?

In 2007 the chickens came home to roost on financial deregulation and the chamber of horrors it had created. The 'credit crunch' was a worldwide phenomenon but it was the offspring of precisely the kind of get-rich-quick mentality that Thatcher had gone out to encourage. It was actually capitalism at its most decadent. Instead of providing goods and services that people actually needed, it dealt in king's ransoms of fictitious capital – that is, paper money not supported by any increase in real wealth, a huge speculative bubble based on cheap credit and the boom in land and house prices, a great financial edifice without any real foundation.

It is likely that Thatcher's father with his Methodist frugality taught his daughter the old maxim of 'neither a borrower nor a lender be'. In fact, capitalism cannot operate without credit but in the hothouse conditions of the 2000s banks were lending recklessly and the 'sub-prime mortgage' had made its appearance. This was a mortgage taken out by a borrower who was a very poor risk. However the lender felt quite secure because one or two possibly dodgy creditors would be more than compensated for by the rest in the general apparently unstoppable rise in house prices. As soon as confidence in credit was broken, the whole edifice fractured and the building tumbled down. Then the capital on which the boom was based was shown to be unreal – to have no substance – to be literally fictitious. Yet this was the ethos of finance capital that Thatcher and those who claimed to be following in her footsteps such as Blair and Brown, had so eagerly embraced. What a contrast to the progressive role that capitalism had played in developing wealth and civilisation back in Victorian times – the very period to which Thatcher constantly referred in such admiring terms. Then huge investments were made in productive capital because there was great confidence that investment now would reap rich rewards in the future. That was genuine wealth-creation – investment in the means of creating even more wealth in the future and from which there were widespread long-term benefits. In the late twentieth and early twenty-first century all that decadent capitalism could do was to turn its back on the productive sector in the search for a quick fix of paper profits. Yet another Thatcher inconsistency – harping back to 'Victorian values' while encouraging an entirely different way of going about things.

Looking after their own

People who would consider that they are not interested in politics and economics will still have judged Thatcher using criteria dependent at least in part on their material circumstances. The Conservative Party ostensibly has as one of its major objectives the protection and furthering of the interests of those who support it. Tory supporters, however, are a very mixed bunch indeed. The Party would never have enjoyed office had it not been able to persuade substantial numbers of lower middle-class and working class people to vote for them. They even obtain votes from those with very little stake in the system including some of the unemployed. Most of these voters are not well-off and yet they ritually turn out to support a party that obtains the bulk of its finances from Big Business and panders to the rich and powerful by protecting the sources of their wealth. The reasons for what superficially seems to be deviant voting behaviour are many and complex and not germane to the current discussion. However we can say with some certainty that the Tories consistently manage to persuade these voters that the policies they will carry out if elected are in the 'national interest', i.e. the interests of all. This phrase has been bandied about as if the reality of it is staring us in the face and is totally beyond question. However the concept of the 'national interest' does not stand up to scrutiny. It is a myth created and perpetuated specifically for the purpose of disguising the reality of where power and influence lies in modern British society and the fact that the vast majority of the population are excluded from any meaningful access to the decision-making processes. The tiny fraction of the population that possesses the lion's share of power is perfectly aware that there is no such thing as the 'national interest' and that the purpose of government and politics as far as they are concerned is to smooth the way for their own further enrichment. This means that not all electoral supporters of the Tory party are equal. Those who are not rich and powerful are basically being taken for a ride; being used as voting fodder. They are the subject of an elaborate and well thought-out confidence trick. Their votes are cynically used to get the Tories into office whereupon the government then proceeds to pursue policies which make the rich richer. On occasion measures which benefit the rest of society may be taken by Tory governments but if they do so that is almost accidental.

The Tories, of course, can never tell the electorate what they really intend to do because if they did, their share of the vote would go into free fall. Mrs Thatcher came into office with the British economy in a deeply troubled state. It was unthinkable that the tasks that needed doing would be approached in the disinterested fashion suggested by the illusory concept of the 'national interest'. Time and time again when British capitalism has been undergoing one of its many crises, politicians, including to their shame Labour Party leaders, have issued calls for everyone to make sacrifices in order to get the economy back on its feet. This is coded language because what is actually being said is, "We're in a mess and you will have to take cuts in your living standards and prospects to get the economy back to a healthy state. For our part we have no intention of belt-tightening so you just shut up and put up."

Thatcher was true to type as a politician by not telling the electorate what was really going on. The effects of her policies by no means spread the pain equally. Her deflationary macroeconomic policies created large-scale unemployment and those who lost their jobs inevitably experienced a significant fall in their income. Industrial productivity increased and as output fell less than employment, there was a boost for profits. Mass unemployment weakened the bargaining power of the less skilled workers whose pay fell relative to that of other groups of earners. Those who owned their own homes or substantial numbers of shares enjoyed something of a bonanza. Between 1960 and 1979 the average annual rise in the price of equities was 5.7 per cent but from 1979 to 1985 it was an unprecedented 17.2 per cent. House prices rose rapidly mainly in parts of southern England but also in selected districts elsewhere. This created an instant 'feel-good factor' as people saw themselves sitting on a small fortune and their mortgage payments represented a smaller fraction of the paper value of their house. We should not give Thatcher all the credit for the rise of share prices which was a worldwide phenomenon but the easing of restrictions on financial institutions which she promoted increased the flow of funds to mortgages and helped to fuel the rise in house prices. These developments certainly made many of those in managerial and professional jobs as well as substantial numbers of skilled workers, better-off. This may have confirmed many of them in their belief that voting Tory made good sense.

Failures include not using North Sea oil to expand demand and the huge waste of human and economic resources consequent on mass unemployment. Also there was a failure to improve education and training in general or to provide greater funding for an enhanced higher education system. Britain's labour force seriously lagged behind competitive nations in its technical know-how.

"Suffer the little children." Suffer indeed as a result of these policies. In 1990 it was estimated that 28 per cent of UK children were living below the poverty line. Under Thatcher's successor as Prime Minister, the figure rose to 30 per cent and by 1997 the UK figure for child poverty was the highest in Europe.

Underpinning Thatcher's economic policies was an unspoken sense that she was engaged in a class struggle where political factors sometimes took precedence over economic ones. Her fundamental task was to facilitate the transfer of wealth from wages and public expenditure to the business community to boost profitability. This in turn was supposed to encourage a rate of investment that would restore the competitiveness of British industry. This transfer could be achieved through persuasion or under duress or a combination of the two. A crucial sub-plot was the necessity of bringing inflation under control. To assist the fight against inflation, she early on supervised a restructuring of exchange-rates despite the harsh impact this was bound to have on the manufacturing sector and jobs therein. Reducing the Public Sector Borrowing Requirement and establishing the concept of 'popular capitalism' seemed to take priority in the drive for privatisation and deregulation over boosting industrial investment and productivity. Where manpower training for the skills needed in this brave new world was concerned, pots of money were thrown particularly at schemes for tackling youth unemployment in preference to sophisticated levels of training in areas such as electronics and communications technology. These developments were pragmatic rather than principled, a quick result being preferred to a longer-term and therefore less spectacular solution of the problem from which she might not be able to extract the credit.

Even Thatcher could not sort Capitalism

Every time capitalism pulls itself out of one of its periodic crises and is enjoying boom conditions, learned and distinguished economists soberly tell us that they have found the magic formula which will ensure that no more crises occur in the future. They do this with such an air of certainty that it seems uncharitable not to believe that they mean what they say. When the next crisis happens, which it always does as certainly as night follows day, the same economists hold their hands up in horror, bemused and totally confused that the impossible and unthinkable has happened once again. Some will admit to having been taken by surprise by the reappearance of crisis and apparently regard the phenomenon as being rather like a tsunami or other natural disaster and every bit as apparently random. Other economists will pretend they had never actually said that the days of crisis were over and they will come up with some explanation for renewed slump conditions that they presumably think sounds plausible.

But whatever is used by way of an 'explanation' never actually explains anything.

Capitalist crises occur as the result of economic forces created by human beings and not as the result of natural forces that cannot be predicted and controlled. The inevitability of crisis is built into the very being of capitalism. Any explanation that does not take cognisance of this inescapable fact is necessarily incomplete. Of course any pro-capitalist economist is bound to be very uncomfortable about this tendency to crisis in his favourite economic system but not even the cleverest of them has ever come up with an effective antidote. Nor will they do so. Just as Canute could not control the tides, so even the cleverest of them cannot eradicate the tendency to crisis.

So what is the fundamental reason why capitalism cannot avoid crisis? Put in the simplest possible terms, every capitalist is in competition with other capitalists. He has to try to keep his costs down and he therefore wants to work his employees for as long and hard as possible, paying them the lowest wages he can get away with. They in turn want the highest wages they can get, the best working conditions, the shortest working day and the longest holidays. This, of course, is the essence of the class struggle in the workplace – the incompatibility of the interests of labour and capital.

Taken as a mass, capitalism in its constant search for more profit and because of its competitive nature, necessarily tries to expand and update the means of production. The outcome is indeed a massive growth of productive capacity but it is not matched by similar growth in demand. The basic problem is that overall the ability to produce goods and services outstrips the ability of the workers to buy those very goods and services that workers like themselves have created. Increasing wages to enhance spending power is not an option because that would reduce profits and capitalists are in business for one thing and one thing only - to make profits.

If companies cannot sell the goods they produce, the bosses will not be able to realise their profit and they are likely to have to close or even destroy the means of production such as factories, offices, plant and machinery and sack the workers involved. The spending power of workers forced into unemployment is obviously reduced so other companies find that they cannot sell what they produce and the whole system faces a crisis of overproduction. This kind of situation has been an inescapable feature of capitalism since the nineteenth century. The most sustained boom that capitalism ever enjoyed was that in the 1950s and 1960s. It led to widespread illusions, even among some socialists, that the tendency of capitalism towards booms and slumps had been finally eradicated. All the ruder the awakening then, in the early 1970s, when it became apparent that the capitalist leopard still possessed the same old spots and all the more desperate were the measures that capitalist economists and politicians proposed in order to deal with the situation.

Couldn't capitalists invest their way out of the crisis? Surely investment in new means of production by the capitalists would stimulate demand? Such investment would lead to the creation of new jobs and workers with jobs would have the money to buy the goods made by other workers – and a virtuous circle would be created. The snag here is the tendency of capitalists not to look over the horizon for what they can't see. Particularly in uncertain times, long-term considerations are always secondary to immediate concerns. The capitalists will only invest it they can expect to realise a profit on a piece of business by actually selling a good or service. If there is too much of a risk attached to investing, especially during a slump, any profit made from previous business will usually be spent or simply left to accumulate interest in the bank.

Capitalism has a cycle of slump and boom but the timing and the duration of these events and of the periods between them cannot be reliably predicted. Nor has any economist found a method of avoiding the cycle although there are various measures that can encourage growth in the economy or partially delay or lessen the effects of slump and recession.

The capitalist system is wasteful and irrational by any standards. Building workers languish on the dole, building materials are left to rot and thousands live in slums and unfit dwellings because there is insufficient profit to be made from building affordable homes. People starve while perfectly good crops are ploughed back into the soil in preference even to giving the produce away free. A thousand other examples could be given. This is the great God 'Market' of which Thatcher, Major, Blair and Brown have made a fetish. It is unplanned and inherently chaotic placing private profit before people's needs and then it has the gall to tell us that this is the best and indeed the only viable form of economic organisation. Anyone who questions it and suggests an alternative to capitalism is stupid, mad or potentially dangerous. Further, when it gets itself into one of its periodic downturns, it tries to convince us that we must all make sacrifices in order to help the good times to return quickly. The problem is that the making of the sacrifices is never shared out proportionate to people's wealth and the burden of doing so invariably falls on the less well-off.

Mrs Thatcher set out her stall to restore the viability and profitability of British capitalism. Statistics on the growth or decline of the GDP, on unemployment, on trends in inflation, investment, living standards, the balance of trade and the creation of new jobs, for example, can all be indicators of the success of Thatcher's and subsequent governments in managing the economy in the short-term. They may point jubilantly to a sizeable fall in inflation or a significant rise in job vacancies as evidence that the economy has turned the corner and growth is once again on the agenda. The problem with pro-capitalist economists and politicians is that they dare not, they cannot, admit the reality of the contradictions and long-term destructive tendencies built into capitalism. This means that for all their huffing and puffing, their self-congratulations when, for a while, things go their way, they are incapable of addressing the root problems of capitalist crisis.

'Small' international economic crises in 1990-1, 2001 and the major ongoing crisis since 2007 are an indication that the neo-liberal policies carried out in Britain by Thatcher and her successors and their equivalents elsewhere have not exorcised the inner demons of capitalism. In 2013 the world is in a classic state of overproduction as goods rot unsold in warehouses and workers rot on the dole in many parts of the world. Most of the 1990s and the first decade of the twentieth century were good times for the advanced capitalist economies. Now the international capitalist class look like skiers, hurtling downhill towards a precipice, blindfolded. A minor pick-up in trade or a few thousand off the dole queue are greeted as if the good days are here again.

That Thatcher was incapable of preventing the long-term decline of British capitalism was unconsciously admitted in 2007 when John Redwood and others of like mind on the right of the Conservative Party produced a report outlining what they thought should be the economic policies of a future Tory government. The programme it should carry out was intended to "…undertake the long-term thinking required to reverse the decline of British competitiveness, and come forward with the policies needed for the new supply side revolution." This was an almost word-perfect replica of the mission that Thatcher set herself. The present unholy alliance under Cameron and Clegg is carrying out policies that are fundamentally little different from those of Thatcher thirty years ago except that then British capitalism had not degenerated quite so far. It is hard not to recall the old saying about history always repeating itself, first time as tragedy, second time as farce.

1. Webster, C. 'The Health Service', in Kavanagh, D. and Seldon, A. (eds), (1989), *The Thatcher Effect: A Decade of Change,* Oxford.
2. Brown, G. (1989), op.cit, p.110.
3. Wilkie, T. 'The Thatcher Effect on Science', in Kavanagh, D. & Seldon, A (1989). op cit.

11. THATCHER AND THE TRADE UNIONS

Trade Unions in the post-war boom

Trade unions had to fight hard in the nineteenth century to gain some degree of recognition under law. The Trades Disputes Act of 1906 acknowledged their legitimacy in collective bargaining with employers and provided trade unionists with legal protection against the possibility of prosecution when they were engaged in official union activities which might otherwise be illegal, for example inducing other workers to break their contracts of employment. This was a significant immunity but experience convinced many trade unions officials and activists that the law and the legal authorities were generally hostile to their aspirations. It was also felt that the news and current affairs media were generally unsympathetic to union interests and that coverage of industrial relations activity was biased towards the employers' point of view. The media seemed to home in gleefully on demarcation disputes involving obstructive activity between members of different unions in the same workplace. They also made much of restrictive practices where unions had used their clout to restrict output and productivity and keep up manning levels. Such practices were not as prevalent as the media suggested and were not balanced by reports of entrenched, outdated practices and incompetence on the part of management.

A familiar feature of industrial relations in the 'consensus' years of the 1950s and 1960s was joint negotiations of a tripartite nature with representatives from the government, from the employers' organisations and senior full-time trade union officials. A cosy little accord had developed whereby discussions took place and policy was fairly amicably arrived at over what became known as 'beer and sandwiches'. There was an unspoken agreement that while each of the parties would have a stance and opportunity to put its case, a conclusion would be reached based on compromise and none of the parties involved would normally want unduly to 'rock the boat'. Class collaboration was the order of the day as the trade union leaders were wined, dined and flattered, those who chose to pursue this approach knowing that if they played their cards right, seats on prestigious public bodies and various official commissions might come their way. Eventually there would be a chance of a knighthood or even a peerage. Some went so far as to become total apostates and they crossed the 'great divide' to find themselves with lucrative directorships on the boards of national and multinational companies. From the point of view of the members, all too often it looked as if the trade union chiefs were mainly concerned with feathering their own nests rather than fighting unequivocally for the interests of their members. Those leaders who succumbed to the allure of the sirens were flattered and simultaneously patronised in the media. The actions of these 'moderate' union leaders were used to confuse and demoralise the rank and file membership.

The salaries and lifestyles that many of the trade union leaders enjoyed made it easy for them to lose touch with the everyday issues, gripes and grievances that their members were experiencing in the workplaces let alone the problems they might have in paying the bills. In this situation tensions often developed between the full-time officers and the lay officials in the workplaces. The convenors, shop stewards, fathers-of-chapel, call them what you will, were their members' points of contact with the unions. In effect, they were the union. They were directly elected by the members, answerable to them for the work they did on their behalf and usually readily available in the workplace, unlike full-time officials, even those who worked at district level. The members looked to their representatives in the workplace to understand, take on board, articulate and resolve their issues with management. On this basis, effective stewards might build up a powerful basis of support where on many matters they could by-pass the full-time officers and resolve issues quickly and effectively. The more the stewards acted as effective advocates close to their members, the more they could become an alternative power base within the unions and might find themselves on a collision course with the full-time union bureaucracy. The latter were usually keen to pour oil on troubled waters. They wanted a quiet life. A natural outcome of this situation could be spontaneous unofficial action at local level and sometimes right across a big company with many plants in different parts of the country because of the networks of stewards that were often established within such companies. The resulting disputes were given the deliberately emotive term 'wildcat strikes' by the media. The phrase originated in the USA.

The 1950s and 1960s were the time of the unexpectedly protracted 'post-war' economic boom. Bulging order books and full employment tipped the balance of power in industrial relations in the unions' favour, other things being equal, especially where there was strong organisation at workplace level or across a company with many sites and strong organised links between the union members on those sites. It is curious how, in the 1970s and 1980s, Thatcher trumpeted the virtues of the market but would not accept that union strength in the years of the boom was itself the result of those self-same market forces.

It was the material conditions of relative growth and prosperity that were the background to a significant rise in the confidence of union members particularly in well-organised workplaces. The bosses needed to get their orders completed and there were no ragged-arsed poor devils at the factory gate begging for jobs – on any terms. The unions were bargaining from a position of relative strength. Not only were the unions often able to negotiate wage rises well above inflation and shorter hours and better conditions, they were frequently in a strong enough position to prevent or at least delay the introduction of new plant and machinery which threatened jobs.

On a national basis, it was largely accepted that trade unions had a right to be involved in the economic decisions of governments in relation to such issues as wages and incomes policies. However, behind the apparent bonhomie of the 'beer and sandwiches' lay a serious decline in the competitiveness of large swathes of British industry. This was partly disguised by the boom economic conditions of the time but as soon as boom turned to recession and slump, questions started to be asked as to why Britain's economic performance lagged so markedly behind that of many of her competitors.

It was the comparatively sluggish economic performance of British industry even in the boom, the growing pressure on profitability, the poor record of investment in new technology and the level of industrial disputes, particularly of an unofficial nature, which made both Conservative and Labour governments start to ask whether legal changes could be effected to make the trade union leaders more responsible for keeping their members' demands, official and especially unofficial, within 'acceptable' bounds. The Donovan Report of 1968 and the subsequent White Paper *In Place of Strife* of 1969, both commissioned by a Labour Government, were the first official recognition that pressure was building up to single out trade unions activity as having a particularly harmful impact on the country's economic performance.

Translated into figures, in 1946 there had been a total of 2,205 strikes with 2.16 million working days lost. In 1950 there were 1,339 strikes and 1.39 million lost working days. In 1960 there were 3,116 strikes with 2.83 million days lost and in 1969 no less than 6.8 million working days lost. These figures paled into insignificance with the figures from the late 1970s, however. In 1977, 10.1 million days were lost and in 1979, 29.5 million. Within these raw figures there were some industries such as automotive engineering, the docks and mining with a particularly troubled record for industrial relations.

Blame the workers

In a world dominated by pro-capitalist ideas, it was easy to blame 'lazy' and 'greedy' workers, 'outdated restrictive practices', 'Luddite attitudes', 'power-crazed' trade unions and 'Communist' activists owing their loyalty to Moscow. The ideological thrust that sought to put the blame on the labour side of the industrial relations equation simply could not accept that there were concrete historical reasons for Britain's particular problems nor that an inescapable factor was the fundamental clash of interests between capital and labour which had, for a period, put labour in a relative position of strength. Even an orthodox economist would have to admit that when labour was scarce, its price was likely to be higher. The ideological hegemony of the time, however, singled out the trade unions to be demonised with the implication that if they were only put in their place, a miraculous revival of Britain's economic prospects would follow.

From the late 1960s there was a systematic campaign throughout the media to vilify organised labour. An impression was created that there was a relatively small number of activists with a sinister political agenda (Communists, Maoists and Trotskyists) who systematically exploited the gullibility of workers in order to disrupt industry and attempt to bring the capitalist economic system to its knees through strikes and go-slows. What form this campaign took and how it operated was the subject of a number of detailed studies by the Glasgow University Media Group in the late 1970s and early 1980s.[1] They showed how the perception became established that the trade unions had become too big for their boots and that it was in the 'national interest' that they should be cut down to size. We were told with unremitting regularity that trade unions were unpopular, that the closed shop was a tyranny, that Labour governments jumped to the tune of power-drunk union barons wielding their block votes at Party Conference, that workers downed tools and brought their workplaces to a halt for the most frivolous of reasons and that picketing was a threat to law and order and to those who did not want to strike because inevitably 'bully-boy' strikers enjoyed using physical threats and intimidation.

This vilification of and attempt to isolate trade unions served the additional useful purpose of being a stick with which to beat the Labour Party and the rest of the political left. It either ignored a number of realities or pretended that they did not exist. One was the sheer number of trade unionists. The membership of unions far exceeded that of any other organisations in the UK. The closed shop was one of the favourite targets of the union-baiters. This arrangement was by no means universal and even where it did exist, most union officials were prepared to make an exception for those workers who objected on moral or religious grounds to being a member of a trade union. Usually an agreement was reached whereby the worker concerned paid the amount of the union sub into an agreed charity or good cause. This did not prevent the media from regularly serving up scare stories about how people of sincere religious conviction were bullied against their conscience into joining a union. A massive silence was maintained about those working in closed shops who, while being allowed to waive their union subs in favour of charitable donations, then accepted the improvements in wages and conditions brought about by the collective bargaining power of the unions. An equally deafening silence drew a veil over the 'closed shops' that existed in the professions and which included such bodies as the Law Society and the British Medical Association. No exceptions on the grounds of conscience were allowed there.

It was alleged that because the affiliated trade unions provided the Labour Party with a majority of its funding, the senior union officials therefore dictated policy to the Parliamentary Party with the block votes they could muster at the annual Labour Party Conference. The leaders of the largest affiliated unions certainly had a major influence within the Labour Party as a whole but since the Second World War it was far more frequently a force for moderation than militancy.

Contrary to the impression that was being created, working people have never gone on strike simply for a whim. They have never wanted the hassle and have had too much to lose, particularly in terms of pay. Despite the strong emotions that may be involved, violence on picket lines between working and striking employees was rare and was much more likely to occur as a result of inept or provocative policing. However the editors and journalists who, day in and day out, presented this sort of material were not concerned about telling the truth or even about balance in their coverage. Most, although not, of course, all of them, were hostile to the trade unions and dismissive of the organised working class and thoroughly enjoyed pouring out this kind of material. In doing so, they were exercising the prerogative of the harlot, well known as being 'power without responsibility'.

The Labour Government 1964-9

Harold Wilson became leader of the Labour Party on the death of Hugh Gaitskell in 1963. Wilson, who had some left-wing credentials, assured the electorate that he intended to employ the latest scientific and technological know-how to set about solving Britain's economic problems but when his 'White Hot Technological Revolution' fizzled out, he cast round and then eagerly snatched at the emerging wisdom which was that the trade unions were to blame for Britain's stuttering economic performance.

Wilson had an on-off relationship with the trade unions and this was emphasised in 1966 when an initial six-month wage freeze was introduced in spite of the opposition of the TUC. As the economy continued its, at best, fitful, progress and increasing mistrust characterised government-union relations, Wilson appointed Barbara Castle to the new post of Secretary for Employment and Productivity in 1968 and gave her responsibility for incomes policy.

Soon afterwards, in June 1968, the Donovan Commission published its report. Donovan suggested that industrial relations, especially in large and complex companies, would be improved if collective bargaining was increasingly carried out at plant level by local management and elected representatives of the employees, i.e. shop stewards. The Commission did not recommend that a legal code be imposed and instead suggested the setting up of an advisory body to be known as the Industrial Relations Commission. To ensure that all employers recognised trade unions, the IRC could be given powers to enforce arbitration where collective bargaining arrangements did not exist.

The Donovan Report met with a lukewarm reception, not least from the trade union leaders who did not like the idea that their importance and influence might be diminished. It did not go far enough for the Conservatives. Nevertheless Barbara Castle went ahead and produced the White Paper, *In Place of Strife*, in January 1969. Much that was in the Donovan Report was simply ignored and the trade unions found the legislative proposals particularly provocative, not liking the idea that they would be required to register, might find their rights to strike threatened and would lose the voluntary basis on which they had operated for almost a century. There was no way that the trade unions as a whole were going to agree to any legislation based on the White Paper and they made that fact abundantly clear to the Cabinet. The Labour Party's electoral fortunes plummeted when it was widely seen as neither able to achieve significant growth in the economy nor deal effectively with the trade unions.

The Conservative Government 1970-4

A Conservative Government led by Edward Heath came to office in June 1970. The experience of the Labour Government's debacle with *In Place of Strife* convinced the incoming government that legislation on industrial relations was a must and the result was the passing in 1971 of the Industrial Relations Act. The National Industrial Relations Court was established and it had the power to adjudicate over most industrial disputes. It was empowered to advise the Secretary for State for Employment to impose a 'cooling-off period' in particularly contentious disputes and it could demand that the unions involved set up a ballot on strike action where it considered that a strike posed a serious threat to the economy. The NIRC could impose fines from £5,000 to £100,000, partly dependent on the number of their members, on unions that carried out what were construed as 'unfair industrial practices'. The so-called 'pre-entry' closed shop was outlawed and the 'post-entry' closed shop replaced by a system whereby a union could gain sole negotiating rights with the agreement of the employer or if it held a secret ballot in which it won the support of a majority of the workforce. Now, written collective agreements were enforceable by law unless they specifically indicated otherwise. A union could be prosecuted through the NIRC if it did not prevent a breach of any such agreement by its members.

Right from the start the Act was contentious not least because it was based on the premise that it was unofficial strikes that were the major bugbear in British industrial relations. There were many that disputed this assertion. It annoyed the full-time officials because it implied that they were failing to control shop floor militancy and it annoyed shop floor militants who did not believe that the job of the officials was to control them. The TUC held rallies against the Act and urged member unions not to register and to boycott the NIRC. The Labour Party pledged that it would repeal the Act when it returned to office. Although some unions did register and were subsequently expelled by the TUC in 1973, the vast majority of the unions, particularly the 'big guns', refused to comply with the new law as it stood.

Before long there was a strong element of farce as most unions did not register, the NIRC was simply ignored, cooling-off periods did not take the sting out of disputes and, when strike ballots were held, much to the chagrin of the Government, the members frequently supported their leaders' recommendations in favour of industrial action. When five dockworkers were arrested and gaoled in July 1972 for ignoring an instruction from the NIRC, the balloon went up. With a national dock strike being threatened, a hitherto largely unknown public servant, the Official Solicitor, suddenly appeared from nowhere and ordered the release of the 'Pentonville Five'. In doing so, he made a complete mockery of the Industrial Relations Act. By the end of 1972 the Act was virtually a dead duck and the number of days lost through industrial action escalated.

The Heath Government had already come under huge pressure when the miners launched a national strike in support of a wage claim early in 1972. To make the strike effective, the NUM revived a largely forgotten tactic. This was the use of flying pickets to try to prevent the movement of coal, particularly to power stations. They won a major symbolic and strategic victory when they effectively closed the Saltley Coke Depot at Birmingham. The Government was totally flummoxed and announced a state of emergency. Before long there were power cuts and a three-day working week to conserve energy. The miners won this confrontation and Heath's strategy to bring the unions to heel lay in total disarray. Heath's Tory Government went down to defeat in the general election in March 1974.

Labour in Office 1974-9

The incoming Labour Government looked positively businesslike by comparison with the utter shambles that had been Heath's government. Senior ministers and trade union leaders were in accord about the desirability of reducing the level of industrial action not least because of the country's continuing dismal economic performance. The Government came up with the idea of the 'Social Contract' which involved getting rid of the Tory's reforms and cordial rather than confrontational working relations with the unions around a voluntary incomes policy predicated on economic growth.

The Social Contract quickly broke down not simply for lack of goodwill but because of the harsh reality of raging price inflation combined with rapidly rising unemployment and a stagnant economy. The Labour Government went on to make large cuts in public spending, part of the price that was paid for a huge loan from the IMF and these cuts resulted in substantial job losses. The trade union leaders began to distance themselves from the Government as they came under pressure from their members angry about the reduced value of their wages. Even though most of the trade union chiefs were willing to support the Government's efforts, there was only so far they could go in trying to persuade their members to accept declining living standards. In the event the TUC in 1978 decided to return to free collective bargaining and to reject further wage restraint. Escalating strike action in the car industry, on the railways, by truck and tanker drivers and local authority workers culminated in what the media with malicious glee dubbed the 'Winter of Discontent'.

The wrath and scorn of the media knew no bounds when the Labour Party and TUC leaders failed to keep the rank-and-file of the unions under control during the period of the Wilson and Callaghan governments. The general election of 1979 brought Thatcher into office. She was able to exploit this ongoing media vendetta against the trade unions but gave it a new and characteristically even more acerbic edge. She seems to have viewed trade unions as one of the least desirable elements of life in a social democracy. Her husband, Denis, went on record saying that trade unions should be abolished. She considered them deeply undemocratic. In reality what could be more democratic than union members voting for a colleague to become a shop steward or workplace representative and that steward holding the position, unpaid, on the basis that he or she could be recalled if the members felt that the steward was no longer fighting effectively for their interests? Thatcher was only a champion of democracy when it suited her and always maintained a deafening silence on the undemocratic anomalies of the electoral system which served her up with three successive electoral victories despite in every case receiving a minority of the votes cast. The opportunities for ordinary people to have any real influence on the processes of political decision-making are strictly limited, even at election time. For most people they consist of voting every few years for a political party which, if it is elected, has little or no intention of implementing the promises it makes during the campaign. Unelected judges, senior civil servants, spin doctors, lobbyists, newspaper owners and editors, executives of multi-national corporations and organisations like the IMF are among those regularly and powerfully influencing the political process without being subjected to any kind of democratic criteria and control. Even the few democratic elements that do exist in the political system are precious. They had to be fought for and need to be defended but they only play a small part in the political decision-making processes of modern Britain.

To the old accusations which she took up and repeated enthusiastically, Thatcher added that the unions were to blame for low productivity, for over-manning and restrictive practices and, in the case of certain public sector workers, of exploiting the fact that their employers had a monopoly of the provision of goods and services in that sector – in other words that they were 'bully boys' holding the public to ransom. They were irresponsible and greedy. Leaving aside at this point whether there was any truth in these allegations, Thatcher was totally incapable of stopping to consider the fact that substantial numbers of stoppages in industry could be explained by poor or incompetent management decisions and/or problems with obsolete plant and equipment. Nor was she big enough as a person or generous enough of spirit to acknowledge that striking workers might actually have justified reasons for withdrawing their labour. Unemployment, Thatcher argued, was directly caused by trade unions and their 'excessive' wage demands not matched by improvements in productivity. As usual, Thatcher was inconsistent. She thought that greed was good when it came to businesses maximising their profits by whatever means, greed was good when citizens were persuaded to buy their own homes and become shareowners but greed was bad when it came to collective bargaining by trade unions for better wages and conditions.

Edging the unions out

Out went the old tripartite 'beer and sandwiches' way of doing things although it was not until 1987 that the trade union leaders were finally shown the door so far as participation in national policy-making on industrial relations was concerned. Thatcher had absolutely no time for the traditional type of 'give-and-take' in negotiations with the unions. The government's hope was that by strictly controlling the money supply and also declaring that it would not rescue 'lame duck' businesses, wage negotiations in the private sector would come to more 'responsible' conclusions. Responsibility in wage negotiations in the public sector could be induced through cash limits to the departments involved. If wage demands were deemed 'excessive' then workers would soon realise that there was a real danger that they would price themselves out of jobs.

Unemployment had its desired effect of inculcating insecurity among workers and of discouraging militancy. Trade union full-time officials became even more concerned to avoid industrial action, particularly any action that could be construed as illegal under new legislation specifically designed for that purpose. Failure to do so could threaten the continued existence of the union because of financial penalties. The National Graphical Association incurred four fines for contempt amounting to £675,000 and eventual sequestration of its funds before it called off its action (illegal under the 1980 Act mentioned below) against Eddie Shah's *Stockport Messenger* Group. Shah, it has to be said, was a willing stooge to take on the power of the print unions, using new legal powers brought in by the Tory government. The National Union of Mineworkers had to pay heavy fines and also suffered sequestration in the 1984-5 dispute. In 1986 the union SOGAT 82 was fined and then had its entire assets sequestrated because the courts upheld the claim that it had illegally disrupted the distribution of newspapers produced by Rupert Murdoch's New International Corporation. In 1985, Murdoch was busy attempting to destroy the power of the print unions in Fleet Street by moving his operations to Wapping and introducing the latest in labour-saving technology. He was ultimately successful but his tussle with the unions had enjoyed the full support of Thatcher and a friendship developed between the two – Murdoch being just the kind of man Thatcher greatly admired. As far
as Thatcher was concerned, it was perfectly acceptable for a multi-millionaire to control a media empire through which he was able to spread his own narrow values and use his considerable power to influence the political process. Ever willing to decry people such as Arthur Scargill for being unrepresentative, she did not bat an eyelid over the fact that Murdoch represented no one but himself and, unlike Scargill, had never had to submit himself to any kind of electoral process.

Thatcher's governments made considerable and highly astute use of new legislation to curtail the power of the trade unions. Between 1979 and 1990 eight acts were passed relating to various aspects of employment law. The 1980 Employment Act ruled that the only picketing that was now legal was that which involved members picketing their own place of work. Secondary picketing such as that witnessed at the Saltley Coke Depot was therefore now illegal, an 80 per cent ballot was required for a closed shop and public funds were made available for secret ballots on strike action. This Act was followed by another Employment Act in 1982. This outlawed the pre-entry closed shop and required an 85 per cent ballot for the establishment of a closed shop. These Acts ended the immunities from civil actions previously enjoyed by the unions and they now became liable for damages if they were held responsible for unlawful industrial action.

The Trade Union Act of 1984 provided legal immunities for trade unions only if they held secret ballots not more than four weeks before proposed industrial action. The Act made money available for executive elections which now became compulsory every five years and it also introduced ballots on political funds. Leaving aside the essential unfairness that the Government should home in on trade union funding for the Labour Party while ignoring the donations to Tory coffers from the potentially far deeper pockets of corporate and individual capitalists, this proved a case of biter bit. The Government's argument that most trade union members did not want to pay a political levy which might be used to support the Labour Party was made to look foolish when secret ballots in 1985 and 1986 decisively indicated the very opposite. All thirty-seven of the unions holding political funds ballotted their members and 83 per cent voted in favour of continuing to support the Labour Party. Needless to say, this crushing response did not make the Government think that they might have got things wrong.

The 1988 Employment Act made various minor changes on closed shops and the election of union officials while yet another Employment Act in 1989 tightened up rules about cases going to Industrial Tribunals, eased regulations about the employment of women and children, exempted employers with fewer than twenty staff from the requirement to include disciplinary procedures in contracts of employment, curtailed time off for training purposes for union lay officials and now required an employee to have two year's continuous service before being entitled to be given written reasons for dismissal. As if this was not enough, a further Employment Act, this time in 1990, returned to the attack and in particular emphasised the requirement that unions disassociate themselves from unofficial industrial action or face financial sanctions.

The Thatcher governments played a clever, calculated game on the issue of trade unions who now found that when they took industrial action, it was with both hands tied behind their backs – which was exactly as intended by the legislation. At all times in the war they were waging with the unions the governments drew on psychological weapons, delivered in politicians' speeches and statements and in their articles in papers and interviews on radio and television. Their denunciations of the trade unions as outdated, selfish, bloody-minded, undemocratic, unpopular, Luddite, even unpatriotic, were eagerly taken up and repeated a million times by the their sycophants and toadies who dominated the mass media. Although these words did not necessarily equate with the actual experience of millions of trade unionists, this wall-to-wall continuous hostility to trade union activity penetrated popular perceptions. If an idea is repeated enough times and presented as fact rather than opinion it gains force and plausibility. When this unremitting battering the unions received was combined with new laws which seemingly doomed industrial action to failure, even some good workplace activists began to believe that they did indeed belong to an isolated, archaic, out-of-touch and unpopular minority and that all they held dear and had fought for was doomed never to be achieved.

At the same time that it was manufacturing this hostile climate of anti-trade union opinion, the first and second Thatcher governments pursued what appeared to be a 'hands-off' policy of not getting directly involved even when there were industrial disputes in the public sector. Superficially, they kept their distance during disputes at British Leyland, British Steel and British Rail, for example. They did not even intervene when the water-workers in 1983 and the miners in 1981 obtained significant concessions without recourse to actual strike action. The Miners' Strike of 1984-5 was largely presented as a dispute between the NUM and the NCB. Where the law was invoked, it was mainly NUM members taking action against their union for allegedly breaking its own rules by not holding a national pre-strike ballot or private businesses claiming damage to trade as a result of the strike. It would be naïve to suppose that they did this entirely off their own bats and that their efforts went unrewarded. This 'hands-off' approach was an illusion. Thatcher and Co had set the parameters for the employers' side in these strikes and they were deeply, if covertly, involved.

Back in the eighteenth century, in his seminal work *The Wealth of Nations*, Adam Smith, the Scottish economist regarded as something of an icon by the pro-capitalist economists of the late twentieth century, had shown that he had a very clear understanding of the basic nature of the class struggle in industrial society. He explained:

What are the common wages of labour, depends everywhere upon the contract usually made between the two parties, whose interests are by no means the same. The workmen desire to get as much as much as possible, the masters to give as little as possible. The former are disposed to combine in order to raise, the latter in order to lower the wages of labour.

Maybe Thatcher read Adam Smith, maybe not. She was, however, well aware of the fundamental clash of interests of capital and labour and she was determined that the interest of capital should prevail.

Trade Unions of the back foot

The trade unions took a frightful battering in these years. Their ability to defend and develop their members' interests was seriously reduced and they lost membership although of course economic and industrial change also contributed considerably to this process. The power of shop stewards and workers' elected representatives declined. It did not help that the leadership both of the Labour Party and of the trade unions seemed incapable of countering the anti-union mood and almost appeared inclined tacitly to accept the truth of the misleading and mendacious propaganda about unions that was being systematically circulated. They should have explained that the Tories' anti-union measures were an integral part of an attempt, hopeless in anything other than the short-term, to restore the fortunes of British capitalism by transferring wealth from the poor to the rich and that the trade unions had the potential power to prevent this process or at least slow it down. Had they put a bold alternative they might have been able to minimise the damage to themselves and to wider society. However, their habits of deference to 'public opinion', i.e. the hostile media, ran deep. They were desperate to appear 'moderate' and 'respectable' but, predictably, when this is their priority, they simply managed to appear weak. The British ruling class can sniff out weakness among the workers' leaders with unerring accuracy and rightly has nothing but contempt for it. Too many workers' leaders thought that Thatcher had won all the arguments and was impregnable. Their gutlessness meant that she was allowed to get away with it.

The unions were then systematically excluded from the official bodies that made and executed economic and industrial relations policy. Union membership fell from over 13 million in 1979 to 10 million in 1986 and losses were particularly heavy in the declining manufacturing industries. The movement was sorely wounded but, happily, not destroyed. The outcome, however, was the most repressive set of laws regarding trade union activity in the western world and it is a total disgrace that Labour Governments under Blair and Brown left this body of legislation intact.

Thatcher's governments made it clear that their ideal was either union-free companies and industries, or single-company unions, with no-strike agreements. Some idea of what they had in mind for industrial relations could be seen by the kind of 'sweetheart' agreements negotiated by Japanese companies like Nissan when starting up operations in this country. It was hoped that these tactics would buy the loyalty of workers who would lay aside for ever old-fashioned ideas of class confrontation and class solidarity, of 'us and them' in industry. With their mortgages and their shares in privatised industry, a new type of worker would be created, each one a stakeholder in capitalist society and, growing ever more prosperous, they would be wholly committed to helping to make capitalism itself prosperous. The Tories who came up with this perspective must have been gratified when their sentiments were repeated by the leaders of unions like the EETPU and AUEW with their talk of 'new realism', a blessed state where the lion and the lamb would lie down together in mental, spiritual and physical harmony and for mutual benefit. 'New Realism' was neither new nor was it realistic. It was tired, discredited old class collaboration and subordination of the interests of labour to those of capital.

Wisely, the Tories decided against attempting to administer a final, fatal blow to the trade unions, much as many of them would have liked to do. They abolished wage councils and minimum wage legislation and moved against the closed shop. They encouraged the use of part-time and casual labour often provided through agencies as a deliberate means of undermining the bargaining power of established unions. Wise heads in government circles (and there were some) clearly thought it prudent not to provoke the unions too far, knowing that even with leaders of the sort just mentioned, they were still potentially a formidable force.

Thatcher's tactics against the unions have to be judged a success from her standpoint. A peak of 4,583 industrial stoppages was reached in 1979. In 1984 that number had fallen to 1,221, resulting in the loss of 27 million working days, a large percentage being as a result of the miner's strike. The number of stoppages fell away dramatically from 1985. In 1990 there were just 630 stoppages with less than two million working days lost and the fall continued through the 1990s. By the time Thatcher left office trade union membership had fallen below 10 million although organic changes in the nature of the economy and of employment explain a substantial part of this loss.

The fight of the Tories to cow the trade unions by emasculating their most powerful wing in the miners was class warfare at its most naked. The results are still felt today. 25 'unprofitable' pits were closed in 1985 and by the end of 1992 a total of 97 had closed.

Those that were left were privatised in 1994 with the terms and conditions of the remaining workforce greatly reduced as indeed were their numbers. Eventually a total of 150 pits were closed and not all of these had been unprofitable. Huge numbers of jobs were lost in mining and associated industries and entire communities virtually destroyed. Such was the bitterness that was created during the strike of 1984-5 that there are still people in the mining districts who have been dancing in the streets when they hear that Thatcher has died.

The productivity of British industry increased as the rate of exploitation of labour intensified. Foreign companies began to see the UK as an attractive place in which to establish new business activities because the British economy could offer a flexible workforce. Not flexible enough, however. In their perennial search for profit many employers have closed or scaled down their operations in the UK and transferred them overseas, particularly to the Asian sub-continent where labour is even cheaper.

1. For example, Philo, G. Hewitt, J. et al, (1982), *Really Bad News,* London.

12. THATCHER AND FOREIGN POLICY

A Greater Role in the World for Britain

Margaret Thatcher sought to restore Britain to the prominent role in international affairs that she had once enjoyed. The Tory Party manifesto for the 1979 election had talked about the aim of 'a strong Britain in a free world'. No one stopped to define 'free'. Although it was an inescapable fact that Britain had lost her once enormous and prestigious empire, Thatcher, like other post-war prime ministers, wanted Britain to continue to play the role of a member at least at the top of the second division of world powers. This, she believed, could be achieved through membership of NATO, through a close and 'special' relationship with the USA, by the possession of an independent nuclear deterrent and, more questionably, membership of the EEC. Playing at the top end of the second division of world diplomatic powers only made sense if the role was underpinned by also being at the top of the second division of world economic powers. It could be argued that Britain in the 1980s was overstretching herself in international diplomatic circles because her relative economic decline meant that she no longer had the financial resources to sustain the military capability that was required for such a role. The expense of maintaining a leading international role and the defence system to go with it could possibly have been put to better use by investment in productive industry.

What were the foreign policy issues likely to face the Thatcher government which took office in 1979? First was the perceived threat from the build-up of conventional and nuclear weapons by the Communist bloc. Thatcher saw herself leading a crusade against what she saw as the expansionist aims of Communism. Second was doing something about the dog's breakfast which British politicians had managed to make in attempting to advocate Britain's interests in the European Community. Third was the situation in what was then Rhodesia where an illegal regime was in power and the country was being wracked by a bloody civil war.

Sub-plots to this were the need to establish exactly what was the role that Britain could play in the international power games that masqueraded as diplomacy and foreign affairs? Her rank as an economic power had diminished relatively so where did that leave her international standing in the 1980s? Did Mrs Thatcher, never seemingly short of self-confidence and a sense of patriotism, think that through the medium of her forceful personality and a revived economy Britain could resume a position towards the very top of the league table of world powers?

Even before she came to office, Thatcher made clear the high priority that she accorded to defence and that she viewed it as a major aspect of foreign policy. She also made it clear that cuts in public spending most definitely did not include reducing expenditure on defence. In becoming known in international circles, she had of course gained the nickname 'The Iron Lady' and she proudly declaimed to anyone who would listen that she was not going to be 'pushed around'. However it was one thing for her to chuck her weight around in the UK where there was an enfeebled opposition and quite another to do in international affairs where there was a good chance that she would come up against someone genuinely tough representing a country with a stronger and healthier economic base.

Every Government wants an Enemy

It is always handy for a government to have enemies overseas. It helps to divert attention away from internal problems and keep people feeling insecure. It is not necessary that the 'enemy' should actually be engaged in hostilities. In fact a threat can be manufactured and proclaimed which is all that is needed for an enemy to exist. Thatcher found her 'enemy without' in the so-called 'Communist' countries of the Soviet bloc. In reality the Communist bloc was almost certainly less aggressively imperialistic than the USA but that mattered little to Thatcher because it was the social and economic system pertaining in these countries that was her real object of hate. They had socialised, planned economies which may not have been functioning very efficiently but while they existed they posed an alternative model to capitalist private ownership. Thatcher made it clear that in her opinion a strong defence policy was the only answer to possible Soviet aggression. Her hawkish attitude towards Russia put her rather out on a limb among European nations at the time. Presumably she never stopped to ask what she thought would induce the Soviets to attack the UK, unless it was because American Cruise Missiles were based here. There were of course parts of the country highly dependent on the maintenance of a strong defence system. Very large numbers of workers are employed in the so-called 'defence' industries. Socialists would argue that the considerable engineering and other skills involved should be diverted into the making of articles that served useful social purposes. No wealth is created and vast amounts of taxpayer's money is spent building an aircraft carrier which is obsolete before it is even launched and whose aircraft might possibly never fire a missile in anger. Arguments about how viable different kinds of weaponry are as deterrents to war will undoubtedly also continue.

Thatcher's views on the so-called 'Communist' states were summed up in a speech in 1990:

> As we peel back the moral squalor of the socialist regimes in Eastern Europe we discover the natural and physical squalor underneath. They exploited nature every bit as ruthlessly as they exploited the people. In their departure, they have left her choking amidst effluent, acid rain and industrial waste.[1]

The pot should not call the kettle black.

A Puppy Dog to US Imperialism

Very early on in her first premiership, Thatcher made it clear that she valued the UK's relationship with the USA more highly than any relationship she might have with the European Community or any countries in it. When the Russians invaded Afghanistan in December 1979, there was an immediate cooling of the already not very cordial relations between the USA and the USSR. The Americans then self-righteously boycotted the Moscow Olympics. With breathtaking double standards, the USA ignored recent aspects of its own foreign policy. We need only cite the cynical US support for the Kurds in Iraq in 1972 followed by the abrupt abandonment of the Kurds to their fate in 1975 and the deaths of several hundreds of their leaders. Before 1974 the US had supported a fascist regime in Portugal until it fell in a bloodless military coup. Systematic subversion by the US of the radical regime in Portugal brought the latter down in 1976 and a CIA-backed regime took over. One more example will suffice to provide an inkling of the extent of the USA's criminal international activity around this time. In 1975 Indonesia invaded East Timor, at that time moving towards independence under a leftist regime. With American diplomatic backing and military hardware, Indonesia invaded and soon overwhelmed East Timor. Amnesty International estimated that by 1989, Indonesian forces had killed some 200,000 people, possibly as much as a third of the East Timor population and the American stooge as Indonesia's ruler, President Suharto, had become distinguished as a mass murderer, bloody even by twentieth-century standards. Thatcher, as a self-proclaimed champion of 'freedom' seems not to have raised one word in protest or criticism when these events occurred, or since. But then double standards always did come easily to Thatcher.

Grenada is a small island, the most southerly of the Windward Islands archipelago. It has a population of around 100,000, little in the way of valuable natural resources and it lies about 100 miles north of Venezuela. A left-wing group had seized power in 1979 only to be ousted by a far more revolutionary grouping in 1983. This coup caused the USA to invade the island shortly afterwards claiming the action as part of their worldwide anti-Communist crusade and in order to prevent the establishment of 'another Cuba'. A full-scale combined operation was launched, resistance was swept aside and the mechanism put in place for a return to constitutional government. Lest any reader cannot believe what is written here, yes, the Americans actually set in motion a return to political legitimacy! Their international interventions frequently overthrow legitimate, democratically-elected governments but it is important to remember that despite what it says, the USA is pragmatic and does not worship democracy per se. It has no particular preference for democratic over totalitarian regimes. Its criterion is whether or not a regime is favourably disposed to the interests of American imperialism. Without turning a hair they will trade with a friendly tyrant even if he is known to be guilty of genocide. However, those regimes that are of a left-wing persuasion, especially if they enjoy popular support, are automatically seen as potentially posing a serious threat.

The heavy-handed action by the USA was immediately condemned by the United Nations as 'a flagrant violation of international law' and similarly by a number of countries with varying political regimes right across the world. The incumbent of the White House at the time was Ronald Reagan with whom Thatcher always claimed she enjoyed a special, close relationship and common purpose. Just after midnight on the day of the invasion, Thatcher contacted Reagan and expressed some concern that an action she claimed she had not known about was being contemplated. Her particular worry was that it was ill-timed coming as it did when there was a row about the location of US Cruise Missiles on British soil. She said that she hoped he would do nothing 'irrevocable'. When she phoned him again twenty minutes later, she was assured by the President that he was not actually contemplating such an invasion. He was being less than frank. He had given the orders and the invasion had already started.

Thatcher seemed remarkably tolerant about this little bit of deceit but then her 'special relationship' with Reagan was very much as a junior partner, to be used or ignored depending on the needs of American imperialism. She had hitched her small British trailer behind his big American tractor and it was he who was most assuredly in the driving seat. He was one of a number of men who she seemed to hold in awe. This subordinate relationship with the USA hardly accorded with her mission of making Britain great again. The USA was infinitely richer and more powerful than the UK and it was going to make certain that any 'special relationship' was first and foremost to America's advantage. Did she not realise that? The real depth of this 'special' relationship is suggested by a poll conducted among young US adults. For the purposes of the poll, a blank map of the world was put in front of the respondents. 65 per cent of them could not place the British Isles anywhere near its correct position and some even put them in the Southern Hemisphere!

The easy-going and low-key concern that Thatcher raised about the invasion of Grenada which, after all, was an independent sovereign member of the Commonwealth, compares starkly with her all-consuming wrath when General Galtieri gave the order for Argentine armed forces to invade the Falkland Islands. There was no political capital to be made by a stand on the former. There was a forthcoming general election to win by giving the Argentine armed forces a good drubbing.

That pugnacious old street-fighter, Denis Healey, who, incidentally, the Tories were very glad did not become Leader of the Labour Party, was quick to point out that the Grenada invasion was not the only occasion on which Thatcher had allowed Reagan to walk all over her. In 1986, the USA drew up plans, illegal under international law, to bomb Tripoli in retaliation for a number of terrorist outrages which they claimed had been authorised by Colonel Gaddafi. France and Spain refused permission for American F-111s to fly over their territory but Thatcher, without reference to the Cabinet, decided to allow these planes to operate from bases in Britain. This decision made the UK very unpopular in European circles but Thatcher justified it on the grounds that it had resulted in a marked decline in terrorist activity attributed to Libya As usual, Thatcher got it wrong. In 1989 a US airliner was blown up over Lockerbie in Scotland killing 289 people in the worst terrorist atrocity of the 1980s. A Libyan was convicted for the offence.

Thatcher stood wholeheartedly for Britain possessing nuclear weapons. She believed, as did many others, that they were a deterrent to war but for her they had another purpose. They were a symbol of national pride and power. In 1983 she chose to renew that deterrent by purchasing the American Trident system but doing Britain down because the US made it clear that they would not allow use of the system without their consent. So much for an *independent* deterrent. The French were far more clever. Their nuclear capacity was tailored to their very specific needs and they did not to go, cap in hand, to the US to ask if they could use it. The boot was on the other foot when Cruise missiles were installed on British soil. The Americans didn't have to ask Britain's political leaders whether they could use them.

The world economy made a recovery after 1981. Although undoubtedly Thatcher would have liked to claim the credit for this, it was a generalised recovery, partly the result of reflationary policies originating in the USA which in turn kick-started demand across the world. Recovery turned into boom as governments, looking as if they were drinking in the last chance saloon, recklessly ran up massive budget and trade deficits. The boom was unsustainable and it collapsed with the financial crash in October 1987. Autarky was not an option for any national government, not even one under Thatcher, and it was impossible to avoid becoming entangled in the travails of international capitalism.

Britain continued to move along subserviently in the slipstream of American imperialism, hardly the role of a 'Great' Britain. It was the previous Labour administration which had agreed to Cruise Missiles being installed on British soil. Thatcher fought a major propaganda war with the peace movement and the other organisations and individuals who were unhappy to see Britain being used by the Americans as something akin to an aircraft carrier permanently moored off the north-west coast of Europe. People were indignant that these missiles were being installed, almost certainly against the wishes of the majority of the population, and were obviously making the UK a prime target in the event of hostilities with Russia. It made people feel extremely vulnerable and it was widely felt that British politicians and especially Thatcher, were being cynically manipulated by the Americans for their own advantage. Thatcherite propaganda homed in on the demonstrators at Greenham Common and Molesworth and depicted them as Soviet sympathisers, as social security scroungers and wasters living in squalid encampments who wouldn't be given the freedom to protest in this way if they lived in Russia, etc, etc

Speaking of Russia, Thatcher thought that in Michael Gorbachev she had found a Russian leader with whom she could do business. She was jubilant about the end of the Cold War and the collapse of the Soviet bloc. For her this was the triumph of capitalism and the victory of good over evil. The reality is that it led to the spread of the most decadent forms of modern capitalism to one of the few areas of the world from which they had previously been excluded. The undemocratic and inefficient bureaucracies of the so-called 'Communist' countries had little going for them but the extension of the 'free market' to embrace their economies was certainly a retrograde development.
She would have liked to take the credit for the extension of market-driven capitalism to Russia, Eastern Europe and even China but the processes which caused this to happen were far bigger than her.

The Westland Affair

Thatcher's determination to do nothing to antagonise the Americans was evident in the Westland Affair in 1985-6. Westland was a smallish but long-standing British company manufacturing helicopters. It was in financial trouble and was the object of a takeover bid by the American helicopter giant, Sikorsky. This was a complicated situation because the board of Westland favoured this bid. However, Michael Heseltine, the Defence Secretary, finding no prospective British buyer, wanted to keep the company's operations at least under European ownership. Against Thatcher's expressed wishes, a consortium of European countries brought together by Heseltine then came up with a bid. Thatcher was determined that Sikorsky was to be the preferred bidder but she and Leon Brittan who was her errand boy, and , as it turned out, fall guy, wanted to assure the partners in the European consortium that they would still be able to bid for British helicopter business. Thatcher won this tussle. Sikorsky got Westland and Heseltine got the hump, resigning shortly afterwards. There may have been more to this than meets the eye because Heseltine was one of the more powerful senior Tory figures and a possible rival for the party leadership. It is likely that Thatcher was glad to see the back of him. He came back later, to deal her a lethal blow.

One result of the Westland affair was to show the way in which the Conservative Party and corporate finance had become integrated. For example, support for the Sikorsky bid came from Hanson Trust and News International, the owners of both being close to Thatcher. Batting on behalf of Westland and the European consortium was GEC. Power games for financial stakes almost incomprehensible to those not involved were being played. Leading figures in earlier Thatcher cabinets such as John Nott and James Prior were involved in the negotiations. They had left politics for even more lucrative posts in the City and the whole business smacked of insider information, cronyism and political patronage.

The details of the affair and the cover-up need not be repeated. Thatcher came out of the affair very badly. She was shown to be incapable of controlling the forceful Heseltine, in Cabinet and elsewhere; the concept of cabinet collective responsibility publicly collapsed; the charitably-inclined would say that Thatcher was economical with the truth when speaking about the matter in the House and she dropped her hapless colleague, Leon Brittan, right in it when he was forced to carry the can for measures taken on her initiative. She survived but it was a close run thing and she largely had Neil Kinnock to thank. He made a complete pig's ear of attacking her in the House. She had been visibly floundering, speaking without confidence and conviction but Kinnock's answering speech was so ineffectual that Thatcher seized her chance, picked herself up and went on the attack once more. Nevertheless her authority was seriously dented and she was clearly on a downward trajectory. Her MPs were becoming increasingly disillusioned with her leadership. Whereas her combative style had once been seen as an asset, now they wanted a more consensual leader. The affair made it very evident that she was as devious as any other senior politician and not fussy as to whom she made scapegoats of so long as she covered her own backside.

Thatcher in Europe

Thatcher was criticised in some circles for concentrating on Britain's relationship with the USA and neglecting those with Europe on the grounds that America's day of unchallenged economic and financial hegemony were over. It followed, therefore, that Britain's interests would have been better served by seeking more cordial relationships with Europe which was where Britain did so much of her international business. She was convinced that West Germany and Europe between them were conspiring to put Britain down but it has to be said that there was very little in her dealings with them which gave them any cause to warm either to her or to British interests. All too often her partners in Europe saw Thatcher as aggressive, xenophobic, bloody-minded and always seeking to throw her weight around. She wore 'The Iron Lady' nickname as a badge of pride but was referred to as 'A Paper Tigress' by Tony Benn when she returned empty-handed from the Dublin Summit in 1980 after having promised to win a rebate on Britain's contribution to the EC budget. It was as if Britain's memories of her former grandeur had trapped Thatcher in an outdated attitude unable to accept the nation no longer had the power and prestige it had once enjoyed. Such an attitude would explain much including her later reluctance to join the European

Monetary System.

Those who closely scrutinised Thatcher's political attitudes over the years saw her do two significant turns on the issue of 'Europe'. As a Cabinet newcomer under Heath in 1970-4 and as the Tory Party leader at the time of the 1975 referendum, she loyally upheld the official Heath-inspired 'pro-European' line. She was not part of Heath's cabal of close associates who were fully aware that the ultimate purpose of the Community was to work towards full political and economic integration. This group knew that it was wise to keep this aim out of the political debate if possible because it was likely to be highly contentious. Therefore they cynically concentrated on all the supposed economic advantages that would follow from joining this enlarged market. It is extremely unlikely that Thatcher was totally unaware of the full implications of membership of the EEC. However as Tory Leader she fronted the campaign for a 'Yes' vote in the 1975 referendum, loftily dismissing claims that the Community was excessively bureaucratic or that membership would swamp national traditions and culture.

This uncritical stance changed when Thatcher became Prime Minister in 1979. By this time concern was widespread about the UK's disproportionate contribution to the EC budget. This dated back to the Luxembourg Treaty of 1970 and reflected France's strong position in the Common Market where she had astutely manoeuvred the Common Agricultural Policy to be basically a subsidy from the other member-states to the French farming industry. Britain's seemingly excessive contribution was because she imported more goods from outside the Community than any other member and import duties were regarded as a resource to be put at the disposal of the Community.

Time and time again she hectored and harangued her colleagues in the European Council on this and other issues. Naturally they found this immensely irritating. On one occasion President Schmidt of West Germany ostentatiously pretended to sleep during one of her rants while on another President Giscard d'Estaing showed his distaste by having his motorcade noisily revving up outside while she was speaking. Thatcher, however, was nothing if not persistent and her war of attrition eventually exhausted the opposition and Britain obtained a rebate at the Fontainebleau Council in 1984. This was by no means the triumph that Thatcher and her supporters claimed at the time because later rule changes pushed through by the French meant that if the UK received extra discretionary funding for any particular project, the rebate would be reduced proportionately.

For all her bombast, Thatcher was frequently outmanoeuvred by her European partners. She preened herself on her 'success' at Fontainebleau and went on to voice her enthusiasm for the 'European project'. She envisaged Britain playing a significant, even a leading role in a Community dedicated to free enterprise. This was not, however, how some of Britain's European partners saw her role and it is clear that Thatcher could not or would not really comprehend what the 'project' was really about, which was ultimate political and economic integration and a single currency. Moves were afoot on the process leading to the Single European Act of 1986 and the Maastricht Treaty on European unity. The reality of what was going on seemed to pass Thatcher by even though it was not exactly done by stealth. She actually sat in a Council meeting and did not demur when a proposal for a Community flag, anthem, common driving licence and health card and other measures building towards a 'common European identity' went through on the nod. Had she dozed off?

She did eventually realise the nature and enormity of the 'project' and just how much sovereignty the UK was going to lose. Having been wrong-footed, and attempting to gloss over her inadequacies, she spoke publicly about the project being little more than the single market, something she still espoused with enthusiasm. It was nothing of the sort and soon Britain soon found itself being bombarded by a mass of EC directives. The business community in particular was squealing and Thatcher was propelled into a new hostile but essentially reactive stance and one of loathing for just about everything European which she did little to hide. By now she had come round to the belief that the resources Britain was required to put into Europe far outweighed whatever benefits she gained from being part of the community. Her new position soon led her into conflict with her sidekick Nigel Lawson, the former Eurosceptic who was a surprise conversion to the view that Britain should join the Exchange Rate Mechanism. He had formed the opinion that tying the value of the pound to that of the strong Deutschmark would assist the fight against inflation. Soon she also fell out with the long-suffering Geoffrey Howe on the European issue. There were other issues with these two ministers and even at the time, some political observers were saying that Thatcher was beginning to lose it. She also found herself becoming increasingly irritated by the French socialist President Delors who made no secret of his intentions to make the Community a vehicle for social reform including a significant extension of workers' rights. Many of the provisions of the EEC's social charter, such as minimum wages, participation for workers in management decisions and widened social provision were anathema to Thatcher and the New Right.

There were some surface signs that the British economy was reviving and after she won her third election in 1987 she got a bit carried away. Encouraged also by what looked like the imminent collapse of the Soviet system in Eastern Europe, she became increasingly bullish about the European Community which she began to characterise as an expensive, bureaucratic and statist monster. At Bruges in September 1988 she delivered a speech castigating the European Community and no one could have been left in doubt as to where she stood. She said, "We have not successfully rolled back the frontiers of the state in Britain, only to see them resumed at a European level, with a European super-state exercising a new dominance from Brussels." As so often happened with Thatcher, what she said was a contradiction of reality. Enormously pleased with herself for having rolled back the frontiers of the British state, when she had actually done the very opposite, she then vented her spleen on the European Community for what she saw as its attempt to impose corporatism on the member countries including Britain. The belligerent tone she adopted in the speech was typical but as so often happened, she was stronger on rhetoric than content. She was concerned about British sovereignty but her speech lacked any concrete proposals for change and only served to rub most of her audience up the wrong way.

By now Thatcher had most definitely lost it. Her former close associates Lawson and Howe had wandered off, disgruntled, into the setting sun and been replaced by the virtually unknown John Major and the avid Europhile Douglas Hurd while the economic 'miracle' was beginning to look like something else after Lawson's parting shot of raising interest rates to 15 per cent.

With insensitivity and ignorance in equal measure, Thatcher chose the bicentennial celebrations of the French Revolution in July 1989 to give the French a lecture on liberty and how much better Britain's record in that department was than that of France. To support her argument she proudly cited Magna Carta despite the fact that it explicitly excluded virtually the entire population from access to even minimum rights on the grounds that were not 'free men'. Small wonder that Thatcher's European counterparts found her immensely irritating, negative and impossible to take seriously. She alone seemed oblivious to this.

In 1990 Delors was going in for the kill on the launch of economic and monetary union and what were euphemistically called 'institutional questions'. Thatcher had few friends and little good will to draw on and found herself, for all her bluster, defeated and with little alternative but to agree to Britain joining the ERM. Her enemies on the Government benches in the Commons of whom there were increasing numbers, were jubilant about her humiliation and her days as Tory Leader and Prime Minister numbered less than ten. Her fall from the dizzy heights was spectacularly rapid.

In a career marred by innumerable blunders and any number of lucky breaks, it was the issues around Europe that made a large contribution to her fall. It would not be unfair to say that Thatcher did not like the European Community, did not like Europeans and did not like their languages, their cultures and their ways of doing things. Thatcher managed to create the impression in Europe that the British were uncooperative and xenophobic, just like their Prime Minister, and this did damage to Britain's relations with her European partners that Thatcher's successors had to work hard to try to put right. As George Urban put it: *…she let it be known that she was speaking for the robust no-nonsense instincts of the great British public, and no continental politician was going to tell her what to think or do.*[2]

The Falklands War is covered elsewhere but for all that Thatcher thought it put her on the world map as a gung-ho leader of strength and determination, the resolution of the conflict in Britain's favour was dependent in US and NATO support and it demonstrated that Britain was no longer strong enough to maintain defence commitments in Europe and the South Atlantic alongside the ability to intervene elsewhere in the world. The realisation of this changed order of things may account for the lack of fuss when agreement was made in December 1984 to hand the economically far more important Hong Kong back to China in 1997.

Sales of Arms

Thatcher's attitude to arms sales was totally unprincipled. In January 1981 she chaired a sub-committee of the Cabinet which decided unilaterally on a highly flexible reinterpretation of the Anglo-American ban on exporting arms to either side in the Iran-Iraq War. Soon afterwards the arms trade subsidiary of the Ministry of Defence was building an integrated weapons complex in Basra and over the ensuing years the 'defence allocation' to Iraq grew, incurring debts of billions of £'s which have never been repaid. It clearly did not matter one iota to Thatcher that Saddam Hussein turned his murderous attentions to slaughtering the Kurds in Iraq using arms sold to him by British companies. In 1993 when giving evidence to the Scott Inquiry, Thatcher pretended that she knew very little about arms sales to Iraq, despite it being international knowledge that encouraging the defence industry to export was a major interest of hers. Not only was she fascinated by military hardware but she had a soft spot for senior officers in full uniform.

Just as morally indefensible were the sales of arms to the likes of King Hussein of Jordan,

President Suharto of Indonesia and General Pinochet of Chile. These deals seem to have been carried through largely on her personal initiative and to have remained surrounded by secrecy. It appears that some arms deals were more for political than business reasons. Credit terms were arranged but the UK never received payment for some transactions.

She was an unashamed admirer of the weapons industry and for an outsider she developed an extremely deep knowledge of the technical specifications and capabilities of different types of weapons systems. Her overseas missions served several purposes. The selling of weaponry to friendly regimes was a way of combating what she saw as Communism's expansionist intentions, as a way of helping British industry and a quid pro quo where foreign aid was concerned because aid might be conditional on agreement to purchase British arms. A small number of favoured companies obtained the lion's share of arms contracts and significantly they tended to be major contributors to Tory Party funds.

Thatcher was not averse to doing deals without consulting those who should have been her political nearest and dearest. For example she clinched a deal to sell military equipment to Saddam Hussein in contravention of her own government's policy. This resulted in blushes all round in 1990 when Saddam invaded Kuwait and Britain found itself engaged in hostilities with a country it had just been helping to arm. Now there were similarities with the Falklands War as Thatcher barnstormed around execrating the actions of her former blue-eyed boy, Saddam Hussein. Another parallel with the Falklands was that Thatcher was once again looking for a diversion from the huge unpopularity of the poll tax and the rising rate of inflation. For all this, she remarkably continued to argue with some passion that a free trade in armaments promoted peace, not war.

Unaccountability and lack of transparency also characterised Thatcher's use of the foreign aid budget. An example was the financing of the Pergau Dam and hydro-electric scheme in Malaysia in return for which agreement was reached that the Malaysians would buy British military hardware. This deal was eventually ruled to be illegal and £65 million had to be returned to the Treasury by which time Thatcher had long since gone. There were, however, allegations of corruption about how public money had been given to the British consortium closely involved with the whole project. Certainly the aid budget was used to finance lucrative projects for British firms such as Balfour Beatty, BICC and GEC who showed their gratitude with generous donations to the Conservative Party.

Double standards were the order of the day in Thatcher's attitude to Israel. She saw Israel as an island of civilised values in a chaotic, shifting sea of hostile Arab nations with very different values and cultures. She denounced the use of terrorism by the PLO but the state of Israel had been founded on the back of terrorist tactics in the late 1940s. Although she frequently claimed that the law was inviolable, typically she failed to denounce the Israeli seizure of Palestinian territory by force in 1967 and its subsequent continuing occupation in flagrant defiance of international law.

South Africa and Rhodesia

South Africa and Rhodesia were white-supremacist regimes based on excluding the majority black populations from access to all important areas of decision-making. The British Empire had also been based on the idea of white or, more specifically, British white supremacy. The racial and cultural attitudes that went with the existence of that empire were deeply-rooted and by no means defunct in Britain in the fourth quarter of the twentieth century. Thatcher's sympathies were very much with the white inhabitants of these states. She had no sympathy for the liberation struggles that were taking place in various African countries and she thought that the leaders of such struggles tended to be terrorists and Communist stooges. She memorably described Nelson Mandela as a 'terrorist'. She admired the old Empire. She was far less enamoured of the Commonwealth.

Although economic sanctions had earlier been imposed on both countries, there were many in the Tory Party at all levels who thought the sanctions should be lifted, and were happy to say so. Thatcher was among them. She thought that the sanctions showed double standards because if economic sanctions were going to be used in an attempt to bring about political change, then there were many other repressive regimes elsewhere which should also have been subjected to them. In one sense this was perfectly true but it was nothing other than sheer unabashed hypocrisy on Thatcher's part because she was perfectly happy for Britain to be on friendly terms with all manner of grotesque totalitarian regimes across the world and to trade with them, making something of a speciality of selling weapons and the materiel of war. Not content with this glaring contradiction, she upped the stakes in bare-faced hypocrisy by stating that the sanctions were also misguided because they were causing economic hardship among the black populations of both countries. Since when did Thatcher have the slightest concern about policies that caused economic hardship to ordinary people? She lost no sleep when, for example, she applied such policies in the mining and iron and steel-manufacturing areas of Britain, encouraging the massive loss of jobs and destruction of entire communities while simultaneously making life more difficult for the vast number of benefit claimants created by the policies of her governments.

Controversially, Thatcher made a point of meeting President Botha when he made a private visit to Britain in 1984. The later President of South Africa, De Klerk, was much more of a realist so far as the future of the Republic was concerned. Thatcher managed to establish a dialogue with him which meant that she was able to extract rather more credit from her dealings with South Africa than she deserved. She remained contemptuous of foreigners. Whites of British origin were top of the food chain. Native Africans were much lower. Thatcher was a 'Little Englander'. When push came to shove, she did not like foreigners, she did not like those who spoke foreign languages and she didn't like being abroad, unless perhaps it was visiting Ronald Reagan during his Presidency. She unashamedly toadied up to him and, anyway, he spoke English as his first language. She lacked the social graces and small talk necessary for oiling the wheels of informal diplomacy. In more formal situations she could act like a bull in a china shop. Her record in international diplomacy was seriously marred. It is no coincidence that she was more popular around the world than she was at home – after all, they didn't have to put up with her on a daily basis. She stood out as an immaculately presented woman among so many grey-suited men and some of the attention she attracted was undoubtedly curiosity about her belligerence, outspokenness and seeming self-assurance. In a television interview, she uttered these memorable words:

Wherever one goes one is recognised, and that happens abroad. You go to the most lonely… far-away places and they will recognise you. 'Mrs Thatcher, Mrs Thatcher, strong leader. Mrs

Thatcher strong'. This is most extraordinary, almost in any language.[3]

Except the language of egotism and self-deception.

1. Speech to the Conservative Central Council, 31 March 1990.
2. Urban, G. (1996), *Diplomacy & Disillusion at the Court of Margaret Thatcher*, London' p.136.
3. Interview on Central TV, 18 June 1986.

13. PUBLIC ORDER AND CIVIL RIGHTS

Enemies within - Enemies everywhere

Despite all her talk of restoring 'freedom' to the British people, Thatcher gave a high priority to strengthening the armoury of the state to deal with disorder. Even she must have realised that although she liked to see herself as a doctor with a bottle marked 'panacea for all Britain's problems', there would be a lot of people who would not want to take the medicine and some might even have to be forced to do so. She soon found that she had her hands full.

In March 1979 Airey Neave, a particularly close associate of Thatcher's, was assassinated by the Irish National Liberation Army. In August 1979 Lord Mountbatten was assassinated and the level of bombing incidents rose sharply. In 1980 the Hunger Strikes began. Their purpose was to win political status for Republican prisoners in the H-blocks in the Maze Prison. The Hunger Strikes were led by Bobby Sands. It was extremely humiliating for the Tory Government when in April 1981 after the sitting MP had died, Sands was elected MP for Fermanagh and South Tyrone. Thatcher absolutely refused to be moved to intervene in the hunger strike despite being besieged by appeals across the political and religious spectrums to show some humanity. Several other hunger strikers also died and eventually the strikes were called off. If Thatcher could be said to have won, then it was no more than a pyrrhic victory. It could be said that Thatcher's handling or mishandling of the hunger strikes boosted Irish Republicanism as a political force.

A challenge of a very different sort came with the riots that broke out in the inner areas of several big cities, including Brixton in London, St Paul's in Bristol and Toxteth in Liverpool. Later they spread to many other towns and cities. Northern Ireland had proved a useful testing ground for new tactics, methods and equipment employed by the police against large and hostile crowds in an urban setting. These were put to use in these riots and some of them later proved handy in dealing with the striking miners.

Nothing is purely accidental in history. Even natural disasters like tsunamis have their causes. The violence, indiscriminate arson and destruction and the looting during the riots were actions that cannot be condoned by socialists but they can only be understood as having material roots in the deprivation, desperation and desolation these places had in common. They were a tragedy waiting to happen and were founded in the economic and social conditions that local people were forced to put up with, a standing indictment of the capitalist economic system in the late twentieth century.

The election of a Tory government under someone as clearly insensitive and coolly callous as Thatcher was not, of course, the reason why the riots occurred but may have had some connection with their timing. The inter-related contributing factors had been accumulating over years in these areas, consistently ignored or neglected by central and local government administrations of both main parties. The wonder is that such riots had not occurred sooner. Clearly just one small spark was all that was needed to set the volatile mix aflame. Although her Government commissioned the Scarman Report after the Brixton riots, Thatcher would have no truck with explanations that mentioned slum-housing, unemployment, poverty, exclusion and heavy-handed racist policing as being major contributory factors. To her the issue lay with a breakdown in public morality and a generalised lack of respect for authority. Abstractions of this sort provide absolutely no explanation at all.

In fact Thatcher had changed her tune. Speaking in the Commons at the time of the riots she initially admitted that unemployment could have been a factor in explaining the riots. A few days later after she seized gratefully on an article in the *Daily Mirror* which 'explained' that the looting which occurred was nothing to do with bad housing, unemployment and zero prospects but was simply the result of 'greed'. In support of its theory, the paper cited the fact that schoolchildren had been seen looting and so unemployment could not possibly be the cause. It was all down to 'greed' – to some kind of original sin to which the poor of the inner cities were particularly susceptible.

Now 'greed' was something that Thatcher knew all about. She earnestly believed in it. It was crucial to her plans for the revival of the British economy. She wanted people to be greedy because she thought greed encouraged the entrepreneurial spirit. Soon afterwards Thatcher visited Toxteth and after she had cruised through Liverpool 8 in her limousine gawping at the natives for all of fifteen minutes, she told reporters that "what was clearly lacking was sense of pride and personal responsibility..." Just for good measure she added that there was a 'lack of discipline' for which the 'permissive society' could be blamed. She simply refused to see any link between crime and social and economic deprivation. Soon afterwards the nation was treated to the saccharine spectacle of the fairytale wedding of Prince Charles and Lady Diana Spencer. Such pageants are useful as brief diversions from harsh reality, as an attempt to make people think that life isn't too bad after all. This one, of course, turned out to be an even bigger sham than most such events.

The Powers and Activities of the Police

Internal security was a considerable preoccupation of the Thatcher administrations. Police numbers were boosted, pay was increased and increasingly sophisticated hardware such as plastic bullets and CS gas deployed to deal with the perceived threats associated with industrial action and urban unrest. There was a significant increase in the use of firearms by the police and a number of regrettable deaths and serious injuries as a result. Several acts were passed which widened police powers and allowed the courts to award longer sentences. The Criminal Justice Act of 1982 brought in new guidance for custodial sentences for offenders under the age of 21. This after so-called 'short sharp shock' detention centres had been set up for young offenders.

The National Reporting Centre handled the coordination of the various police forces in the miners' strike of 1984-5 to such effect that it was widely thought that it would provide the model for the organisational base of a future national police force. The government steered away from this particular option. The role of the police in the miners' strike had, however, seen them used for overtly political purposes as a strike-breaking force. The courts imposed demanding bail terms on strikers to prevent them moving round freely to expedite the strike effort. For many, and not just those involved in the strike, serious concerns were raised about the alleged impartiality of the police and the courts.

For someone engaged in supposedly removing obstacles to 'freedom', Thatcher's governments were remarkably authoritarian. Bad police officers of whom there were too many, buoyed up by their enhanced pay and state of the art equipment, swaggered around housing schemes and districts where virtually everyone had poverty in common, intimidating and sometimes roughing up individuals. They seemed to make a speciality of picking on black teenagers and young men. It was the perceived racism of the police that was a major factor leading to the inner-city riots. The media hastened to make it appear that the ringleaders were criminally-inclined black benefit claimants but those out on the streets venting their anger and frustration crossed ethnic and racial barriers and plenty, of course, were not welfare claimants. The majority, however, were seriously disaffected. They could see how little Thatcher's Britain had to offer them.

The Public Order Act of 1986 made severe restrictions on the democratic rights to march, to meet in the open air and to picket. Spontaneous marches and demonstrations were made illegal and failure to notify the authorities in advance of these activities rendered the organisers liable to criminal proceedings. The police were given wide discretionary powers to reroute and curtail marches and outdoor assemblies if they thought that they might be unduly disruptive or could lead to serious damage to property or were intended to be intimidating. A number of other criminal offences associated with demonstration and other forms of public protest were introduced or existing ones strengthened. These ranged from 'riot' which carried a ten-year maximum custodial sentence through violent disorder, affray, threatening behaviour to disorderly conduct.

New Prevention of Terrorism Acts were passed in 1984 and 1989 which strengthened and made existing legislation more draconian. Suspects could be held without charge for up to seven days, remaining silent could attract criminal charges while exclusion orders deprived those on whom they were served of the right to move around the UK or to live where they wished.

The Police and Criminal Evidence Act of 1984 was a wide-ranging piece of legislation that was the result of right-wing concerns that extra measures were needed to counteract the seemingly inexorable rise of crime. It was also the outcome of a strong lobbying process by the police to the effect that they needed more powers. The Act extended police powers to stop and search and enter premises and considerably widened their power to arrest without warrant. At the same time it extended the period for which suspects could be detained without charge to 96 hours maximum. PACE did nothing to reduce crime. Nor did it allay concerns about illegal police violence and other forms of abuse. Out of 13,147 complaints against the police which were received by the Police Complaints Authority established under PACE, only 156 resulted in disciplinary charges being brought against police officers.

In November and December 1982, six terrorist suspects were shot dead by the Royal Ulster Constabulary. Five of the victims had been unarmed. It was alleged that the RUC was operating a 'shoot to kill policy'. Four members of the RUC were charged with murder and acquitted. It was revealed in court, however, that the defendants had been instructed to lie in their official statements so as to conceal the nature of the special police operations. In 1984, John Stalker, a Deputy Chief Constable from the mainland, was appointed to investigate the shootings and the activities of the RUC. In September 1985 he submitted an interim report recommending the prosecution of eleven police officers. He also asked for access to a secret tape recording which he believed could be crucial in bringing further charges against other police officers. These charges would include perjury and possibly murder and attempted murder. This was seriously putting the cat among the pigeons when Stalker was suddenly taken off the investigation. Dirty tricks were in the air as various allegations suddenly started flying around about Stalker although he was later exonerated. His version of events was that he had been too close to being able to publicise a major scandal in the police which would have named senior names and put the RUC in an extremely unfavourable light. Stalker subsequently claimed that even if there was not an official 'shoot to kill' policy, informally there was a tendency towards shooting suspects rather than arresting them. Early in 1988 the Attorney-General that there would be no further action in respect of the shootings. He added that although evidence had been gathered made the RUC officers liable to prosecution for perverting the course of justice, a decision had been made not to go ahead for reasons of 'public interest' and 'national security'. Needless to say, the public was not allowed to know why it was not in their interest to proceed against the officers. Stalker and his investigations were now officially off the radar but the taste left behind was a dyspeptic one of police officers closing ranks to obstruct pursuit of the truth, of officers nefariously engaged in criminal activities and impenetrable secrecy about the activities of the state purporting to act on behalf of the 'public interest'.

Thatcher had many spats with the BBC but in 1988 she also managed to get into one with the independent company, Thames Television. The company was making a programme called 'Death on the Rock' about the killing of three IRA terrorists by the SAS. The TV company argued that they were simply trying to establish the truth and were within their rights to do so. The government countered this by saying that it was not in the public interest that the programme should be broadcast. Three terrorists had definitely planned to explode a bomb at a military ceremony in Gibraltar. This intention was known by the security services who had had them under covert surveillance and who gunned them down, killing all three. Geoffrey Howe made a statement that they were shot when they were seen reaching for their weapons. It was quickly proved that they were actually unarmed and this revelation only confirmed what many people were thinking which was that the security forces were operating a 'shoot to kill' policy. The government was unable to stop the programme being broadcast and it went out on air on 28 April 1988. Thatcher was enraged. She was known for her frequent statements that the rule of law was inviolable but the shooting was illegal. While Thatcher fulminated, an inquiry ruled that Thames Television was well within its rights to broadcast the film and that the media was perfectly entitled to subject government activity to close scrutiny of this sort.

Thatcher's Perceptions

Thatcher liked to promote herself as strong on law and order but it is impossible to escape the impression that what she really meant was strong on countering public disorder. That is where she thought the real threat lay. People in her circumstances never walked the streets and could retire at night to the security of their gated estates. While the police may have got all tooled up to deal with flying pickets or rioting youths and they worked out sophisticated tactics to deal with such contingencies, crime continued to rise unabated.

On a number of occasions Thatcher made clear her aversion to people coming to settle in this country, especially if they were black. During the 1979 general election campaign, while being interviewed for television, she picked up a few cheap votes when she said: *The moment a minority threatens to become a big one, people get frightened. The British character has done so much for democracy, for law, that if there is any fear that it might be swamped, people are going to react and be rather hostile to those coming in.* They were said to be feeding 'alien' ideas into traditional British culture, whatever that is and the immigration rules were tightened up. Thatcher was deliberately playing the racist card here and encouraging precious little of the harmony that she assured the world she would bring when she stood in Downing Street as the new Prime Minister in 1979.

The Tories have a history of cleverly but unscrupulously exploiting populism in order to play on the insecurities of sections of the working class and the lower middle classes. They did so notoriously in the late nineteenth century, deliberately fanning the flames of existing hostility to both Irish and Jewish immigrants. They have waved a 'tough on immigration' flag ever since when they have thought it would win them easy votes. Likewise they used a 'tough on crime' ploy after carefully orchestrating fears that crime was going out of control. Increases in crime they may have been partly ascribable to policies implemented by the Tories themselves when they were in office.

It is a great shame that no one took her up on what exactly she meant when she said that the British character had done so much for democracy and for law. Democratic rights have remained severely limited in Britain and even those that exist had to be fought for, often by people being prepared to take action outside the law, risking punishment in doing so. Even fewer democratic rights were enjoyed by the native people of British dominions across the world where Britain systematically and ferociously suppressed opposition, stooping to genocide on occasions. As for the law, it was to be applied when it suited and flouted when deemed necessary. Thatcher turned a blind eye, for example, to the ferocious and excessive use of violence by the police against miners and their families during the strike of 1984-5. Few people believe that all British citizens are genuinely equal before the law.

It is significant that one perception of the Tories at this time was that they were so right-wing politically that substantial numbers who might otherwise have supported the National Front in elections felt that their votes were going to a good place when they plumped for the Conservatives instead. Tory policies were solidly reactionary and stood much more chance of being implemented by a Tory government because the National Front did not have a cat's chance in hell of winning a parliamentary seat let alone of being elected into office.

Thatcher saw whole sections of the population as a threat. The poor and benefit claimants were another such group. They were told to pull themselves together and find work. There were too many of them and some of them were making fraudulent claims so more fraud detection officers were appointed at exactly the same time that the number of officers investigating tax evasion by the rich was being cut. A culture of snitching was encouraged as ordinary citizens were urged to inform on neighbours who they thought might be benefit cheats. If the government had been really sincere in wanting to find people who were not fulfilling their obligations as citizens, they would have gone after those rich enough to be able to pay fancy accountants to come up with ways in which they could avoid paying any direct taxes at all. This, of course, would never have happened. The Tories did not want to offend their friends. During the Thatcher years, spending on law and order rose by 53.3%.

Thatcher had a deep suspicion that there were 'reds under the bed' in the Civil Service. She took the entirely undemocratic (and unjustified) step of banning trade union membership among the workforce at General Communications Headquarters (GCHQ) at Cheltenham. There was a certain irony because this 'listening post' by its very nature used illicit, illegal and anti-democratic methods in order, of course, to preserve democracy, transparency and the rule of law. The Government's claim was that membership of a union and the possibility that trade union members might take industrial action posed a threat to the efficient operations of GCHQ and thereby also a threat to national security. The implication was the totally scurrilous one that active trade union members were potential traitors.

In 1984 with Thatcher's full approval the Crown prosecuted Sarah Tisdall, a junior civil servant who had passed on classified documents about Cruise Missiles at Greenham Common to *The Guardian* newspaper. She received a six-month custodial sentence. Clive Ponting was a middle-ranking civil servant at the Ministry of Defence. He leaked information to the maverick Labour MP Tam Dalyell that Michael Heseltine had misled Parliament while attempting to cover up the fact that Mrs Thatcher had provided him with inaccurate information about the sinking of the 'General Belgrano' during the Falklands campaign. Ponting was prosecuted under the Official Secrets Act but to Thatcher's great chagrin, he was acquitted in February 1985. The jury, against the judge's direction, decided that it was in the public interest for the information which Ponting disclosed to have been made known.

Thatcher threw her authoritarian weight around once again when she used every means at her disposal to try to block publication in 1985 of the book usually known as *Spycatcher*. This contained the memoirs of Peter Wright, a retired MI5 officer. In it, Wright spilt the beans about various decidedly shady aspects of governmental 'security' policy. It was an instant hit when published first in Australia. It was available for sale in the USA, in the Irish Republic and the Continent and inevitably its revelations had become common currency across the UK. Thatcher was incandescent about what she regarded as Wright's disloyalty as if honour was uppermost in the minds of 'spooks'. The more she ranted and raved, the more she attracted attention to the book which of course became a bestseller. Even Thatcher had to bow to the inevitable when the book was published but in the mean time she had merely
made herself look stubborn, petty and vindictive.

Censorship and Secrecy

Among the armoury of a repressive state is censorship and secrecy. Censorship controls the flow of information available in the public domain. Secrecy hides sinister or mistaken actions of the state. Thatcher's governments were good at both.

In 1986-7 the investigative journalist Duncan Campbell who was employed by the *New Statesman* made a series of six programmes collectively called *Secret Society*. One of these was about the Zircon satellite and the thrust of the programme's argument was that the government had reneged on a promise it made to the Public Accounts Committee and misled Parliament over the existence and cost of the satellite. The programme was banned and so the *New Statesman* went ahead and published the story. Then the Government acted. The Attorney-General obtained an injunction against Campbell. Special Branch officers raided the offices of the *New Statesman* and searched Campbell's home at night, having broken down the door to gain access. Shortly afterwards Special Branch officers raided BBC Scotland in Glasgow and seized all the films in the *Secret Society* series. For his part, Campbell insisted that the information about Zircon was gained from material already in the public arena and that the only item that he thought might be helpful to a foreign power he had had no intention of publishing. Although the programme was eventually shown in 1988, these events looked like a government-sponsored campaign to browbeat the media. The conditions of secrecy and lack of public accountability in which the Special Branch was able to operate were of great concern and it emerged that inquiries by the Home Affairs Committee of the House of Commons into the Special Branch had come up against a wall of intentional obfuscation masquerading as 'the interests of national security'. Another programme in the series, titled *Cabinet* which highlighted how the Government manipulated the news, has never been shown.

In December 1987 the Attorney-General once again used an injunction, in this case to stop the first of three BBC radio programmes called *My Country, Right or Wrong*. This series was pretty tame and included interviews with former members of MI5, MI6 and ex-employees of GCHQ, none of whom were going to blow any serious whistles. What was most sinister about this injunction was its wide-ranging brief. It banned the BBC from broadcasting any programme which contained interviews with existing or past members of the security and intelligence services and using any information provided by them. The ban was lifted in May 1988.

In October 1988 The then Home Secretary, Douglas Hurd, without any prior notice, banned interviews with 'terrorists' and their supporters in Northern Ireland including Sinn Fein which had 56 councillors and one MP. This move attracted criticism from many quarters, mainly on the grounds that it prohibited free expression, deprived the public of information it needed in coming to reasoned decisions and that it marked a further extension of state censorship. So all-embracing was this ban that President Botha declared that he would welcome a similar measure in South Africa. Thatcher, characteristically unrepentant, stated that civil liberties had to be suspended in the war against terrorism.

Privacy and Confidentiality

Ideally public life would be open, transparent and accountable and private life closed to government and other forms of scrutiny. In reality successive governments (not just Tory) have presided over the accumulation of ever-increasing amounts of personal and private information by organisations of the state ostensibly existing to safeguard the interests of the public. Even in the 1980s, increasingly sophisticated electronic and other methods were being used by government to intrude covertly into the lives of growing numbers both of individuals and a wide variety of organisations, doing so using the dubious excuse that it was 'in the interests of the state'. The nature of this 'official' activity is of course shrouded in secrecy but in October 1988 *The Observer* produced a report on the huge increase in phone-tapping that had occurred in the previous decade and which had been implemented without the scrutiny or approval of Parliament. This report claimed that British Telecom had increased the number of its operatives engaged in phone-tapping by 50 per cent since 1980 and that about 30,000 taps were taking place each year.

In 1985 Cathy Massiter, an ex-MI5 agent, revealed on television how the then National Council for Civil Liberties (now Liberty), many trade unions and the peace movement were officially considered to be subversive and therefore were subjected to routine covert surveillance by Special Branch and other arms of the security services. She revealed that, for example, Michael Heseltine, while Defence Secretary, had had the phones of prominent CND members tapped.

Despite her rhetoric, Thatcher was far from being a freedom-loving Prime Minister engaged in rolling back the sphere of the state's activity. Under her tutelage, there was a significant increase in the state's powers of coercion and control of the population and a corresponding reduction in civil liberties. For Thatcher it was all about restoring 'authority' but never stopping to question on what authority was based and, if consent was declining as she believed, initiating a serious analysis of reasons why this was occurring.

Thatcher was always disappointed that two free votes in the Commons in 1979 and 1983 did not bring about the restoration of the death penalty. Sentencing was made more severe and the biggest prison building programme ever was embarked upon. Under Thatcher crime continued to rise and violent crime doubled between 1981 and 1997. Clear-up rates reached an all-time low. Theft accounted for more than half of reported crimes. She could never understand why and blamed just about anything and everybody while never getting anywhere near the complex mix of inter-related and interacting factors including contemporary material conditions that were the major cause. Her mindset simply would not permit her to do so.

14. THATCHER AND LOCAL GOVERNMENT

Changing Attitudes to Local Government

After the Second World War, the Conservatives tended to see local government as a potential check on over-zealous, centralising, power-hungry Labour governments. On an issue like comprehensive secondary education, for examples, the Tories believed it was a matter to be left to the decision of each local authority and they pictured Labour's desire for the inauguration of a nationwide comprehensive system as typical of that Party's bureaucratic centralising tendency and of its drive towards what they thought of as the kind of rigid uniformity associated with Soviet Russia.

This Conservative attitude persisted until the mid-1970s when the desire for financial retrenchment, given the serious problems facing the British economy, meant that a long, hard look was taken at the state of local government. The spending of local authorities was thought to be going way out of control, rates were rising apparently inexorably and a number of left-wing Labour-led local authorities had embarked on various initiatives that were widely portrayed as controversial or in some cases even crackpot. Such initiatives were often expensive and the Conservatives found an echo among rate-payers when they asked whether they were getting value for money from the services of local government. A constant litany of Thatcher's was that local government spending was increasing in real terms, year by year. This was simply untrue. In 1979 when Thatcher first came to office, local government spent £24.5 billion or 28.3 per cent of public sector expenditure. In 1983, local government cost £23.9 billion or 26.3 per cent of public expenditure.

The Labour Party and Local Government

Labour Party activists had gained control of some large urban authorities and were using them as a medium for implementing what might be described as 'municipal socialist' policies. Getting socialist policies carried through Parliament was regarded as either a ponderous and hopelessly slow process or a virtually impossible one. Local government was therefore seen as an arena in which relatively rapid gains could be made by the Left on issues dear to the heart, particularly of a new type of Labour councillor. Gone was the old proud 'gas and water' form of municipal socialism implemented largely by Liberal and later by Labour-held councils composed mostly of working men, horny-handed, down-to-earth sons of toil without airs and graces or much in the way of formal education. Such men could be highly conservative, sometimes reactionary in many of their social and political attitudes. Even those who were socialist class fighters schooled in hard years of industrial conflict could be guilty of what was now being termed as 'political incorrectness'. They were increasingly being replaced by younger, more middle-class, professional, often university-educated activists who were frequently graduates in the Arts and Social Sciences and many of whom were themselves part of the growing workforce employed in local government. Thatcher loathed such people with a passion, deriding them as the 'chattering classes'.

From 1979 some town halls therefore began to be seen as a means through which grass roots socialists could challenge Thatcherite central government. Manchester and Liverpool City Councils were to the fore along with the Greater London Council and a number of London boroughs such as Lambeth. The political views and priorities of these activists reflected the increasingly pluralistic and multi-cultural nature of British society. Especially in London these activists emphasised a number of political concepts which were relatively new to the political agenda. They included issues around equal opportunity, gender and race. They took these up because they certainly needed addressing but often did so in a way that made them easy targets for lampooning, especially by the tabloid press who lumped them together as the activities of the 'loony left'. There were lurid but totally fallacious stories such as that about little children at school being taught nursery rhymes with words like "baa baa, green sheep" so as to avoid any racialist connotations. Much was made of left-wing councils dispersing money with reckless abandon to refuges for battered women, to gay and lesbian groups, to anti-racist groups and other 'unworthy causes' but, at least as far as the GLC was concerned, spending on minority groups only amounted to about 2 per cent of all its expenditure.

It is worth noting that aspects of gay rights such as lowering the age of consent, a demand once thought to be the prerogative of the 'loony left', is now political orthodoxy.

Thatcher throws down a Challenge

Ideas do not have to be true for them to gain credence if repeated sufficiently often in the media. This nonsense about the so-called loony left added fuel to a growing general Conservative Party critique of local government. Councillors were not representative, it was claimed, because frequently they were elected on derisory turnouts. (It didn't matter so much if the councillors were Tory). Many voters were local government employees who had a vested interest in councils increasing their spending. The tenants of council houses likewise had a vested interest in subsidised rates. Some of the services provided by local authorities were monopolistic and of poor quality, it was alleged. There was too much bureaucracy and too much waste. Left-wing controlled councils were criminally prodigal with ratepayers' money and so it went on… In reality, central government spending was growing considerably more quickly that of local government.

The Greater London Council was the product of gerrymandering by the Tories in 1964 when they had extended the old London County Council boundaries by subsuming mainly affluent outer suburbs that were Tory heartlands in an effort to counter the inner-city boroughs where voters were much more likely to favour Labour. To their chagrin the first election to the GLC produced a Labour majority and the Tories had to wait until 1967 to obtain a majority themselves. The GLC was fine from the Tories' point of view when it was under their control but they then found a thousand and one reasons for criticising it when it fell under Labour control. A particular hate figure for the Tories was the Labour Leader of the GLC Ken Livingstone, a rather maverick left-wing socialist but a skilful publicist. Thatcher was absolutely incensed that Livingstone took great delight in reminding the country's parliamentarians as well as huge numbers of commuters, trippers and tourists about just how many Londoners were currently unemployed. He had the figures constantly updated and emblazoned in huge letters on the roof of what was then County Hall, just across the Thames from the Houses of Parliament.

It has already been said that Thatcherism was a jigsaw in which the pieces all related to each other. In local government Thatcher found a fruitful issue which fitted in neatly with others with which she was concerned. By tackling the alleged problems of local government, she was able to appeal to the middle-class and the skilled working class. They were repeatedly told that they deserved value for money and certainly did not want to have to pay for any of the nonsense associated with political correctness. Thatcher was able to appear as the champion of the individual against the increasingly oppressive power of the state albeit in this case the local rather the national state. Under the guise of giving better value for money she was able to initiate the privatisation or outsourcing of municipal services and, as an added bonus, she was able to have a swipe at the Labour Party and the political left in general in addition, of course, to weakening some well-established bases of trade union activity in local government. Soon Thatcher and various recalcitrant councils were on a collision course. Even she could not have envisaged the political and legal battles that would be fought over the ensuing years, the Acts of Parliament that would be needed in order for her to get her own way and the eventual creation of a very different system of local government. Nor did she know that local government was eventually to prove to be her Nemesis.

In 1980 the Local Government Planning and Land Act gave central government powers to decide the size of the spending totals of each local authority. Many authorities continued as if this Act did not exist so the government then introduced penalties in the form of reduced central government grant for those authorities which exceeded their targets. Invariably Labour-controlled, these authorities then raised the money they felt they needed in order to fulfil their obligations by increasing household and business rates. Some refused to set a legal rate or used creative accounting methods to raise the additional money. By this time Thatcher had steam coming out of her ears and she now decided to inflict a lethal blow on these defiant authorities. The 1982 Housing Finance Act abolished the right of authorities to set a supplementary rate and this was followed by the 1984 Rates Act which allowed the government to limit the spending and the rates of those authorities that Whitehall considered were deliberately overspending. Even rate-capping was not a complete success so Thatcher, by now quite clearly having lost it and simply incandescent with rage and frustration, abolished the rates system in 1988 and introduced the Community Charge. This was no more and no less than a poll tax. Clearly Thatcher had not gone to the history books to learn about the fate of previous attempts to introduce a poll tax or, if she had, was so arrogant that she did not think that the lessons of the past applied to her.

Battling it out

Relations between central and local government hit an all-time low during Thatcher's tenure of office. Her response of course was not to stop and question whether she and her government had perhaps got things wrong. Even some Tory-held local authorities were deeply unhappy about her approach to local government. For Thatcher, the councils were being deliberately obstreperous and many of them were nests of socialism. If they would not toe the line, they would be destroyed or at the very least cut down to size. In the 1983 election manifesto, the Tories promised to abolish the GLC and the six metropolitan councils. Some of the functions of these councils were to be taken out of the jurisdiction of local government altogether. An example was transport. Their powers were now to be given to agencies far less accountable to democratic control by the local electorate. A battle royal ensued putting the government in an extremely unfavourable light but the abolition went ahead in 1986. No forms of democratic decision-making were going to be allowed to get in Thatcher's way despite very large numbers of people across the political spectrum wanting these local authorities to continue in existence.

Of all the Labour-held councils who challenged Thatcher, the most determined (and therefore the most troublesome from her point of view) was the Liverpool City Council. Labour took over the governance of the city in the local elections of May 1983. The Marxist 'Militant Tendency' had a strong base in the Liverpool labour movement, built up over decades of painstaking local activity. Several Labour councillors supported Militant or were strongly sympathetic. The effective leader of the City Council was the sharp-suited, fast-talking and combative Militant Supporter, Derek Hatton. The Labour group on the Council had come to office promising that they would create jobs and tackle the City's appalling housing problems. They were determined that they were not going to carry out the dirty work of the government and betray the interests of those who had elected them into office. The Council was desperately short of money so it set a budget to enable it to meet its promises and launched a campaign demanding extra funding to support its programme. It was adamant that it would not make any of the Council's labour force redundant nor would it increase the rates.

From the start the City Council was on a collision course with the Thatcher Government as, indeed, were several other councils although, one by one, they succumbed to the huge pressure they were being put under and eventually Liverpool stood alone in defiance. The Council had a sufficient popular base in the City to set up a campaign with mass support and they forced the government to make some concessions in early 1984. This did not represent a change of heart by the Tories but was because the start of the miner's strike meant that the government did not want to become embroiled in two tough fights at once. It was only a brief respite because the City was soon in the financial mire once again. To avoid total bankruptcy, loans were obtained from foreign banks.

A massive and totally one-sided media campaign was launched to blacken the City Council and Hatton in particular as a dress-rehearsal for the even more vicious pillorying of Arthur Scargill and the NUM which was to follow shortly afterwards. More in hope than expectation, the Council tried to generate support from the hierarchy of the Labour Party but Neil Kinnock was revelling in his new role as Party Leader and his apostasy in which he had moved with such mercurial speed from the left to the right of the Party. Now, engaged in showing how 'moderate' and 'responsible' he would be if he ever became Prime Minister (he never did), he ditched all pretence of being a socialist and echoed the capitalist press by launching a bitter attack on the Liverpool Councillors and demanding the expulsion of all Militant supporters not only from the Liverpool District Labour Party but from the rest of the Labour Party as well. This was music to the ears of the government and the media as Kinnock warmed to his task of doing their dirty work for them.

There is an old adage in the labour movement that a defeat for one is a defeat for all and that the strength of the movement lies in its unity. While large numbers of rank-and-file trade union activists and Labour Party members and others across the country supported the stand of the Liverpool City Council, the government, the media and most of the Labour Party leaders to their great shame used every means at their disposal to weaken the resolve of the Liverpool councillors. They could not break them politically and so the government eventually had recourse to using the District Auditor and the courts to surcharge, bankrupt and disqualify them. This defeat smoothed the way for the same dishonourable triumvirate of government, media and labour leaders (because the latter refused to lend their support) to return to action soon afterwards with their sights trained on the miners.

At each step in the acrimonious interaction between central and local government, voices on the Left had been raised criticising the actions of the Thatcher government. A major thrust in these criticisms was that, far from being evidence that the boundaries of the state were being rolled back, the government's actions represented a serious erosion of representative democracy at local level. They greatly diminished the powers and responsibilities of local authorities and strengthened the powers of central government, giving the lie to Thatcher's claims that she wanted to hand power back to the people. Policing and education policies, for example, now came increasingly under central government auspices and therefore less responsive to local needs. Urban Development Corporations were set up by the government with the ostensible purpose of regenerating decayed inner city districts. They were dominated by big business and largely unanswerable to the electors via the local authorities in which they were situated. Fly-by-night companies opened up operations in these enterprise zones gorging themselves on handouts of public money and the legal evasion of many of the normal planning regulations. Frequently they took the money, stuck around just long enough to keep up appearances and then ran.

The imposition of rate-capping on local councils, the reduction in the Rate Support Grant, the bringing in of opt-out schemes for schools, the battles with Liverpool City Council and the abolition of the Greater London Council and the Metropolitan Councils together represented a serious diminution of local democracy and a corresponding rise in the power of central government. For Mrs Thatcher, central government knew best. She did not so much reform local government as destroy it.

Although the selling-off of council houses at discount prices was undoubtedly a popular policy, it was argued that the cream of the stock was being sold so cheaply that public assets were being wantonly squandered partly for Thatcher's own dogmatic reasons and also as a gimmick to gain short-term electoral support. Since local authority house-building programmes were almost at a standstill, the Thatcher initiative was having a serious impact on those either unwilling or unable to rent with many being thrown on the tender mercies of rack-renting landlords in the private sector.

The question of how best to raise the money needed to fund the operations of local government had dogged the political agenda for a century or more. How could the burden of paying for local services be distributed as equitably as possible and how could the payments themselves be collected effectively? A number of reviews of the rates system were carried out from the mid-1970s. They all acknowledged dissatisfaction with the existing system but made no recommendation about how to replace it with a different and better one.

The thinking of the New Right was that everyone who benefitted from the services provided by local government should contribute to the cost of providing those services while at the same time local authorities should be more accountable for what they did with the money they received from local ratepayers. As we have seen, Thatcher was convinced that there were various maverick councils that were blithely spending their revenue on any number of ridiculous and wasteful schemes which represented nothing but their own hare-brained prejudices and priorities. What, then, was to be done?

Controversially, Thatcher plumped for a new system which, to her intense irritation, immediately attracted the opprobrious nickname 'poll tax' because with very few exceptions, it required every resident to make an equal contribution to paying for the local authority's services. Exceptions were only made for some on very low incomes including full-time students. Thatcher argued that this new system would make local residents more interested in how their money was spent and therefore more likely to participate in local government elections with a beneficial result on local democracy. This sounded very fine and dandy but was accompanied by the government making an assessment of each particular authority's needs. They would be rewarded with extra grants if the level of their community tax was below the figure that the government had set for them. Equally, they would be penalised with cuts in funding if they set a tax at a figure above that determined by the government. In effect, this meant that local authorities were damned if they did and damned if they didn't. The Community Charge was another, perhaps the most ill-conceived, of Thatcher's many bloomers. Myopically, she claimed that it would stimulate participation in the politics of local government. In practice its effect was enormously to enhance the power of central government and to diminish local democracy. Fortunately, it was short-lived.

Many experienced Tories had serious misgivings about the Community Charge or poll tax, arguing that it would be seen as an extremely unfair and inequitable tax, favouring the rich since it had the be paid by every adult householder irrespective of their income and actual ability to pay. The commitment to the Community Charge was included in the Conservative manifesto for the 1987 election and Thatcher had had to fight her corner all the way to get her pet scheme incorporated in the manifesto. Nigel Lawson had predicted that the poll tax would be 'completely unworkable and politically catastrophic' and Michael Heseltine referring to the proposal to enforce the capping of local authority expenditure, called it 'an act of centralised power outside our experience'. Even they could not have predicted the furore it created. Demonstrations organised by the Anti-Poll Tax Union led to violent confrontations in council chambers and out on the streets. Across society from dowager duchesses to people on the dole, it was hated and many refused to pay, being prepared to go to prison rather than to do so. Public anger culminated in a monster demonstration in London on 31 March 1990. Predictably, Thatcher could not accept that everyone else was right and only she and a few die-hards were wrong. Maggie had lost her touch.

15. THATCHER AND THE NATIONAL QUESTION

Ireland had been a running ulcer in the British body politic since the seventeenth century. An artificial and unsatisfactory settlement was imposed on the Irish in 1920 which created the Catholic-dominated Irish Free State and a Protestant-dominated mini-state in the north of the island. Ulster had home rule and was governed at that time from Stormont. The bulk of Northern Ireland's population was Catholic but gerrymandering ensured that the Protestants had more-or-less a monopoly of political power. The entire population of the North was economically disadvantaged by comparison with those who lived on the mainland but the Catholic part of the population suffered particular discrimination. It was somehow symptomatic of the retrogressive nature of life in Northern Ireland that the birching of young offenders was not abolished until the 1980s. Its abolition on the mainland had taken place earlier and among the most vociferous opponents of this was none other than Thatcher herself. Now there's a surprise!

The 1920 settlement was not really even a compromise. It managed to please just about no one but it took the Irish question off the top of the political agenda for a period. Because of its essentially unsatisfactory nature, it was inevitable that the issues involved would sooner or later force themselves back into prominence. After several reasonably peaceful decades, they did so with a vengeance in the late 1960s when the Civil Rights Movement came to the fore. The violence generated in Ireland on both sides of the sectarian divide and by the security forces and the various inter-related economic, social and political issues and problems were a dominant and inescapable factor in British politics throughout the Thatcher years.

Constitutionally, Northern Ireland was a curiosity. It had by now become directly ruled from Westminster. There were fewer MPs per head of the population in the six counties than in mainland Britain. Its history of terrorist violence meant that political rights and liberties were restricted compared with those on the mainland. The Official Ulster Unionists MPs could usually be relied upon to vote with the Tories. The other Ulster MPs were regarded by the Tories as mavericks or worse. Thatcher never seemed to be quite at home with the Unionists despite the essentially reactionary nature of their ideas and policies.

It is difficult to avoid the conclusion that Thatcher accorded Northern Ireland as little attention as she could get away with, having limited understanding of the deeply-rooted issues involved and scant sympathy for those living in the province and caught up in its problems. Like all bourgeois politicians, she found the problems of Northern Ireland ultimately insoluble on the basis of capitalism. When she came to office in 1979, the 'troubles' had been going on for ten years. Violence, murder and terrorism were features of everyday life in a part of the UK and they spilt over onto the mainland on many occasions. During the time that Thatcher was in office, no fewer than 850 people were killed as a result of terrorist action. In 1980 and 1981 Republican prisoners went on hunger strike while attempting to regain the political status such prisoners had had before 1976. It was typical that the Thatcher-led Government was officially not prepared to intervene, making much of the courage of its stance in the face of this 'moral blackmail'. It made nothing of the courage of the ten hunger strikers who underwent the appalling agonies of starving to death for a cause they believed in. The hunger strikers may have died, the hunger strikes may have eventually been called off but the issue was a propaganda coup for Irish nationalism. The British government managed to look to the outside world like an oppressive colonial power occupying Northern Ireland against the wishes of its population.

Actually Thatcher's government had not been entirely candid about its position on the hunger strikes because behind-the-scenes discussions had taken place with republican leaders in an attempt to bring the strike to an end. This had nothing to do with humane motives but was because Britain's international image was being seriously damaged. It was therefore an attempt at damage limitation but further damage was of course inflicted when it became known that these secret talks had been held despite the government's robust statements that it would not give in to what it described as 'moral blackmail'.

Thatcher seemed incapable of, or unwilling to get to grips with, the kind of detailed information that any Prime Minister could reasonably be expected to take on board concerning a part of the country for which he or she was responsible and which was undergoing the problems that Ireland was experiencing. She continuously referred to making minor adjustments to the border so that all Catholics could reside in the Republic and all Protestants comfortably bed down together in the North. Reminded time and time again that people of both religions were widely scattered through both the Republic and the North and that this 'solution' was a non-starter, she never seemed able to grasp this simple fact.

On the matter of Northern Ireland, Thatcher's interests seemed to be mainly focused on the issue of terrorism. Some of her close associates, most notably Airey Neave, were killed or injured by republican terrorists and she herself narrowly escaped death when the IRA exploded a bomb close to her hotel room during the Tory Conference at Brighton in 1984. She seemingly saw terrorism manifesting itself right across the world as the enemy of what she regarded as 'democracy' but despite it occupying such a prominent place in her consciousness, she conspicuously failed to come up with any policies to eradicate a political tactic which she so obviously found so repugnant. It is possible that the Brighton bomb marked a watershed in Thatcher's life. Her narrow escape not surprisingly seemed to affect her and she perhaps lost some of her 'edge' from that time. She was also surrounded by greater security which caused her to be become even more distanced from reality.

The lack of clarity which Thatcher brought to the question of Northern Ireland was made clear by the Anglo-Irish Agreement devised in 1985. The purpose of the agreement was ostensibly to give the Irish Republic some say in the affairs of Northern Ireland but it never actually defined how this was to be applied in practice. Thatcher insisted that the meetings at which the negotiations took place for the agreement should be behind closed doors and would not be minuted. This cloak-and-dagger ploy further alienated her from the Ulster Unionists who, of course, were totally hostile to the idea of allowing the Republic even the slightest say in the governance of the Six Counties. 100,000 of them turned out in a rally in Belfast to let Thatcher know what they thought.

For all that Thatcher liked everyone to think what an innovative, radical and brave politician she was, there was very little that deserved any of those adjectives in her policies for Northern Ireland. The life of the province was blighted by very high levels of unemployment, far worse for the Catholics but by no means negligible among the Protestants. Pragmatically it made sense to throw money at the problem and what industrial employment remained in Northern Ireland's ravaged economy was supported by sizeable government subsidies. In 1972 government subsidies totalled £100 million. In 1988-9 this figure had risen to £1.6 billion. Some central Thatcherite policies were never of much significance in Northern Ireland. Her assault on the powers of the local authorities and on local democracy on the mainland was not replicated there because direct rule had already stripped local government of much of its power. The selling of council housing was a non-starter. Significantly there was no poll tax in Northern Ireland. It is difficult to escape the impression that Thatcher was playing politicians' games in Northern Ireland. 'Keeping a low profile' and 'out of sight, out of mind' were hardly the policies of a courageous and decisive Prime Minister.

Nor did Thatcher enjoy particularly happy relationships with that significant proportion of the mainland population that viewed themselves as Welsh or Scottish. In Wales nonconformist traditions went with an aversion to the Conservatives and had deep roots in many communities. Although de-industrialisation had been taking place for years, strong Labourist ways of viewing the world meant that the iron-producing and coal-mining districts were no-go areas for the Tories even before the miner's strike. However the Tories had some support in certain more affluent or rural parts of the principality and picked up a few seats in the 1983 election. By the time she was on her way out antipathy to her and her policies was rising sharply. This may have had something to do with a rise of anti-English sentiment in general. Perhaps Thatcher personified what many Welsh people saw as the very worst of English personal characteristics. There was something of an economic recovery in South Wales in the late 1980s as foreign companies were persuaded with various grants and concessions to start up operations there but it only looked like good times were back when a comparison was made with the early 1980s when Welsh heavy industry had taken such a battering.

Scotland was the same but different. There had for long been some concentrated centres of support for the Conservatives in Scotland. Important senior members of the Party were from Scotland including the recent Prime Minister, Sir Alec Douglas-Home. However Thatcher and her policies cut little ice in Scotland and support for the Tories fell away throughout the 1980s. After the 1983 general election, elsewhere something of a triumph for Thatcher, only eleven Conservative MPs remained in Scotland. Percentage-wise, fewer Scots were persuaded to buy shares or their council houses.

Thatcher had even less understanding of the mindsets and everyday realities of the Welsh and the Scottish than she did of the ordinary people of England. In 1988 she attended the Scottish Cup Final held at Hampden Park, Glasgow between Celtic and Dundee, one of her more unexpected acts. Her appearance in one of the expensive parts of the ground was greeted with thousands of fans waving specially printed red cards and gesticulating towards her box. Her first instinct was to be flattered to be the object of so much attention. She was soon disabused. Typically, given the extremely narrow social circles in which she moved, she had not previously known that red cards were shown for a sending off. She certainly knew by the time the Scottish football fans had finished with her. It was her one and only visit to the Scottish Cup Final.

Any ambitious member of Thatcher's government knew that he was well out of favour if he was given the Welsh, Scottish or Northern Ireland portfolios. Thatcher used these roles to remind anyone she thought was getting ideas above their station just who was boss. She then enjoyed watching such marginalised ministers slug it out with each other as they tried to do the best for the areas under their jurisdiction within the limited resources that were made available. Such cavalier treatment suggested that Thatcher had a marked lack of esteem for the inhabitants of those parts of the British Isles.

It should be remembered that Thatcherism was an English phenomenon. Her governments enjoyed even less of an electoral majority in Wales, Scotland or Northern Ireland than they did in England. The heartlands of Thatcherite support were in the affluent Home Counties and south-east and in various pockets of above average affluence in leafier areas of the provinces such as parts of Cheshire and Warwickshire and some other shires. She and her policies were less well received in the large conurbations and former seats of heavy industry especially in the North of England. Despite her claims that she wanted to restore a sense of practical and positive unity to the United Kingdom, her policies were deeply and damagingly divisive and it is hard to escape the conclusion that this was often intentional. When the purpose of her economic policy was primarily to boost the flagging profits and prospects of British capitalism by transferring wealth from those on average and lower incomes to the better-off and positively rich, hostility was only to be expected. The encouragement of existing and even the creation of new divisions among the people of the UK was a tactic she employed in trying to achieve her aims. It had little to do with the harmony that she promised when she made her famous set-piece speech outside No.10 Downing Street on becoming Prime Minister on 4 May 1979. The intent expressed in this speech, if we are to believe that she meant what she was saying, was negated by her every action over the next decade or more.

The old 'One Nation Toryism' now became under Thatcher the politics of two nations. Those who unequivocally benefitted from the policies she carried out were 'on board'. Adding to their existing wealth or acquiring and accruing considerably more wealth and the power that goes with mega-bucks, they were the small minority who openly made a fetish out of the concepts of 'freedom', acquistiveness, self-interest and 'the market'. Other layers of society saw some definite improvements in their economic situation but the benefits, if that is the right word, of Thatcherite policies were by no means spread evenly. The particular slant put on neo-liberal economic policy by Thatcher created cleavages along the lines of what she perceived as productive versus parasitic and also between rich and poor, North and South and employed and unemployed. These policies led to friction between the selected and favoured socio-economic groups and those who were even further marginalised. The latter included large swathes of the ethnic minority population, single parents, the elderly on state pensions and the unemployed, particularly away from the South-east of England and many of those in the inner-cities through the UK.

Revelling in his role of elder statesman, Harold Macmillan in his maiden speech in the House of Lords on 13 November 1984 as Earl of Stockton chastised Thatcher by implication:

There is a growing division in our comparatively prosperous society between the South and the North and Midlands which are ailing, that cannot be allowed to continue. There is a general sense of tension... I can only describe as wicked the hatred that has been introduced, and which is to be found among different types of people today. Not merely an intellectual but a moral effort is required to get rid of it.

Thatcher set herself the task of restructuring and revitalising the British economy along post-Fordist lines. She adopted an accumulation strategy involving the deregulation of private capital, substantial privatisation of the public sector and the introduction of commercial criteria into various remaining public sector activities. New technologies, products and services were encouraged and a new dual labour market created in which a small high-waged skilled core was counterposed to a low-waged, largely unskilled and 'flexible' mass workforce frequently slipping into and out of employment, being at the mercy of the vagaries of the economy..

It seems to have mattered little to Thatcher how much damage was done in pursuit of these aims. Her policies did not work. She proved totally incapable of putting the fortunes of British capitalism back on a firm, sound and lasting foundation. This is evident by the myriad of problems which the Tory-dominated Coalition government is impotently attempting to deal with in the second decade of the twenty-first century, many of which have roots that can be traced back to Thatcher's policies in the 1980s. So much for the hope and harmony she promised.

16. THE THATCHER STYLE

As a socialist the author is less interested in historical figures as personalities and more concerned with what such people said and did to promote the material and class interests they represent, consciously or otherwise. It is important to try to establish their influence as historical figures, agents of change operating within sets of circumstances which they have not themselves created but which they can intervene in and alter. Thatcher had an extremely high opinion of the role she played in history. Her style cannot be ignored as an historical factor but she was not an autonomous historical agent. Thatcherism was an instinct, a series of moral values and an approach to leadership. Rarely has one individual so much set his or her stamp on the era of their political leadership.

Myths and Misunderstandings

It would be absurd to deny that Mrs Thatcher was the dominant figure in British politics in the 1980s. The contention here, however, is that she was allowed to get away with a great deal because of ineffectual opposition, that vast amounts of what has been written and said in her defence or by way of praise is vacuous, superficial and often simply wrong and that many of those qualities that have been taken as her strengths were in fact serious weaknesses when manifested in someone in the position of a prime minister. Rarely in history has a figure of such great historical significance been surrounded by so many myths, misunderstandings and mendacities that have taken root and flourished as indisputable 'facts' which it has become almost heretical to question. The other modern British historical figure who comes to mind in a similar respect is Winston Churchill.

There are a few facts which cannot be denied. She was the first woman Prime Minister of an advanced western country, the first woman to lead the Conservative Party – a bastion of male supremacy and she was the first leader since Lord Liverpool in the 1820s to win three elections in a row. She was also the first British political leader to give her name, even while she was still alive, to an 'ism,' this being the distinctive, totally unmistakeable style she employed in all her political dealings be it when she was bellowing like a fishwife at the opposition benches in the House, bullying and berating Cabinet colleagues, purring in the presence of President Reagan or patronising the presenter and the viewers in a television interview.

The woman was a hotchpotch of contradictions. She presented herself as having come from a poor background which she had not and having sympathy for the poor which she did not. When referring to the working class, she unashamedly described it as something from which a person with any sense or drive would want to escape. She came from a medium-sized country town in the East Midlands when it suited her but her mindset was firmly centred in London. She grew up in a fiercely Methodist milieu to which she referred admiringly in later life while being an Anglican by practice and rejecting the precepts of

Methodism. When Tory leader and later Prime Minister, she eulogised her father but put distance as she could between herself and Grantham and she rarely went back. She seemed more devoted to him when he was dead than while he had been alive but he constituted a useful icon to which she could refer when it suited her purpose. She prattled on about 'family values' while having been brought up in a family where the mother seems to have been little more than a cipher and her early childhood was dominated by her father's mother who by all accounts was formidably strong-willed. Her own marriage seems to have had a strong element of convenience in it and her children do not seem to have shown any great affection for her. Her errant son could do no wrong yet he was the very antithesis of all the values she purported to uphold.

She was somewhat ingenuous when offering herself as an example of merit, of having risen without anyone to give her a leg-up. Her upbringing was 'comfortable' rather than well-off. Her father was sufficiently ambitious for his younger daughter and well-off to allow her an extra year at school to prepare for entry to Oxford. He had the means to provide special tuition in Latin which was necessary for entry but he also was sufficiently nuanced from the social point of view to pay for her to have elocution lessons. She herself was definite that it was Oxford she wanted because she regarded it as more prestigious than Cambridge and she chose to apply to do a Chemistry degree not through any particular love or aptitude for the subject but on the basis that her chances of securing a place were stronger because few girls applied to read that subject. Later on she was able to study to be a barrister because her husband was wealthy enough to pay for her to do so.

Tory Opponents

Even important figures in the Tory Party found Thatcher intolerable. Julian Critchley and Sir Ian Gilmour were old-fashioned Tories or 'wets' who crossed swords with her on a number of occasions. Critchley commented scathingly, *Mrs Thatcher is didactic, tart and obstinate. Her economic policies are 'Thatcherite' rather than Conservative, for her treasury team have placed the Public Sector Borrowing Requirement up on a pedestal... We are suffering from 'A' level economics. In consequence of this new ideology, economics have been elevated above politics.*

Sir Ian Gilmour with customary suaveness lectured the Cambridge Union to this effect: *Conservatives dislike what Wordsworth called 'Upstart Theory', that is to say, overarching abstract systems of ideas or ideologies, which purport to embody immutable truths that are infallible guides to political behaviour. They believe instead that political theory should be firmly grounded in practice. So far as Conservatives are concerned, there is an important distinction between theory and ideology.*

On a less cerebral level, Norman St John Stevas who Thatcher dumped and who then found a natural niche as a kind of pompous and unconscious court jester, was fond of coining nicknames for his political mistress. One was 'The Blessed Margaret' and another was 'Attila the Hen'. He did not like her either.

Saying one thing and doing another

Mrs Thatcher believed that she had the resolve and the moral strength to implement the unpopular, painful but necessary policies from which other recent political leaders had shied away. She firmly believed and constantly declared that she possessed a cohesive set of solutions with which to undertake the urgent task of reinvigorating the British economy and that these were based on thought-out political principles. She was fond of saying 'we' when she meant 'me' but said it as if she was speaking on behalf of the mass of decent, sensibly-thinking people who could not but agree with her. She never publicly described her task as being that of restoring the profitability of British capitalism. In someone claiming to speak it the way it was, this lack of candour was understandable since it would have involved explaining that this task required transferring wealth and resources from money and social wages to the business sector with no certainty, except in her own mind, that short-term pain would lead to long-term gain. Although some of her policies were unashamedly populist such as the sale of council houses, she might not have stayed in office so long had she been completely frank about what her economic policies really entailed.

For Thatcher the pursuit of economic individualism was a major virtue. In 1988 she said, "…we are actually encouraging the best in human nature," This could be rephrased as, 'We are encouraging the individual pursuit of greed and avarice and self-interest'. This reality sits uneasily alongside the moral dimension that Thatcher claimed for her 'mission'. Was she unaware of this contradiction or did she simply chose to ignore it? If she was unaware that showed a serious lack of understanding. If she ignored the contradiction then she was by no means the 'straight-talker' she claimed to be. The sheer stupidity of which she was capable was amply demonstrated by her asinine comment, "every citizen aspires to a conservatory." Perhaps her statement, "We are a grandmother," was even more idiotic.

Few people have been Thatcher's equal in their ability to turn reality upside down. She believed that social inequality was desirable, that it was a force for good in a vigorous entrepreneurial society. To be high in the hierarchy was a recognition of and reward for success. To be low in the pecking order was the result of personal failure and lack of effort. If people were poor, it was their own fault. On one occasion she said, "… poverty is not material but behavioural." In 1978 she uttered these kind and thoughtful words, "…there may be poverty because they don't know how to budget, don't know how to spend their earnings, but now you are left with the really hard fundamental personality defect." So the poor suffered from a deficiency of character. So people who worked hard all their lives doing jobs essential to society but for which they were poorly-paid were, according to her, feckless and feeble. The utter nastiness of this little piece of Social Darwinism should perhaps not surprise us. It acted as a justification for the low pay of which Thatcher was such a fan. Thatcher neither knew nor cared about what low pay meant to those on the receiving end of it. On several occasions she dismissed the idea that there was any genuine poverty in Britain as a figment of fevered socialist imaginations. For Thatcher, the worth of a person was demonstrated by what he or she owned.

Despite her many utterances about how people should show a bit of moral fibre and pull themselves up by their own bootlaces, social mobility remained severely limited, partly as a result of policies carried out by Thatcher's own governments. The share of wealth going to the poorest 10 per cent of the population fell by around one-fifth between 1979 and 1996. If you were born rich, her economic policies meant that you were likely to stay rich. Born poor, the odds were on that that is how you stayed. In 1979 there were an estimated 5 million people in the UK living in poverty. By 1992 this figure had become 14 million. This looks like downward social mobility! Even those who bought and then quickly sold a clutch of shares or who bought their council houses at a discount did not become rich in any real sense of the word. Upward social mobility was an attractive prospect if it meant being able to enjoy more of the good things of life – having the choices not available to the poor but it was no more than a dream for millions of working and unemployed people. Thatcher deplored everything to do with the working class, except of course the profits they produced for capitalism and the essential services they provided to keep the economy going. In making such a merit of upward social aspiration she was mocking the reality of everyday life for the bulk of the working class in the 1980s.

Her appeal to the aspirant working class, especially in the relatively prosperous parts of the south-east and the Home Counties where it may have struck more of a chord, was intentionally divisive. Even there for many it remained little more than an illusion. In the old industrial and mining districts with less of a middle class, this appeal cut much less ice. She was incapable of understanding that workers did not automatically become middle class just by owning their own homes, having a foreign package holiday and enjoying a spot of DIY. Manual workers in the automotive industry in the 1950s and 1960s often owned their own homes. So did miners. They knew that they owed their relatively good wages, terms and conditions of employment to their preparedness to use their collective bargaining strength as workers.

Her curious morality was essential to any understanding of Thatcher's view of the world. In 1977 she wrote: *… a moral being is one who exercises his own judgement in choice. In so far as a citizen's right and duty to choose is taken away by the state, the party, or the union, his moral faculties atrophy and he becomes a moral cripple.*

As a typical neo-liberal, Thatcher was somewhat selective in the choice of historical phenomena on which she drew to support her 'mission'. Her skewed version of 'Victorian Values' has already been commented on. She chose simply to ignore the fact that Britain's mid-nineteenth century world domination, based on a century or more of massive accumulation of capital, owed much to the use of violence and abuse of human rights that inevitably went with its major involvement in international slavery. She also ignored the genocide and plunder involved in the creation of the British Empire. Equally absent from Thatcher's utterances were references to the blighted industrial environments, the brutal workplace discipline, the premature death, industrial diseases and injury, the general squalor and misery and outright exploitation of working people on which Britain's rise to world domination as 'the workshop of the world' were based. These are only a few among the many questions that could be raised about the moral and ethical basis of British capitalism.

Again, Thatcher as a neo-liberal was wont to talk about how private property was the lifeblood of a free society. What about that sizeable percentage of society consisting of people who had no property? Does that mean that they are not free? What is the exact nature of the 'freedom' that the citizen gains when he or she start buying the council house in which they live or purchases a modest portfolio of shares in a couple of privatised utility companies? Freedom is not just the absence of coercion. Freedom, among other things, is the ability to make choices. In Thatcher's ideal of capitalism, all were free but some were freer than others. In reality there is little freedom for those with limited means – they have few choices available to them. Thatcher had no qualms about this and indeed made a virtue of inequality.

For someone who valued inequality so highly, it was totally inconsistent for Thatcher to dismiss talk of the existence of class. She called class a 'communist concept' but saying that was not enough for it simply to disappear. Thatcher did not want a classless society. She stood four-square in the defence of a system based on gross inequalities of access to wealth and power. The rich and powerful minority did not necessarily owe what they had to hard work on their part or because they made an especially useful contribution to society. Wealth and merit were by no means synonymous.

Thatcher clearly got off on the aura of 'wealth creation' which she thought entrepreneurs exuded and many of them found their efforts rewarded when they received baubles and gongs in the Honours Lists, especially if they contributed generously to the Conservative Party. Not all of them had necessarily been too fastidious in how they had come by their riches. Some were just speculators and asset-strippers. One or two had engaged in activities which brought them to the attention of the law. It speaks volumes for Thatcher's view of the world that such people were held up for public recognition as 'successes'. How on earth did Thatcher square her admiration for such people with the nonconformist values of her father to which she constantly referred in reverential terms? What was it about, say, a millionaire whose riches were based on building up a chain of casinos, which made that person of greater merit than, say, a miner or a paramedic? Not since the Maundy Gregory scandals of the 1920s had honours been disbursed with such abandon on the one hand and with such selectivity on the other. The other side of this bare-faced favouritism was the failure to recognise people who were not Tories or had somehow got on the wrong side of the lady. One such was John Harvey Jones, very successful in his time as Chairman of ICI. He was known not to be a supporter of the Conservatives but, even worse, in 1981 he had told Thatcher to her face that the policies of her government were ruining British industry. She had a long memory and a vindictive streak.

The activities of the Thatcher ministries could raise serious concerns about the legitimacy of government. None of her governments enjoyed the support of more than a third of the electorate and in all cases more people voted against the Conservatives than for them. We know that the quirks of the first-past-the-post electoral system frequently allow such anomalies to arise but seldom has there been a Prime Minister who simply dismissed such piffling objections and was convinced that she had public approval for all the policies her governments enacted. This was not necessarily true. Mention was made previously of large-scale unease about the privatisation of the utilities. 79 per cent disapproved of the privatisation of water, a figure identical to those who did not want the Greater London Council to be abolished. 71 per cent were opposed to the Poll Tax and 69 per cent thought the banning of trade unions at GCHQ was wrong. It could be argued that Thatcher never had a democratic mandate in any meaningful sense of the word.

Tory policy has always been contained a strong element of divide-and-rule. This plumbed new depths in the Thatcher days. In order to fragment possible opposition and to discourage and demoralise those who were most likely to be hardest hit by her policies, a war of ideas was launched, the object of which was to encourage the slightly better-off sections of the working class to dump on those on the rungs below them in the social hierarchy. An example of this was the demonisation of single parent families. Newspapers like the *Daily Mail* gleefully circulated stories about how thousands of no-hoper teenage girls were going around deliberately getting themselves pregnant so that their local authorities would be forced to find them accommodation. The thrust of these stories was that their greed and sexual laxity were enabling them to jump the housing queues at the expense of people more deserving of being allocated social housing. Hard evidence of extensive practices of this sort was always hard to come by. Such stories did not contain an explanation as to why council waiting lists were so long – and growing. At other times they returned to the hardy perennial of the benefits culture and how there was a huge underclass of semi-criminalised long-term spongers living off the taxes paid by the hard work of the rest of society. The paper's investigative journalists loved nothing better than digging the dirt on those least able to fight their corner and obtain redress.

"This lady's not for turning' is a phrase always associated with Thatcher but it is all part of the mythology. She carried out U-turns on many occasions when she found it expedient. For example she oversaw a generous settlement of the miners' pay claim in 1981 in contravention of her stated rejection of pay policies but as part of her strategy of making preparations for a showdown with the NUM when the government was ready for it. Likewise for all her talk about not helping 'lame duck' businesses, she threw money at the steel industry and at British Leyland because it seemed the advisable thing to do in view of the circumstances of the time.

While a fierce ideological commitment to capitalism underpinned Mrs Thatcher's view of the world, it was not backed up by any sense of principle and she acted pragmatically in response events as much as any other politician with an eye to the next election.

Hitting out with her Handbag

Thatcher was impatient, abrasive, confrontational, overbearing and rarely prepared to listen to or even consider views that conflicted with her own. She acted as though anybody or anything at variance with her own viewpoint was absurd and pathetic or deserved simply to be steamrollered out of existence. She had the skill not so much to win arguments as to somehow gloss over them or dismiss them from her presence in a way which suggested that any sensible person would realise that there was in fact nothing to argue about. She preached and moralised, was bossy and was sometimes likened to a querulous girls' boarding school headmistress.

She was hugely impatient with institutions like the civil service whose byzantine procedures seemed to be designed to prevent rather than expedite meaningful activity. The civil service was the epitome of the things she hated. She saw it as parasitic, leeching off the efforts of those who created wealth. It was oversized, bureaucratic complacent, obstructive, self-serving, self-satisfied and self-protective. As one veteran Tory backbencher said, "She cannot see an institution without hitting it with her handbag."

One institution she did not attempt to bash with her handbag was the monarchy. She was in awe of it. Here was another of Thatcher's contradictions. The monarchy is continuing living evidence of a hierarchical society based not on 'merit', whatever that means, but purely on heredity. It is a throwback to medieval feudalism and to the kind of primitive society in which monarchs believed that they had the right to ride roughshod over their subjects, pretending that they had the endorsement of the Almighty for this kind of oppression. The monarchy is the highest rung in a class-ridden social system and the complete antithesis of what Thatcher claimed so vehemently to advocate – a society where people advanced by making the most of their talents. British monarchs have a totally unreal life experience, surrounded as they are by flunkeys rushing to answer their every call, completely insulated from the everyday grind of working or, all too often in today's Britain, of being jobless and without prospects and not knowing how to make ends meet. Wherever they go, they are fawned upon, people genuflect at their feet and they are treated with exaggerated respect. As they go about their public duties, they are only allowed to see the carefully choreographed best of everything and have only the haziest idea of what life is like for the majority of their 'subjects'.

The monarchy is an ongoing soap opera tolerated by the rich and powerful because it provides a solid underpinning or social cement considered essential for the continuance of social stability. Despite being such tangible evidence of the existence of class differences and gross inequalities, it is portrayed as being something standing above issues of class and politics, impartial and independent. It is portrayed as a symbol of continuity and tradition, as an institution that somehow binds the nation together and to which all citizens should accord respect and reverence. The monarchy is an institution designed to implant feelings of deference to authority. Little is made of the fact that the monarch still has certain residual anti-democratic powers which could be called upon in defence of the status quo in the event of major social upheavals.

A tradition has developed whereby the Queen normally gives a weekly audience to the Prime Minister. Rumours used to abound concerning Thatcher and this weekly meeting. The general belief is that Thatcher regarded it as something of an unwanted intrusion in her busy diary and that the Queen did not welcome the ritual either. Thatcher's social gaucheness made her ill-at-ease with the Queen who was equally uncomfortable even if she was more gracious about it. When Thatcher jetted around the world on diplomatic missions, comments followed wherever she went that she comported herself far more like a Queen than Mrs Windsor did when engaged in similar duties. Thatcher craved power and attention. The Queen craved neither. It is not surprising that theirs' was not a cordial relationship.

Thatcher was less deferential in her relationships with another ancient and hallowed institution, the Church of England. Thatcher was incapable of leaving things alone and those around her were driven to distraction by her constant interference and inability to let people get on with what they did perfectly well. Her predecessors in the role of Prime Minister had made little use of their powers of episcopal appointment but Thatcher had no such qualms. She used the opportunity to give vent to her strong personal likes and dislikes. The Bishop of Stepney, Jim Thompson, was widely thought of as a candidate for preferment but his left-wing views found an enemy in Mrs Thatcher who steadfastly ignored repeated recommendations for his advancement. On several occasions she referred to the need to keep politics out of religion and did so while not turning a hair in drawing on her own political sympathies when employing the powers of patronage so far as these appointments were concerned.

The obsessive belief in her personal correctness was a serious weakness in a politician who made decisions affecting millions of people. Her combative style often irritated or alienated other members of the Tory Party. One senior colleague wrote in his diary after a shadow cabinet, "Margaret wants to fight. But what about?" This apparent desire to launch herself at windmills like Don Quixote helps to explain why many of her associates lost confidence in her as she increasingly seemed to part company with reality, wanting to fight battles that had already been fought or did not need fighting. Her readiness openly to berate colleagues and others who seemed indecisive, weak or apparently did not know what they were talking about could be cruel. Like any bully she soon learned whom she could and could not pick on with impunity. She was frequently ill-mannered and boorish and the cavalier fashion in which she often treated her junior colleagues made it hard for them to assert themselves for fear of getting a lashing from her tongue. She became more dominant as she got older by which time most of her ministers, colleagues and others usually found excuses not to tell her things they knew she wouldn't like. She was seemingly incapable of relaxing and seemed to find it a weakness in others if they did so.

Ruthlessness is maybe a requirement for politicians and Thatcher had it in bucket-loads. In order to get her own way in the Government, she manipulated or created sub-committees of the Cabinet and filled them with the people she knew would come to the decisions that she wanted. She reallocated or reshuffled ministers totally without mercy and it was obvious that she often gave more credence to unelected political advisors than to her own ministers. It was this tendency that caused Nigel Lawson eventually to resign in 1989 as Chancellor because he felt his role was being usurped by Professor Alan Walters. To get what she wanted she appointed sympathisers to senior roles in the Civil Service and on quangos, challenging the practice of impartiality on such matters. When people were being considered for appointments she would ask, "Is he one of us?" She skilfully wooed those who controlled large sections of the printed media and as a result was virtually able to be guaranteed space and favourable coverage when she wanted it and she unashamedly used patronage to build up a layer of sycophants in politics, the media and elsewhere who would jump when she snapped her fingers because they owned their position and their futures to keeping in her good books. Thatcher, of course, was not unique in exercising powers of patronage but did so more unashamedly than most and to an extent that might raise questions about her integrity.

Thatcher and the 'Trickle-down' Theory

Thatcher was comfortable in the company of entrepreneurs, apparently plain-speaking and unpretentious businessmen who she regarded as 'wealth-creators'. It would be possible to take issue with this description. Under capitalism 'wealth creation' is dependent on the applied labour of the worker in the productive process and on the essentially exploitative relationship that this entails. The word 'exploitative' is not used in an emotional or moralistic way but simply to explain the essential nature of the workings of capitalism. Entrepreneurs with their capital are therefore only one part of the process of wealth-creation and capital itself is dead without the application of living human labour. Those men with whom she was most at ease seem to have been from southern or south-eastern England, from an urban upbringing, probably the first in their family to go to university, self-made, aggressive and often Jewish. She gorged on the attention and flattery of such men. Other close associates, however, did not necessarily fit into this pattern. She had a long and close association, for example, with Woodrow Wyatt. A renegade escapee from the Labour Party, his compulsion for lechery was only exceeded by his snobbery and his seemingly bottomless reserves of sycophancy. For all that she claimed to be a meritocrat, she went all weak at the knees in the company of a genuine aristocrat. One such was Lord Carrington, her early Foreign Secretary who epitomised the political establishment which she claimed to scorn. He was a patrician to the core, an intelligent man who knew exactly how to play Mrs Thatcher.

Her own family encapsulated some of her contradictions. She was brought up in a family in which her father emphasised the virtues of hard work, thrift, respectability, saving for the future and helping the less fortunate but her son, Mark, was involved in any number of ventures, most of them dodgy. He was found guilty of helping to finance an intended coup in Equatorial Guinea for which he was given a four-year suspended sentence by a South African court and fined about US$560,000. The maverick Labour MP, Tam Dalyell, claimed that Mark Thatcher got rake-offs from the massive Al-Yamamah arms contracts. Mark remorselessly used the Thatcher name when engaged in his many nefarious business deals and his mother was well aware of this and, presumably, gave it her blessing. She purported to believe in meritocracy but her son seemed totally bereft of merit or any other saving graces and was the complete opposite of everything she claimed to stand for. Thatcher doted on him and would never hear a bad word said about Mark even when he managed to get himself lost in the African desert and people put their lives at risk in a huge and expensive search and rescue mission paid for out of public funds.

The theory that entrepreneurs should be given every freedom to maximise their business activities so that the wealth they create 'trickles down' to the rest of society in terms of jobs and wages has little basis in reality. In fact some of those who Thatcher admired were the total opposite of wealth creators – they were parasitic asset strippers who systematically laid waste to the forces of production, to jobs and to peoples' lives in the search for a quick paper profit. She remarked: ... *wealth creators have a tendency to acquire wealth in the process of creating it for others*. Entrepreneurs of the sort she admired were in business for one reason and one reason only – to make as much profit as possible. How much of the wealth that resulted from the workers' efforts actually trickled down to the less well-off depended on a whole range of factors but capitalists are concerned with their own enrichment or those of the shareholders if they have them. The class struggle is the outcome of the conflict between capital and labour as to how the profit accumulated is shared out, in other words, how the wealth created is distributed. If the wealth really trickled down, there would be less need for a struggle by those who are not wealthy.

Thatcher, the Petit Bourgeois

Mrs Thatcher was not a Conservative Party grandee in the style of recent Prime Ministers such as Eden, Macmillan or Home, all of whom seem to have emerged from a deeply-rooted self-perpetuating oligarchy or political establishment of old-fashioned 'One-Nation Tories'. They believed that social obligations were a necessary part of Conservatism. Such men came from one or more of the traditional breeding grounds of senior Tories – business, land or a political dynasty. Already a dying breed in the Party, they obviously upheld the supremacy of capitalism and the maintenance of the status quo but larded their aristocratic hauteur with helpings of *noblesse oblige*. No such considerations influenced

Thatcher – she was the *petit bourgeois* red in tooth and claw and her view of social dynamics was very much the primeval one of sink or swim. No handouts had been available for her father as he went about the difficult task of running his small grocery business in Grantham before the Second World War. He was always diligent, independent and respectable – the embodiment of the values that Thatcher claimed to admire and cherish. There is some irony in Thatcher boasting that no one had ever given her father a leg-up when she, of course, had married a millionaire, a lucky break which was immensely helpful in the development of her own political career. She never had to face the financial and logistical issues of childcare that can make life so difficult for working women on lower incomes. Her vaunted belief in the sanctity of the family was curious. She never allowed her children to be obstacles to her political ambitions and some of her policies led to familial fragmentation in wider society. Another contradiction flowed from the fact that on a personal basis Thatcher was rather prim and puritanical yet the untrammelled commercialism over which she presided encouraged and witnessed an explosion of pornography. Still, it was a free market.

Her petit bourgeois provenance meant that what she said and did resonated with large numbers of Tory Party members in the constituencies and of course loyal lower middle-class and upwardly aspirant working class Tory voters who shared her social background. She was, after all as she was so fond of saying, a grocer's daughter. When she inveighed against direct taxation, public spending, the 'unproductive and bloated' public sector, the 'selfish bully boy' trade unions and spoke sympathetically about tax relief for home owners and small investors, about encouraging farmers and small businesses and bringing back respect for authority with more police visible on the streets, the members and her followers outside the Party recognised her as one of their own.

Labour MPs made a hate figure of Thatcher without really being able to develop a sharp critique or pose a plausible socialist alternative to the ideas she put forward. Roy Hattersley accused her of 'a ruthless electoral strategy' which exploited the economic betterment of 55 per cent of the population while 'ignoring the 45 per cent whose conditions have deteriorated'. Peter Shore claimed that she had brought a new rancour into class struggle (his words), having 'distributed opportunities and income without a blush in favour of those who are already on the top' while simultaneously reducing the benefits payable to those at the bottom. Michael Meacher condemned 'a system of values in which the rich were cosseted and the poor were penalised, in which competitiveness is exhorted without any regard for the losers'. These criticisms were entirely justified but we have to ask why a far more powerful and sustained campaign of challenging her and calling her to account was not launched by the Labour Party. Thatcher put the Opposition on the defensive but only because they allowed her to do so.

Thatcher had (and still has) the ability to polarise opinion and for all those who seemingly admired her for being outspoken, brave and persistent, others could be found who thought her divisive, intolerant, condescending and without compassion. Image was all-important for a political leader and early on in her career it was decided that she desperately needed a new and markedly softer one if she was going effectively to win hearts and minds. One journalist memorably likened her voice to 'a cat sliding down a blackboard.' Another one described it as '…some devilish Roedean water torture'. The image-changers never really did a successful job on her. Out went the egotistical, aggressive, strident and unresponsive persona to be replaced by – a hectoring, patronising, self-righteous and shrill alter ego. Thatcher liked to be remembered as being the lady who was not for turning. As far as her image was concerned she was the lady who was definitely not for softening.

Morality and Freedom

One of the most irksome aspects of Thatcher's time in office was the readiness with which she held forth publicly on a variety of issues and infused what she said with a quasi-religious moral fervour. Even before she was Prime Minister, she declaimed: *In our philosophy the purpose of the life of the individual is not to be the servant of the state and its objectives but to make the best of his talents and qualities. The sense of being self-reliant, of playing a role within the family, or owning one's own property, of paying one's way, are all part of the spiritual ballast which maintains responsible citizenship...*[1] Leaving aside the sexist nature of this statement, how could she dare to prattle on about people making the best of their talents and qualities when she was bent on using unemployment as an instrument of economic policy? As an outcome of her attempts to restore the health of British capitalism, millions were left to rot on the dole, a heinous squandering of their talents and desire to make a contribution. How many families were torn apart as a result of the divisive policies pursued by Thatcher's governments in the 1980s? Far from 'owning one's property', how many people were rendered homeless or forced to live in substandard accommodation because of the unwillingness of capitalism to provide sufficient affordable housing and the selling off of the cream of the council housing stock? Hard to pay your way when you lose your job. Lots of miners never worked again when the pits closed. The true price of home ownership was revealed by an unprecedented number of homes being repossessed by their real owners – the building societies and banks. We could go on. So much for the 'spiritual ballast' which maintains 'responsible citizenship'. Does anybody know what spiritual ballast actually is?

Another word Thatcher readily bandied about was 'freedom'. Liberty and freedom were taken away from people, she said, when taxes were high, when bureaucracy stifled initiative and enterprise and prevented people from following enlightened self-interest. This is a one-sided view of freedom based on the concept that freedom merely consists of an absence of restraint. A counter-argument could be advanced that freedom and liberty can only exist on the basis of positive rights. In an advanced economy like Britain today, jobs should be a right and not a privilege, an affordable home a right and not a privilege, a decent pension is a right and so is a comprehensive health service free at the point of delivery. The poor are much less 'free' than the rich because the choices available to them are far more limited. Deeply rooted in the Thatcherite concept of 'freedom' is the freedom of the rich and powerful to continue enjoying lives of comfort and genuine freedom of choice. The inherited wealth of some of them means that they have never had to work in their lives as their assets simply go on accruing more riches. The Tory Party has always stood in defence of hereditary privilege, a concept which clearly obstructs the range of choices of those from less well-off backgrounds. The idea of hereditary privilege sits uneasily alongside the nonconformist diligence that was part of Thatcher's spiritual upbringing. During the 1983 election campaign she told an audience, "The heart of the

Christian message is that each person has the right to choose." In practice that right is only as reality for those with enough money to afford choices. There were many losers under Thatcherism. They included the unemployed; state pensioners; single parents – often female; those in low-paid casual employment – often female and young people for whom the future seemed to hold few positive prospects. They didn't have many choices or much freedom.

One issue on which Thatcher had (relatively) little to say was the environment. She seemed to think that environmental issues were about litter, graffiti and vandalised empty buildings. As far as she was concerned, these phenomena were symptoms of declining values and could be tackled through the moral rearmament that she claimed was part of her economic programme.

She gave readers the benefits of her home-spun view of the world in an interview with the *Financial Times* when she said;

In my young day there was not such a thing as a Coca-Cola can. We had bottles and we saved them and we took them back and got one penny returns...[2]

She had nothing but contempt for organisations like Greenpeace and thought of environmental activists as contemptible, decadent, anti-capitalist anarchists. Presumably if she ever gave any thought to the innumerable environmental problems mounting up in the world, her solution would have been to leave capitalism alone to maximise its profits and it would soon get round to tackling and dealing with any outstanding issues or problems. Left to itself, capitalism would not do this in a million years.

She had complete faith in nuclear power which totally blinded her to its dangers – both the hazards of potential accidents and the long-term danger of storing nuclear waste. She simply brushed aside the catastrophic explosion at Chernobyl in the Soviet Union in 1986 with the comment that such an incident could never happen in the UK because of the stringent safety codes in place. This remark was uttered as a statement of fact whereas it was only a statement of opinion and an ill-informed one at that.

Thatcher made occasional references to environmental matters especially around 1988 at the time when British scientists claimed to have discovered a huge and ominous hole in the Earth's ozone layer. This, of course, was not the product of natural processes but the result of international capitalism's irresponsible destruction of the finite bounty of the earth while in hot pursuit of profit. Her inability to see any wrong in capitalism meant that she was incapable of making an objective analysis of the problems that it created. She contented herself with expressing the view that concerns about the future of the planet were greatly exaggerated and by doing so kept in the good books of the USA.

Thatcher was a passionate advocate of the private motor car. Railway trains she thought of as dirty, old-fashioned and a bit socialist. The car, by comparison, was the symbol of individual freedom and we were all supposed to worship it. Between 1980 and 1990 the number of private cars on Britain's roads rose from 16.5 million to 22.8 million, i.e. by nearly 40 per cent. By contrast several European countries, less crowded than the UK, invested in fast, modern railway systems in the 1980s in the knowledge that rail was a more environmentally friendly and more ecologically efficient way of moving people and goods.

Did she really believe these things?

Thatcher had a great capacity for self-delusion. In February 1983 she told an interviewer: *What I am desperately trying to do is create one nation, with everyone being a man of property, or having the opportunity to be a man of property.* Apart from another curious all-embracing reference to the male gender, her statement was simply nonsensical. Her policies were utterly divisive, setting North against South, home owners against those in the rented sector, employed against the jobless and dipping her toe in the mire of racism. She was no 'One-Nation' Tory in the Disraeli tradition. Greed, material accumulation and selfishness were exalted. Success was synonymous with making money but social mobility increased little, if at all. The rich got richer, a few ruthless and unscrupulous individuals made it rich, not infrequently at the expense of others, plenty of worthy people worked hard all their lives only to see their hopes of bettering themselves evaporating in Thatcher's Britain and of course, the poor remained poor. In fact they became poorer as the proportion of total wealth going to the rich increased during the Thatcher years. In the 1990s the average household income rose by 36 per cent. The top 10 per cent increased their income by 62 per cent. That of the bottom 10 per cent fell by 17 per cent.

Margaret Thatcher made it as an exhibit at Madame Tussaud's waxworks in the mid-1980s and by 1986 it was reported that she was the political figure on display that people most wanted to see. She was already a lady of legend because visitors ranked her second only to Adolf Hitler in the 'Hate and Fear' category. This piquant juxtaposition of perceptions neatly sums up the duality which was such a feature of her personality, her ideas and her political activity. The values she espoused so vehemently were those of the daughter of a small shopkeeper in a medium-sized market town surrounded by an agricultural hinterland. She felt that she was speaking up for small businesses, the self-employed and the small saver, those who did not have trade unions to fight their battles for them. Although she never realised it, this was a contradictory role. Reduced to essentials, her historical role was the attempt to restore the profitability and competitiveness of British capitalism. But the British economy was dominated by massive business corporations which in growing so big and powerful had mercilessly crushed underfoot the *petit bourgeois* she claimed to speak for. What price the small backstreet grocer in Grantham versus Tesco? The interests of the multi-nationals and those of the small businesses for which she claimed to speak were diametrically opposed and she could not serve both interests at the same time. It can only be assumed that, as usual, she was unaware of the essentially contradictory nature of the task she had set herself.

"Economics are the method: the object is to change the heart and soul." This was one of Thatcher's favourite incantations and it provides a window illuminating the way in which she laced her economic arguments with ethical considerations. She was strongly committed to reversing the growth of collectivism – to her mind tantamount to socialism – in post-war Britain. Instead individual values were to be encouraged by bringing about a reduction in the power of the state and the extent to which it intervened in the economic affairs of the nation. She also believed that a higher moral climate could be achieved by promoting sound money, providing incentives to entrepreneurial enterprise, retuning state-owned businesses and services to the private sector and assisting hard-working, respectable citizens to gain a stake in society particularly through home-ownership. Just how the pursuit of these policies of worshipping materialism would miraculously effect a large-scale moral transformation for the better was never explained in any detail.

As mentioned earlier, the family was an institution which Thatcher seemed to revere, at least in the abstract but as often seems to have happened with her, practice did not necessarily quite square up with the theory. She said that she thought a woman's place was in the home. In view of her own situation this was highly ironic but as the economy picked up, employers wanted female labour because it was cheap and 'flexible' and she could not blind herself to this. During the years of economic recession many of the cuts in social services and benefits fell most heavily on working-class women such as those who were single parents. Thatcher had very little time for such women and absolutely no understanding of the problems they faced. For her and her associates the only real family was the nuclear two-parent family, the parents of course being married. However this was the late twentieth century and many people chose to bring up children in alternative ways.

Unemployment and, where there were jobs, long hours and awkward shifts could play havoc with domestic arrangements and many marriages and long-term partnerships broke up because of the stresses and strains set in motion by the impact of the policies of Thatcher's governments. Employers wanted female workers but were not prepared to put necessary facilities such as crèches in place. Cuts in social service budgets had the effect of returning some functions such as care for the elderly back to the family. The rosy picture painted by the Tories of Mum and Dad with their 2.4 children in their comfortable semi in Surbiton was a long way from the reality, for example, of an elderly couple trying to eke out an existence on the state pension, both having worked hard all their lives and where the wife of 70 was attempting to care for her older husband who was suffering from dementia and needed constant attention at a time when social services were being cut back.

Destroying Socialism

For Thatcher, socialists were envious, divisive and destructive creatures who were incapable of understanding that it was through individual enterprise and the pursuit of self-interest that the wealth that benefited society as a whole was created. She was pathologically incapable of understanding that capitalism is essentially amoral – ultimately all is subordinated to the profit motive. While socialists recognise capitalism as an economic system that historically has been enormously dynamic and progressive in developing the means of creating wealth, they would argue that its success lay in harnessing aggression, greed, ruthlessness and self-interest to create over time a society in which a tiny minority of the population enjoyed most of the wealth, power and good things of life. Socialism has a higher practical and moral purpose. A democratic, planned economy would first of all move to satisfy everyone's basic needs, something which capitalism has never been able to do even in an advanced country like Britain. It would then go on to facilitate the democratically-planned creation of wealth on an unprecedented scale in a society where all would have the opportunity to make the most of their talents and, as Marx said, where it would be 'from each according to his abilities, to each according to his needs'.

Thatcher boasted that three successive governments under her premiership would 'kill off Socialism'. She might as well have tried to bail out the ocean with a teaspoon. It is unhistorical to see capitalism as anything other than just one stage in humankind's material development of culture and civilisation. Each earlier stage gave way to a higher and more efficient way of creating wealth and a new culture associated with that stage. Capitalism contains within itself contradictory forces and processes which are the seeds of its own destruction. Compared to previous cultures, it has had a short life of only a few centuries but, as with its predecessor, feudalism, it will not wither or simply fade away. As we can see today in the events of the last few years, it will stumble along from one crisis to another dragging society backwards into barbarism unless the working class, especially in the advanced economies, consciously move to replace it with socialism, the next and necessarily higher stage in the evolution of society. We can be entirely confident that in the future, people will look back at the early twenty-first century and ponder the question as to why their ancestors tolerated for so long such an inefficient and inequitable way of producing, distributing and exchanging wealth.

The 'killing off of Socialism' which Thatcher boasted about referred to the Labour Party. At grass roots level the Party has always attracted substantial numbers of sincere socialists, often with different perspectives about how and when socialism should be achieved; the party after all, has always been a broad church. When she talked about 'killing off socialism' it was the leadership, direction and policy of the Party that she was referring to. The Blair administration that came to office on a landslide in 1997 got straight on with continuing and widening out the neo-liberal economic policies of its Tory predecessors while sailing under false colours by calling themselves 'New Labour'. The direction the new government intended to follow was clear when within a few days of talking office Blair, to his eternal shame, invited Mrs Thatcher to Downing Street for private discussions on various political policies. No previous Labour Prime Minister had plumbed similar depths, fawning at the feet of an avowed enemy of all that the Labour Party should stand for. How she must have chortled to herself as she was whisked away in her limousine. She had Blair's number and knew that capitalism was safe in his hands. Her glee club agreed. A year into the first Blair administration the 'Economist' slightly grudgingly conceded '…judging by his record so far Mr Blair is a pretty good Tory after all'. The arch right-wing think tank the Adam Smith Institute positively purred as it described New Labour as a 'genuine conservative party'.

Her limited understanding however did not allow her to grasp the fact that having a 'Labour' toy boy at no.10 was not the same thing as eradicating the objective conditions which will cause people to turn to socialist ideas as an alternative to the horrors that capitalism by its very existence inflicts on so many people on this planet.

The Dictatorship of the State

In the course of supposedly rolling back the boundaries of the state in the name of freedom, Thatcher presided over a very marked trend towards centralisation and the widening and strengthening of the authority of the state. When she left office the intrusion of the state into the lives of the people had grown considerably and has continued to do so under the neo-Thatcherite policies of her successors. Thatcher and Blair between them took Britain down the road to an elective dictatorship.

An example of growing authoritarianism could be seen in education. In 1978 James Callaghan when Prime Minister had initiated a debate on teaching standards and the curriculum. Concern had been expressed about the decline of effective discipline in schools, about the supposed relaxed attitude to discipline of many teachers and, so it was alleged, the excessively left-wing propensities of a substantial minority of teachers. It was also claimed that many teachers were incompetent. It was argued that large numbers of young people left school illiterate and innumerate and lacking the attitudes and skills necessary for success in the world of employment. A lot of public money was being thrown at education and thoroughgoing reform was necessary to ensure better value for the taxpayer, it was claimed. The tactics employed were clever in that they implied that there was a consensus among right-minded people about the need for root-and-branch reform. What was really going on was a drive to make education more responsive to the needs of Big Business.

The reformers set about their task by removing the compulsion for local authorities to reorganise secondary education along comprehensive lines; allowing parents to express preferences for the school they wished their child to attend: the appointment of parents and teachers to governing bodies, and the assisted places scheme allowing parents with few financial resources the opportunity to send their offspring to an expensive school in the private sector. The next stage in reform was aimed at undermining the role of teachers. The DES was given more control over teacher training; 'underperforming' teachers were named and shamed with the publication of reports by HMIs and teachers' pay, terms and conditions of employment were unilaterally altered to their disadvantage. Central government increasingly dictated the nature and content of the curriculum. Later on local authorities lost their monopoly of public education provision, head teachers were given more powers and so it went on. The Teachers' Pay and Conditions Act (1987) gave unprecedented power to the senior minister with responsibility for education and completely contradicted the concept of rolling back the state.

Changes in higher education funding were intended to ensure that universities and polytechnics concentrated on teaching and research construed by the Government as 'meeting national needs'. This was a euphemism for inculcating uncritical and unquestioning support for enterprise and capitalism in the minds of young people. The reduced funding available to the University Grants Committee was allocated in favour of the older-established supposedly better universities. The irony was that this was at the expense of newer universities which were more likely to offer the science-based, business and vocational course of which Thatcher approved.

The harmful impact of the reforms to higher education during the Thatcher years even generated criticism from those who were otherwise among Thatcher's staunchest supporters. Examples were Brian Cox, editor of the notorious education Black Papers in the late 1960s, Max Beloff, Principal of the free-enterprise Buckingham University and Kingsley Amis, the novelist who, by this time, had completed his trajectory across the political spectrum from left to right.

We were told that this was part of the nation's necessary moral regeneration. The outcome of these changes was greater inequality, a more demoralised profession and equally large numbers of young people still leaving full-time education with very low literacy, numeracy and life skills. Their choices were strictly limited. So much for their 'freedom'. It is worth mentioning that Thatcher often stated that politics had no place in the classroom. This sat uncomfortably alongside the sight of her handing out 'I love Maggie' hats to children at a school she was visiting during the 1987 election campaign.

R.H. Tawney in *Religion and the Rise of Capitalism* (1926) wrote that there is "no touchstone, except the treatment of childhood, which reveals the true character of a social philosophy more clearly than the spirit in which it regards the misfortunes of those of its members who fall by the way". The values underlying Thatcherism were incompatible with this criterion. Its over-emphasis on the virtues of self-reliance and thrift incited contempt for those not able to be independent or caught in a poverty trap such as the old, the unemployed, the low-paid and those on various benefits. The structure of British society was such that the accident of birth was still the main determinant of wealth or poverty. No career open to all the talents was created during the Thatcher years and many of those she admired as role-models of merit were ruthless entrepreneurs engaged in what were essentially parasitical business activities who, in enriching themselves, made certain that as little as possible of this wealth ever trickled down to anybody. On the other hand, there were plenty of hard-working, self-reliant and thrifty people doing essential jobs on low wages who found themselves being blamed and stigmatised by Thatcher and the New Right for the fact that they were poor.

Thatcher, Blair and Brown between them left Britain's people reeling under the impact and the burden of greater taxation, increasingly restrictive laws, more rules and regulations, less genuine accountability on the part of central government, more inspectors and snoopers, more weasel words about 'transparency', more forms and formalities and much less individual freedom.

There's Nothing as cold as Charity

Speeches by Thatcher were laced with references to how wonderful the Victorian age was. This was an age which sent small children down the pits and up narrow chimney flues in the houses of the rich. It was an age in which working people were old by the time they were in their mid-thirties, if they lived that long. It was an age when women were denied social and political rights. Admittedly it was also an age of extremely valuable social reforms. These were not handed down willingly, however, but had to be fought for by the very kind of people that Thatcher and her associates would have been opposed to had they been alive at the time. The reforms were not entirely altruistic because their intention was to try to ensure minimum standards of health and education for the working class who were, after all, the goose that lay the golden egg so far as profit-making was concerned. It was an age which would have denied Mrs Thatcher the opportunity to enter politics and rise to the Olympian heights of Prime Minister and would have done so for no better reason than because she was a mere woman. To become leader of the Tory Party and then the first woman Prime Minister of Britain was a remarkable feat but she did nothing to advance the situation of women in general. She only ever appointed one woman to the Cabinet and even her stay was a short one.

After the election of 1987 in which she had been extremely lucky that, despite her government's record and unpopularity, Kinnock had been unable to pose an effective critique or alternative, Thatcher gave an interview to 'Woman's Own'. In this interview, she came up with one of her best-known aphorisms:

There is no such thing as society. There are individual men and women, and there are families. And no Government can do anything except through people, and people must look to themselves. It's our duty to look after ourselves and then to look after our neighbour.[3]

The view stated here contrasts sharply with her utterance in 1977 when she said, "Man is a social creature, born into family, class, community, nation, brought up in mutual dependence…" [4]

She went on to say that individuals contributing to charity constituted a more virtuous and beneficial option than collective provision via taxation. This statement itself may beggar belief but she then went on to assert that the richer the wealthy became, the more they could fulfil their social responsibility by giving to charity. Remember that Thatcher argued that if people were needy, it was their fault – they hadn't worked hard enough nor made the most of their opportunities. So those who have fallen by the wayside were to be allowed to scramble for the crumbs that fell from the rich man's table. Some of the rich do engage in philanthropic activity, it is true. Some like to do so in the full flare of publicity because they think it is good for their personal image or the businesses associated with their name. Others do so far more covertly. However any young boy or girl who has ever done a paper round will remember that the Christmas tips tended to be far more generous in the working-class areas of their round than the districts inhabited by the upwardly-aspirant middle class or the definitely already-rich.

Oscar Wilde got it in one when he said that the existence of charity prolongs the evils it attempts to mitigate. At best the charitable efforts of the rich constitute a drop in the ocean and do nothing to tackle the causes of poverty, need and inequality of opportunity. Thatcher's idea has more recently been shared and expanded by David Cameron with his vacuous concept of the 'Big Society'.

She should have been pilloried

Thatcher could sometimes display what, at best, was wanton ignorance and at worst culpable bigotry and prejudice. In March 1988 she made a reference to events in Northern Ireland saying, "There seems to be no depths to which these people will not sink." Those she referred to so disparagingly were specifically the working class Catholics of West Belfast. Thatcher tried to portray the troubles in Northern Ireland as a mindless and pointless tribal conflict. In fact the people she was talking about and their ancestors have had to put up with generations of discrimination and exclusion at the hands of the Protestant minority in this part of Britain. The situation in Northern Ireland was the direct result of the policies of British imperialism back in 1921 when in a desperate attempt to solve the Irish 'problem', the government had created the Catholic-dominated Irish Free State and a Protestant-dominated mini-state in the north. By doing so they managed to create more problems than they solved. The poverty, the discrimination and the continuing tensions between Catholics and Protestants were the result. To dismiss them as she did was disgraceful.

Thatcher once said something to the effect that anybody over the age of 30 who used buses was a 'failure'. Such a statement shows monumental insensitivity, ignorance, stupidity, prejudice and sheer nastiness in equal measures. Buses are used primarily but not exclusively by working-class people. These are the fire-fighters who would risk their lives to rescue her in a conflagration; these are the water-workers who process her excreta; these are the lorry drivers who service the supermarkets where her food is bought; these are the nurses who tend her when she is sick; these are the men and women without whose efforts nothing happens in the economy and society grinds to a halt. They are the salt of the earth. How did she dare to turn her spiteful contempt on such people? Thatcher needed them far more than they needed her.

Thatcher was not and never pretended to be, an intellectual. Generally, the British are not impressed by intellectuals or intellectualism. Thatcher never came across as cool and detached, weighing up the various options in a dispassionate, rational way. She went with her raw, gut feelings. For much of her period in office she was unpopular as the opinion polls showed but for all that she was an effective practitioner of the politician's skills, developing a style which contributed greatly to her winning three consecutive general elections. She seemed direct, seemed to have the courage of her undoubted convictions and an unswerving confidence in the efficacy of her policies. However, her style might not have been so effective in the old days of the rough-and-ready knockabout street corner hustings where she would have simply been shouted down. Now in the new, carefully controlled and less confrontational television-dominated election campaigns, she had conditions that were much more favourable for the display of her particular style.

One of Thatcher's pet hates was the BBC. She loathed the fact that it was state-funded. As far as she was concerned woolly-minded and sanctimonious lefties were writing its programmes in an attempt to undermine decent Christian values and to belittle the business ethic.

She saw it, as a nationalised industry, subsidised, anti-commercial and self-righteous; like the universities, she believed, it poisoned the national debate with woolly liberalism and moral permissiveness at the taxpayers' expense.[5]

Presumably she approved as perfectly right and natural the fact that the British media was overwhelmingly right-wing. That the BBC was one of the few mediums that were available for the sceptically-minded to use in pursuit of the grand old British tradition of questioning and dissent cut no ice with her. She saw to it that new governors when they were appointed were largely drawn from the kind of people she approved of. Her prejudice against the BBC was so intense that even the 'The Sunday Telegraph' accused her of pursuing a vendetta! Denis Thatcher once said, "Of course, everybody at the BBC's a Trotskyist."[6] The problem with Denis was that if anybody else had made such a crass statement it would have been thought that he was joking.
In his case he actually meant it.

By your Friends

A particular favourite of Thatcher's was Rupert Murdoch. In pursuit of her desire to ensure that the media was in 'safe' hands, he helped him to acquire *The Times* and *Sunday Times* in 1981. She connived at efforts made by others to ensure that Murdoch's acquisitions were not referred, as they should have been, to the Monopolies and Mergers Commission. One good turn deserves another and soon, despite Murdoch's assurances of editorial independence, he saw to it that these papers were rooting for Maggie. She saw nothing anomalous or essentially anti-democratic about one extremely rich and powerful man using the media that he owned to disseminate his views of the world and how it should be as if they were facts. Likewise she allowed Murdoch to acquire a monopoly of satellite television, another move not referred to the Monopolies Commission. Thatcher was fully in support of Murdoch's battle against the print unions and the transfer of his operations from Fleet Street to Wapping. She chose to turn a blind eye to the soft porn, sleaze, crassness and general banality of Murdoch's 'Sun' and 'News of the World' titles so long as they rallied to her support. Thatcher was by no means fussy about those she had as her friends.

The louche Robert Maxwell was another gun-toting entrepreneur who Thatcher admired. He bought the *Daily Mirror* in 1984. This move was supported by Thatcher who told one of the newspaper's correspondents, "A dose of Maxwell will do you good." She said that in the full knowledge that the Department of Trade had ruled in 1971 that Maxwell was unfit to run a public company.

It was not only about her friendships with certain foreign men like Reagan and Pinochet that questions could be asked about Thatcher. Far from being 'iron', she was more like putty when it came to being handled by the likes of Cecil Parkinson and Jeffrey Archer. The first was a smooth-talking and highly ambitious social climber who enjoyed looking and sounding more patrician than those from genuinely patrician backgrounds. The second was transparently an arrogant and devious bounder who would have made a very successful snake-oil salesman. Parkinson's ambitions for the highest political office after a meteoric rise under the patronage of Thatcher were dished when it was revealed that he had had a long-term extra-marital affair. His mistress, Sarah Keays, was expecting his child. He retired to the back benches hoping to return to ministerial office when the dust had settled. It is thought that Thatcher had known about the infidelity before it became common knowledge and was disappointed that her protégé had been indiscreet enough to be found out.. At Thatcher's behest he did later stage a return to the front benches but he had enemies in the party and the rising star John Major made no secret of his dislike for Parkinson. He was too closely associated with Thatcher and, probably wisely, he left office when she was ousted. In 2001 it emerged that although he had paid for the child's education and upbringing, he had never seen her nor even as much as given her a Christmas present. He was widely denounced as heartless when it became known that the child had severe learning difficulties. It was also revealed that he had repeatedly promised Ms Keays that he would leave his wife and as frequently reneged on his promise. The writer is not judging Parkinson on his morals but making the point that the Tory Party has always proudly claimed to stand as the defender of family values. Thatcher herself made a great point of the moral and social virtues of the family. While loyalty is an admirable quality, it is either hypocritical or inconsistent to say one thing and do another but then, as we have seen, this was a common trait with Thatcher.

The British honours system is a curious animal because it made a 'Right Honourable' out of Jeffrey Archer, late of HMP Belmarsh and a number of other establishments where he resided during the Queen's Pleasure. Silk purses and sow's ears come quickly to mind. This gentleman led what can only be described as a varied and multi-faceted life and his curriculum vita would have made interesting reading as a piece of fiction even more imaginative than Archer's own literary efforts. Whatever he did and wherever he went, it seems he was dogged by disparaging rumours and accusations. It was even alleged that he had used false references in order to obtain a place in higher education. Dodgy financial dealings seem to have been his particular forte and he often appeared to have material possessions and a lifestyle that were incompatible with the relatively low-paid occupations he ostensibly pursued. Questions about his probity followed wherever his nose for business took him, be it charity fund-raising or dodgy share deals. He was eventually convicted of perjury for which he served time although some people thought that the conditions under which he was detained were less onerous than might have been expected for the very serious crime for which he had been convicted. He was another of Thatcher's blue-eyed boys and it was on the basis of her patronage that he became Deputy Chairman of the Tory Party, much to the horror of those party grandees who thought he was an upstart and a chancer. People are known by the company they keep and friendships are a reflection of character. Her regard for someone like Archer might cause some people seriously to call her judgement into question. Mind you, this was the woman who called Nelson Mandela a terrorist and whose husband, Denis, sniggered as he referred to native South Africans as 'coons'.

No one should swallow the myth about 'The lady is not for turning'. We do not know whether a speechwriter came up with this phrase for her or whether she was adlibbing when these words first passed her lips. Either way, it was a smart sound byte but it gave a very misleading impression of a politician who was actually far more pragmatic than she would have liked to admit. In her early years she talked constantly about monetarism only for the word and the practices it involved quietly to slide away as she abandoned them later on. An early thrust to reduce inflation made considerable headway and she let everyone know it but was much quieter on the same subject when the level of inflation began creeping up once more. Her promises drastically to reduce public spending needed constant modification in the light of her inability to deliver, and so it went on. She could not work miracles and she had no choice but to turn or bend with the wind when the situation required it. She never succeeded in her avowed intention of reducing the share of GDP consumed by the state.

The image of Thatcher never lived up to the reality. She had a distinctive style and modus operandi, thankfully very much of her own, built upon and around a carefully cultivated image supported up by equally carefully created myths. Some of her most devoted admirers claimed that she saved the nation. How could one person do that? From what did she save it? David Cameron has spoken about 'Broken Britain'. Her policies did not create an economic miracle and they initiated processes taken up by her successors which led Cameron to use this very apt phrase although he did so as a politician's gibe against New Labour and was only unconsciously speaking the truth.

History is unlikely to be kind to Margaret Thatcher.

1. Speech delivered at Zurich in 1977 quoted in Kavanagh, D. (1990), *Thatcherism and British Politics: The End of Consensus,* Oxford, p.295
2. Interview in *Financial Times,* 11 December 1989.
3. Interview in *Woman's Own,* 31 October 1987.
4. Thatcher in *Ian Macleod Memorial Lecture,* 4 July 1977.
5. Campbell (2004), op.cit. p.401.
6. Quoted in Cole, J. (1995), *As it seemed to me*, London, p.346.

17. DECLINE AND FALL

There was a growing feeling in her last few years in high office that Thatcher was losing it. This feeling was widespread in the Conservative Party, evident elsewhere in the House and a constant talking point among political commentators. It certainly accelerated after, and in spite of, her third successive election victory in 1987, and it seemed as though she and the mission she had set herself were still running full steam ahead but not fully under control and having no idea where they were going. Even her fans (and she always had some hard-core faithfuls) felt that she was beginning to lose her touch – that what they had first thought of as fresh and innovative about her approach was now beginning to look tarnished and careworn. The more charitably-inclined perhaps thought that she had done what she had to do. Politicians should never overstay their welcome. While it might be politic to go gracefully earlier rather than to stay and to be pushed later when things started going seriously wrong, would Thatcher ever leave centre-stage voluntarily?

As she went into political decline, Thatcher's growing inability to see herself as others saw her, to recognise and acknowledge her faults and increasingly lose touch with reality was clearly demonstrated when she told a close political associate, "They say I am arrogant, I am the least arrogant person there is."

Certainly some people had much to thank her for. The long-term rich had never had it so good. Since most seriously rich people had inherited their wealth and because a certain level of wealth simply generates more riches without any effort on the part of its owner, Thatcher's 'achievement' of further enriching this narrow layer of society stood at odds with her stated aims of rewarding merit and hard work. There was also a significant layer of *nouveaux riche* who had come by wealth as a result of financial deregulation or by the exercise of the kind of rapacious entrepreneurial enterprise that Thatcher had strongly encouraged. Many of them were asset-strippers, traders, dealers and speculators who made paper millions often at the push of a button on a keyboard but whose activities actually produced no real wealth. This was the day of the 'yuppie' frequently behaving loutishly and flaunting his or her ability to consume conspicuously. They were dubious exemplars of the morality and hard work that Thatcher claimed to champion.

Thatcher had increasingly lost touch with reality, being cocooned from the everyday experiences of ordinary people by an entourage of aides, understrappers and security personnel. Her public appearances were arranged and choreographed so as to avoid unpleasantness and embarrassment because throughout the period of her premiership, hostile demonstrators, even if only in small numbers, often gathered in order to let her know what they thought of her. A team of advisors carefully selected the information that she was fed with, knowing that they were in for a hard time if they brought her news that she did not want to hear. Thatcher had little respect for the fact that the bearer of bad news was just a messenger.

In her later years, she got through ministers at a remarkable rate, if anything becoming more ruthless as her confidence in the rightness of her policies hardened. The casualty rate kept everyone on their toes but even minor peccadilloes on the part of ministers or aspiring up-and-comers could be enough for them to get the black spot from Thatcher. She could be disloyal even to those with whom she had worked closely and reasonably amicably and so those in the Government were kept in a permanent state of anxiety and insecurity, fearing what would happen if they got it wrong. She had her favourites, thereby encouraging sycophancy and she was amenable to flirting and flattery although her understrappers had to learn quickly how to identify her moods and know when it was time to keep a low profile. They lived and worked on a knife edge, anxious not to catch the eye of their increasingly cantankerous and irrational mistress when she was not having a good day.

As she went into decline, she had those kinds of days more frequently. She proposed to end the BBC monopoly on public-service broadcasting and was forced into a U-turn by the sustained opposition not only of the media but large numbers of her political colleagues. Her attempt to cut down on football hooliganism by the introduction of identity cards proved to be a fiasco. So did her creation of a student loans company for this quickly went bankrupt. The Child Support Agency was set up in an attempt to make parents meet their financial obligations to their children where families had split up. Intended to save public money, it proved expensive and inefficient and became something of a standing joke before it was abolished in 2006.

Thatcher's proverbial luck was beginning to run out. Although she could not directly take the blame, a number of disasters occurred which somehow seemed to be the products of or associated with the brave new world which she had so forcefully championed and of which she was so proud. First the ostentatiously-named *Herald of Free Enterprise* ferry sank in 1987 with 187 deaths, an accident resulting from the owning company's desire to maximise its profits by cutting down on turn round times, streamlining procedures and reducing crew numbers. There were serious rail disasters at Kings Cross in 1987 and at Clapham in 1988. A Thames pleasure boat, the *Marchioness* was in collision in 1989 and sank with many deaths. 1989 also saw the disaster at Hillsborough stadium in Sheffield where 96 Liverpool FC fans were crushed to death. Police incompetence was a major factor but the *Sun* newspaper to its eternal shame blamed drunken Liverpool fans who it claimed rifled through the pockets of their dead mates. Memories are long on Merseyside and many people there will still not buy the paper.

It was understandable that many sought to blame these events on the 'get rich quick mentality' which had been forced on the nation in the Thatcher years. The chickens were coming home to roost on deregulation, staffing cuts and lack of investment on the country's infrastructure. As A.N. Wilson said:

Unless we all decide to vote Labour… we may face a dud future with dud trains, dud libraries, dud museums, dud hospitals and the poor getting poorer – sans eyes, sans teeth, sans everything.[1]

Thatcher had made her years of administration so personal and had been so given to boasting about how successful she had been that it was not surprising that she then had to take much of the rap when things started going seriously wrong. Evidence of sleaze and seedy scandals only added to the tarnished image of both Thatcher and the Tory government.

That Thatcher managed to fall out openly with some of her previous closest associates presaged her political decline. Well publicised and acrimonious resignations of leading figures of the stature of Nigel Lawson and Sir Geoffrey Howe in 1989 and 1990 respectively strongly suggested that the wheels were coming off. By now even some people thought of as being as totally Thatcherite as Norman Tebbitt had distanced themselves from her. Cabinet reshuffles were frequent enough to be taken as evidence of serious malaise at senior levels of the Party. There were six cabinet reshuffles in fifteen months as her career as Prime Minister went into free fall.

Thatcher's nemesis was, of course, the Community Charge (her name) which became commonly and abusively known as the 'poll tax'. This aroused controversy right from the time it was first mentioned publicly in 1985. It may have been evidence that Thatcher was approaching her sell-by-date because it was a policy that was inevitably unpopular across a wide spectrum of society, including many of those middle-class elements who were normally the bedrock of support for the Tories and indeed there were many leading Tories who were hostile to it. There was, almost, unbelievably, a demonstration against the tax in posh Maidenhead!

A uniform rate was charged on every adult resident in a local government district irrespective of their ability to pay. A millionaire, a benefit claimant and a pensioner all paid the same amount just as they all had the same vote but was it perfect equality? It was the complete opposite. The poll tax bill for a millionaire might represent one-thousandth of his annual income whereas for a low-paid worker it obviously represented a far higher percentage. Her advisers warned her against it but she regarded it as the flagship policy of what turned out to be her last administration. It was a typical Tory tax – regressive and therefore inherently unfair and it provoked riots with many people risking prosecution rather than paying the tax. Some people went to prison but had their convictions overturned on appeal – this was messy and harmful for the Government's credibility. Some councils reported non-payment levels as high as 50%. Thatcher defended the poll tax on the grounds that it gave all the residents in a local authority area a direct interest in ensuring 'good housekeeping' or value for money and, in effect, becoming involved in exercising much greater control over their local council. The poll tax was one mistake too many for Thatcher and time was rapidly running out for her. For someone who proudly boasted that she knew what people wanted, this was an awful tactical mistake because the people told her exactly what she could do with the tax. Nevertheless, Thatcher remained convinced that she had been right on the merits of the community tax. This was not just stubborness, it was pig-headed stupidity. She was right and everyone else was wrong. The estimated cost of setting up and then abolishing the poll tax was £20 billion.

> Nothing did more than the poll tax to precipitate Mrs Thatcher's downfall. It seemed to epitomise the least attractive aspects of her political personality – a hard-faced inegalitarianism combined with a pig-headed authoritarianism – and at the same time it demonstrated a fatal loss of political judgment.[2]

One of the major bones of contention in the Tory Party was the question of the European Union and the role Britain was to play in it. No ruling class is ever totally homogeneous and although the role of the Tories was to promote the interests of the ruling class via Parliament, some MPs supported the industrial wing which was keen to sell in Europe and therefore were conciliatory on the issue. Others were supportive of the financial sector which was trading in sterling and wanted good relationships with the USA. By her posturing, her patronising and her belligerence, she did little to raise Britain's standing in the world. She was correctly thought of as having made the UK increasingly subservient to the USA, the latter's aggressive imperialism making it unpopular in many parts of the world. She was disliked by many politicians on the Continent who believed that she willfully refused to engage constructively in matters of European concern.

Cracks and fissures were visibly opening up in the Tory Party. The very public disaffection and then resignation of Michael Heseltine after the Westland Affair unquestionably caused head-shaking in the Party's inner circles. Tory MPs and ministers were becoming increasingly irritated by Thatcher's growing habit of 'going public' on matters which were best kept private and doing so entirely off her own bat. Further evidence of disenchantment came in 1989 when, for the first time in the fourteen years that Thatcher had led the Party, an MP came forward to challenge her leadership. This upstart was a rather eccentric figure by the name of Sir Anthony Meyer. He did not constitute a serious threat but it was the fact that he stood at all which was significant. He may have received only thirty-three votes but it was impossible under the circumstances to construe this as meaning anything other than the reality that there were at least thirty-three Tory MPs who had simply had enough of Thatcher.

In 1990 a general election was imminent, Labour was well ahead in the opinion polls and it was inevitable that there would be widespread discussions among the cognoscenti in exclusive West End clubs, in the bars of SW1 pubs, on private golf courses and even in draughty corridors in the Palace of Westminster about the wisdom or otherwise of going into that election with Thatcher as Tory leader. Had she become an electoral liability? If she was ousted, was there anyone else who was likely to lead them to victory at a time when the Tory Government was looking tired and the electorate seemed jaded with them. The challenge when it came was from the formidable, energetic and highly ambitious Michael Heseltine. The reality was that Thatcher's authority in the Party was ebbing away visibly and there were a large number of MPs in marginal constituencies looking anxiously over their shoulders, not enamoured by the prospect that they might have to pick up a UB40 and sign on down the Social. The omens suggested by the opinion polls were not favourable about another Tory election victory.

In the event, Thatcher gained 204 votes in the first round, Heseltine gaining 152. Even those close to her said, if not quite so directly, that she should go because the chances of her winning the second round were almost non-existent. She was angry and embittered by what she thought was the personal disloyalty of so many Tory MPs but was quite unable to see that for some of them it was less a personal issue than a career one In some cases it was probably both. While she had her enemies in the Party, those MPs as a whole felt that Thatcher had fought her battles and many admired her for doing so. They saw her as a good battling leader but did not think she had anywhere to go now, was no longer the right person to take the country forward. They feared for their careers if she remained leader. As

Michael Cockerell wrote:

> With the lack of new battles to fight, the Prime Minister's combative virtues were being received as vices: her determination was perceived as stubbornness; her single-mindedness as inflexibility and her strong will as an inability to listen.[3]

Sir Geoffrey Howe resigned as Deputy Prime Minister on 1 November 1990. He was seen as one of Thatcher's staunchest supporters but she had systematically and publicly humiliated him over the years. His patience finally ran out and he had had enough when she refused to agree a timetable for Britain to join the European single currency. Shortly afterwards he made his feelings known in an unexpectedly rancorous speech in the Commons and it was this chain of events which sealed the fate of Thatcher's premiership. Heseltine then followed up, like Brutus, delivering the death-blow by challenging her leadership. Her cabinet were unsympathetic and the world was soon treated to the sight of a tearful Margaret Thatcher leaving No.10, Downing Street, having resigned as Prime Minister and Leader of the Conservative Party. She considered herself to have been brought down by perfidious and unworthy peers and seemed completely bemused by the speed and the direction that events had taken. The standing of the Tory Party in the polls shot up overnight under the new leadership of John Major, perceived as a far more reasonable person than Thatcher. However Thatcher need not have worried. Her policies continued. It was just that her colleagues had decided it was better for them to continue without her. She had become a political liability. We should always remember that it was not the electorate who gave Thatcher her marching orders. It was her colleagues who assassinated her. Although they had a strong sense of political self-preservation, they clearly did not share the unalloyed belief in her unique rightness that was such a leitmotif of Thatcher.

To the end, Thatcher was unable to take on board the fact that perhaps she had got things wrong. She regarded the advice of senior colleagues to step down after the first ballot as "treachery with a smile on its face." She thought that they were being disloyal but she never stopped to think how little loyalty she had ever shown to those for whom she no longer had any use or for those who disagreed with her or even those who might be highly able but could possibly pose a threat in the future.

She was the only one seemingly incapable of grasping the reality of her headlong fall. The situation was summed up by political commentator Robert Harris. He wrote:

> The crisis is entirely the responsibility of the Prime Minister: of her addiction to power, of her arrogance, of the contempt with which she treats her colleagues... For more than a decade, the Prime Minister has abused the power of her office to undermine and crush anyone who opposed her. She has now achieved what one presumes is her idea of state of grace: to be the only member of the 1979 cabinet still in government. No other leader in British political history has behaved in such a fashion. Her style is the substance of the crisis...she will destroy any minister who crosses her; ...she lacks the common sense and even, dare one say it, the common decency to preside over a talented cabinet; she has become a menace to our system of government and to our national interest; she is, in sum, unfit to rule.[4]

As she left Downing Street for the last time she said, "...we're very happy that we leave the United Kingdom in a very, very much better state than when we came eleven and a half years ago." This was mere delusion; simply untrue. The policies applied during her terms in office had created the start of 'Broken Britain'. When the news of her fall broke, cheers resounded across the land and people danced in the streets.

By the time she went, people had been worn down by her remorseless desire to interfere, to control and find someone or something new to fight. It was good riddance. Nigel Lawson put it succinctly:

Her ceaselessly confrontational style became – in the view of her long-suffering colleagues who had tried to pick up the pieces after her bravura perfomances – counterproductive.[5]

The statement that Thatcher was popular is a myth, nothing more. Even many of those who thought she was administering some much-needed medicine did not like her because there was simply not much about her that was likeable. While too much credibility should not be invested in opinion polls, they clearly showed that she was personally unpopular for most of her premiership and that some flagship policies like attacking the unions, privatisation of the utilities, tax-cuts for the rich and, of course, the poll-tax never enjoyed popular support even with the media throwing their weight behind them. Many of those who counted themselves as materially better-off as a result of the Thatcher years felt those same years had seen the encouragement of undesirable, unethical and antisocial attitudes and practices. They were uneasy with the blatant worship of money and wealth no matter how it was obtained.

Despite her apparently championing freedom and the small state, she is indelibly associated with a command economy with formidably increased areas of centralised jurisdiction. On numerous occasions she derided the 'nanny state' but she was the greatest nanny of all and not a benevolent one at that. Her governments were devoted to dismantling the state and yet they ended up greatly strengthening it. She was an authoritarian and that approach to government was continued and enhanced by Blair and Brown. They continued to privatise and reform the public services as if they were on a carousel which continued to whirl round uncontrollably. They seemed to accept that there was no alternative to the perpetual motion of this carousel but this motion has left society dizzy and exhausted. Even the current Coalition government has the same sense of the job not yet being done and more reform and change needed – to achieve what? Will we know when or if we get there? Will it be any better? If so, for whom?

Has there ever been a time since the achievement of universal suffrage when so many people have so strongly distrusted politicians and felt so powerless to change things, that they are virtually disfranchised? From Thatcher's time onwards there have been widespread feelings that just about every aspect of public life is incompetently run or tainted in some way; that no one actually knows what is going on or how to control what is happening. The environmental decay, the shortage of affordable housing, the continuing closure of what is left of manufacturing industry, the rundown of public services, the growing dole queues, the bleak and uncertain future facing youth, the obscene arrogance personified by the pay and perks arrogated to themselves by bankers and many senior executives, the public pensions scams – all these breed cynicism and resignation at the same time. Diversions are continually being created – a royal wedding here, a royal jubilee there, even the Olympic Games and we are told that they give us the 'feel good factor'. We'll be have a royal baby next but who's kidding? None of these have anything to do with the grim reality of everyday life for millions of people in modern Britain. The market, the trickledown of wealth from enterprise to the poor and the benefits of the enterprise culture – all have been revealed as nothing more than chimeras.

Britain rose from fifteenth in 1980 to top in 1999 of the OECD table of countries rated for 'economic freedom' and 'entrepreneurial welcome'. By any standards this was a remarkable turn round and other countries gazed on this transformation enviously and decided to try emulating the kind of measures associated with Thatcher. The world of international capitalism had experienced an unpleasant shock with the end of the post-war boom and was forced to re-evaluate and make some changes in a politically rightward direction in a new post-industrial world.

Thatcher referred in euphoric and exaggerated terms to the impact she thought she had had in the world:

So popular is our policy that it's being taken up all over the world. From France to the Philippines, from Jamaica to Japan, from Malaysia to Mexico, from Sri Lanka to Singapore, privatisation is on the move... The policies we have pioneered are catching on in country after country. We Conservatives believe in popular capitalism, believe in a property-owning democracy. And it works! [6]

The USA, Australia, New Zealand, some South American countries and a few elsewhere carried out some policies the inspiration for which might be traceable to Thatcher. She may have been seen by some as a role model but she no more than anyone else was capable of resolving the internal contradictions of capitalism and the world currently faces a future of intense uncertainty because of those contradictions and which neo-liberalism if anything exacerbated. Thatcher was desperate for Thatcherism to live on after her departure from active politics. It did, and the current Coalition Government is floundering around ineptly and incompetently trying to solve the problems of capitalism bequeathed from and made worse by Thatcher and her successors.

1. Interview in *The Spectator*, 11 May 1989.
2. Campbell (2004), op.cit. p.562.
3. Cockerell, M. (1988), *Live from Number 10: The Inside Story of Prime Ministers and Television*, London, p.307.
4. Harris, R. 'Thatcher is now for burning – win or lose', *Sunday Times*, 18 November 1990.
5. Lawson, N. (1992), op.cit. p.898.
6. Speech to the Conservative Party Conference, 10 October 1986.

18. CONCLUSIONS

Thatcher was in absolutely no doubt when she left office that the British economy was in a far healthier state than it had been when she assumed office eleven and a half years earlier but then she would say that. She said more. During her years in office, Britain, she claimed, had experienced "a total industrial and commercial transformation" accompanied by a "colossal increase in efficiency of our manufacturing industries." As the well-known popular philosopher Dr Joad was given to saying, "It all depends what you mean by…"

1989 marked the end of Thatcher's last full term as Prime Minister so it is an appropriate time to make some assessment of what her governments actually achieved. The following points are drawn, where possible, from official statistics and ministerial answers in *Hansard*. Unfortunately, a caveat needs to be applied at this stage. Government statistics became increasingly unreliable during her period in office. 'Cooking the books' is a phrase that comes to mind and lest that be thought of as being unduly cynical, a degree of scepticism is understandable given that almost 30 different yardsticks were applied to the production of official statistics concerning unemployment. Some other data series simply ceased to be made public. An example was the Low Income Family Statistics. Had they continued to be published, it is unlikely that they would have shed a favourable light on Thatcher's achievements.

Inflation rose from 10.3 per cent in May 1979 and peaked at about 18 per cent in 1980. It then fell quite dramatically to 3.4 per cent in 1986 after which its trend was once more upwards. It would be wrong to ascribe the fall in inflation to some magical nostrum of Thatcher or her Chancellor. Inflation fell in all the major economies of the world at least partly because of a short-term fall in commodity prices. By 1989, however, the UK's inflation was about twice the average of the leading industrial countries. Energy prices for consumers rose by inflation-busting rates and customers of privatised water supplies on average paid 22 per cent more in 1989 than they had in 1988.

Britain's share of world trade fell by 15 per cent between 1979 and 1986 which was a larger share than that experienced by any other major industrial country. In 1988 the deficit in the balance of payments was larger than any in the previous forty years, amounting to 4 per cent of GDP. A £5 billion surplus in the export of manufactured goods over imports in 1978 had become a £14.4 billion deficit in 1988. Without the contribution of North Sea Oil the deficit in the balance of payments would have amounted to at least 6 per cent of GDP. Even Thatcher could not take credit for the bonanza extracted from under the cold, grey waters of the North Sea!

A key component of Thatcherism was the reduction of public spending in an attempt to reduce interest rates. A Public Sector Borrowing Requirement of £10 billion in 1979-80 became a debt repayment of £14 billion in 1988. Between 1986 and 1988 UK interest rates were the highest of any major industrial countries. In January 1989, for example, they were 8 points higher than Japan and 4 points higher than the USA. Mortgage rates were never less than 9.5 per cent from 1978 to 1989 and, if inflation is taken into account, real interest rates in the UK in 1989 were at their highest level since the Napoleonic Wars.

The UK economy grew less than other major economies in the Thatcher years. Even with North Sea oil, economic growth under the Tories was slower than it had been under the Labour Government of 1974 to 1979. It averaged just 1.8 per cent per annum compared with 2.5 per cent under Labour. In 1987 and 1988 there was a short-lived surge when GDP grew by over 4 per cent in both years which was faster than any other major industrial country. The rate of growth then began to fall away again. Manufacturing output fell by 14 per cent between 1979 and 1981 and did not return to its 1979 level until 1987. Over those years manufacturing output rose in Japan by 38 per cent, in the USA by 25 per cent and in West Germany by 12 per cent. As would be expected, Britain's share of manufacturing exports in world trade fell. Given that there was economic growth under Thatcher, albeit sluggish, that growth was largely concentrated in south-eastern England. The heartlands of the old manufacturing and extractive industries saw precious little growth. It was an echo of Disraeli's 'Two Nations'.

The productivity of manufacturing industry rose by over 4 per cent per annum between 1979 and 1988 which was the fastest growth rate of all the major economies. It was largely the result of intensifying the rate of exploitation of the labour force by shedding jobs and forcing down the terms and conditions of those still in work. In spite of this 'success', the UK remained in the bottom six of the European industrial productivity tables. Investment in the UK economy, crucial to the task of creating the basis for sustained recovery, was less than that of any of her major international competitors and half of that in Japan, for example. Between 1979 and 1987 investment in the UK rose by just 9 per cent which was less than half as fast as consumer spending. At the end of 1988, manufacturing investment was still below its level in 1979. Investment in public infrastructure such as schools, hospitals and roads fell by 50 per cent between 1979 and 1988.

Over the same years, consumer credit, including mortgages, doubled in real terms. Over 100,000 families lost their homes because they were unable to maintain their mortgage payments and repossessions by lenders rose by 800 per cent. More than 60,000 people were declared bankrupt which was double the normal rate. Not to be outdone, the annual rate of companies going into liquidation also doubled.

Nearly two million jobs were lost between 1979 and 1983, a very high proportion of them in manufacturing. By September 1987 the number of employed was close to where it had been in 1979 but a large percentage of them were service sector part-time and low-paid jobs. Many of these were located in the South-East and in the Midlands and were predominantly taken by women, thereby accentuating their tendency to be in low-paid jobs. Unemployment reached a peak of 13 per cent in July 1986. Rates of unemployment in the North-West, the North, In Wales, Scotland and Northern Ireland were twice that in the South-East and they fell more slowly.

The 1970s saw a narrowing of the gap between the earnings of the lowest tenth of full-time workers and the highest tenth. Under Thatcher this desirable trend was reversed. As far as the lowest tenth of male workers were concerned, their wages increased in real terms by 6 per cent between 1979 and 1987 while the earnings of the highest tenth grew by 30 per cent.

Britain's training programme performed dismally compared to those of her major competitors. In what was then West Germany only 21 per cent of the workforce had no occupational qualifications in 1989 whereas in the UK the figure was 66 per cent. The Tory Governments abolished the statutory industry training boards and what had been the Manpower Services Commission, passing over the responsibility for training to the employers. In 1986-7 employers spent just 0.6 per cent of GNP on training. Skills shortages in 1988 were slightly higher than they had been in 1979.

Inequalities in the distribution of income increased substantially between 1979 and 1988. If we take income as consisting of pay, dividends, pensions and benefits, over the period from 1979 to 1986 the average real income of all households taken together increased by 12 per cent. However only the richest 30 per cent of households exceeded this average. The top 1 per cent of households enjoyed a rise of 55 per cent while the top 10 per cent did not do too badly with 31 per cent. The poorest 40 per cent of households suffered an actual decline in real income. The poorest tenth lost 8 per cent of their 1979 income. Behind these raw statistics lay further disadvantage in unemployment and low pay experienced by ethnic minorities.

Poverty increased sharply in Thatcher's Britain. In 1985 it was estimated that 17 per cent of the population were living at or below the official poverty line. This was an increase of 55 per cent since Thatcher became Prime Minister. The number of children in poverty nearly doubled and by 1985, two-thirds of disabled people were living at or below the official poverty line. In the same year, it was estimated that 28 per cent of the population were in poverty or on its margins. By contrast, by 1989 the richest 1 per cent of the UK population owned one-fifth of the total marketable wealth of the country. 'Wealth' is here defined as houses, land, other physical assets, company shares, life insurance policies, cash and other financial assets but not pension rights. On this definition, the richest 2 per cent owned more than the bottom 75 per cent. The trend to greater equality of wealth which was apparent between 1966 and 1980 was reversed.

In 1988-9 British taxpayers paid £20 billion less in income tax than they would have paid under the 1978-9 income-tax rates. However 23 per cent of this income-tax saving went to the top 1 per cent, each of whom gained an average of £22,680 per year. This cool little tax cut they enjoyed was a larger sum of money than the income of 95 per cent of the taxpaying population. However, by 1988 most British families were paying a greater share of their income in taxes than they did in 1979. This was because of increases in national Insurance and VAT, the effect of which is to redistribute the tax burden from the better-off to the worse-off. Hence an average family with two children paid only 35.1 per cent of its income in taxes in 1978-9, by 1988-9 it found itself paying 37.3 per cent. The level of State retirement pensions fell, relative to earnings after the Government cut the link between pensions and earnings in 1980 and relying on a state pension became more-or-less synonymous with living in poverty.

The lives of ordinary people in British society were blighted in other ways by the neo-liberal policies of Thatcher's governments. The crime rate rose significantly from 1979. Reported notifiable offences rose from 2.7 million in 1980 to 3.9 in 1987, an increase of 45 per cent. Armed robberies tripled from under 1,000 to 3,000 a year. Spending on the police rose by 30 per cent and the number of police officers increased by 9.5 per cent but the average clear-up rate for all crimes fell from 40 per cent in 1980 to 33 per cent in 1987 creating a feeling that crime was out of control. Meanwhile the prison population had grown to a record 50,400 in 1988. This was the highest both in relative and absolute terms in the EEC as the government impotently floundered around trying to stem the rising tide of crime by throwing the relatively small number of those brought to justice into overcrowded gaols.

Not only were Thatcher's governments making a mess of the present, they were mucking up the future as well. From 1982-3 to 1989, they cut capital spending on education by about 10 per cent in real terms. Teachers became increasingly disillusioned and in many places were in seriously short supply. Many older school buildings suffered from lack of maintenance and in some schools class numbers escalated to unmanageable numbers. Higher education did not escape and total funding fell by 5 per cent between 1982-3 and 1986-7.

The number of families categorised as homeless doubled from 56,750 in 1979 to 112,400 in 1987. Single homeless people were not included in official statistics. In 1987 an estimated 25,000-40,000 young people were sleeping rough in London alone. One estimate is that there were 150,000 young single homeless in 1988. Meanwhile the number of all new houses completed in the UK fell by 17 per cent. Local authority new housing completions fell by 75 per cent and over 1 million public-sector homes were sold. Between 1983-7 local authority waiting lists rose by 170 per cent. The cost to the exchequer of mortgage tax relief doubled in real terms in 1987-8 when it began to be phased out.

Poverty was bad for the health in Thatcher's Britain. Between 1979 and 1986, 285 NHS hospitals closed and a further 126 at least partly closed. This could cause serious problems by pushing up transport costs for the poor. The number of hospital beds was cut by 14 per cent or 50,470. The number of acute beds was reduced by 19,000. Hospital waiting lists rose from 628,000 in 1979 to over 700,000 in 1987. Inequalities in health and life expectancy between manual and non-manual workers increased. Prescription charges rose by 577 per cent in real terms and by 1,200 per cent in cash terms.

Incidents of water pollution rose by 69 per cent between 1980 and 1987. In the latter years it was estimated that about 50 per cent of Britain's beaches were seriously polluted, not least with raw sewage. Public transport was run down. What used to be British Rail saw its fixed asset investment fall from 24 per cent from 1977-8 to 1988. Expenditure on track and signalling fell by 14 per cent while air pollution created by road vehicles rose by 16 per cent.

These are just some of the criteria by which Thatcher's record should be judged. Did Thatcher's policies create the conditions for future sustained economic growth? Did they restore the long-term profitability of British business? Did they reverse Britain's relative decline as a world economic power? Since for Thatcher economic and moral issues were interlinked, did she succeed in sparking a renewed sense of national purpose? Did her admonitions help to stimulate a revival in the morale and mores of the British population? On a different plane, did she manage to turn round Britain's previously flagging prestige so that the UK came once more to be regarded as a serious major player in international diplomatic circles?

Thatcher always said there would be no gain without pain. The pain was enormous but Thatcher and the motley crew with which she surrounded herself ensured that the pain was not shared equally. Or the gain, for that matter.

For the interlinked components of Thatcher's economic policies to work, the power of the trade unions had to be severely reduced. The miners were the vanguard of the organised labour movement and they could not have been defeated had the government not used high levels of unemployment as a means for reducing workers' willingness to give the miners support during the 1984-5 strike. Likewise, privatisation was predicated on being able to defeat strongly entrenched union organization in the public sector. This was a key component of her strategy and she met with considerable success in implementing it on such a large scale precisely because she had been able to put the trade unions on the back foot. She initiated a marked shift in the balance of power in industrial relations. It is a matter of opinion as to whether this shift has benefited Britain in the long-term.

There may often be a marked difference between people's objective economic situation and their subjective assessment or perception of how governments are serving their needs. At their most crass, eulogies for Thatcher say that she struck a chord with the public and was hugely admired for her courage in being prepared to take what were accepted as being tough but necessary measures. It simply wasn't true. For much of her time in office, she was highly unpopular if opinion polls are to be believed. Overall they placed her as the second most unpopular UK prime minister of the twentieth century. On occasions she topped the table. Especially towards the end of the 1980s it was clear that the word 'Thatcherism' was increasingly evoking unpleasant and negative reactions. She did not win hearts and minds in the manner so frequently suggested despite such sustained efforts by the bulk of the media to create that impression. Even with the constant barrage of propaganda telling the electorate that Maggie was doing it right, large numbers of voters remained suspicious or sceptical of free-market values and they wished to maintain essential social and welfare services even if that meant an increase in taxes. They also tended to contrast unfavourably the individualism and acquisitiveness associated with Thatcherism to the 'old-fashioned', more caring community values and mutual support which they believed should underpin society.

We have noted how for Thatcher there was a critical link between economics and morality. She set out her stall not only to reinvigorate the British economy but to install a new and higher sense of purpose in the British people. Needless to say, she was convinced in her own mind that she achieved this laudable aim and that New Right ideas and attitudes had taken root and were prospering in Britain's new and improved collective consciousness. But just how popular were policies to cut the trade unions down to size, privatise large sectors of business, reduce benefit and welfare and sell off council housing without building replacements at affordable rents, for example? An opinion poll in 1989 showed that 64 per cent of respondents believed that the government was not achieving its job of providing jobs and a decent standard of living for all. Only 14 per cent favoured more privatisation and 38 per cent actually wanted more nationalisation. Support for the work being done by trade unions had risen from 56 per cent in 1979-80 to 70 per cent in 1987-8. 55 per cent preferred a society which emphasised social and collective provision of welfare as opposed to 40 per cent who plumped for self-help. No less than 83 per cent were unhappy with the slashing of local authority council house building programmes. Even after the Falklands War, a poll in 1985 showed that 42 per cent of respondents had less pride in Britain then five years earlier. 32 per cent thought that Britain's status in the world was in decline. Despite the rhetoric, Thatcher did not win the hearts and minds of the British population.

In the mass of eulogistic propaganda that was churned out about her grit and determination, little was made of the fact that she enjoyed extraordinary luck during her political career. She was lucky to be the Leader of the Conservatives in the 1979 general election when Labour was so discredited by presiding over the so-called 'Winter of Discontent'. She was lucky that John Smith died prematurely and that the Labour Party leaders who followed, Michael Foot and Neil Kinnock, were such ineffectual opponents. The fortuitous bonanza of North Sea oil pumped income into the Treasury and considerably widened the economic options available to her. Unlike her predecessor Heath, she benefitted from an international fall in commodity prices and this helped her to keep inflation relatively under control. The opportunities offered by Argentina's invasion of the Falklands just fell into her lap like a ripe plum. She enjoyed good fortune by escaping the fallout from the Westland affair even though several statements she made in Parliament were described as 'highly misleading' at best. She was lucky to survive the bomb which was intended to do for her in the hotel on the Brighton sea front. She was lucky that the SDP appeared on the scene to split the anti-Tory vote and she was lucky to benefit from a voting system which gave her victory in three consecutive elections despite the fact that each time more people voted against her party than for it.

Political surveys concluded that while a substantial core of the electorate thought that their own material position had improved since Thatcher had come into office they felt somewhat shame-faced about admitting this. The material factor helps to explain why they kept re-electing a Thatcher government although of course there was a distinct lack of credible alternatives put forward by opposition parties. Thatcher was extremely lucky to have Michael Foot and Neil Kinnock leading the Opposition. Foot looked old and tired and she was usually able to run rings round Kinnock for all his bombast. The Labour Party leadership seemed too obsessed with internal problems of its own making to be taken seriously. The fact that it was engaged in witch-hunts of Marxists and others on the left at a time that mass unemployment returned and the social services, NHS and trade unions were under sustained attack was evidence of the extent of the political degeneration of the Party's leadership. Foot never looked like a potential Prime Minister and Kinnock, who was clearly avid for the job, had little credibility except in his own perception of himself. The absurd quirks of the British electoral system dished up three successive general election wins for Thatcher although the votes cast for the Tories in all those elections were hardly a ringing endorsement of her policies. The arrival of the SDP on the scene effectively split the opposing forces.

The Tory Party lost something when it got rid of Thatcher as leader. The present author is obviously no great fan but he recognises how she so dominated the Party that whoever and whatever followed was bound to constitute an anti-climax. Her presence was so enormous that her preferred successor, John Major, inevitably looked diminutive by comparison. Even the unexpected victory in the 1992 general election did little to dispel a kind of tiredness or ennui that seems to have run through the Party. The Tories then managed to go through four leaders and lose three elections between 1997 and 2005. Clearly there was a serious malaise at the heart of Toryism. An examination of these years is rather outside our terms of reference but it does provoke speculation as to whether Thatcher was in any way responsible. For several years the Tories under Thatcher had looked unstoppable yet even before she had been forced out of office, serious fissures were opening up and at the centre of them, as might be expected, was conflict about the role and the future of Thatcher and Thatcherism – as well as the related, longstanding bugbear of the Party's stance on Europe. The Party had not been in a healthy state when Thatcher took over the leadership but a recovery to a considerably more robust condition followed, only for Thatcher to be ousted with the Tory Party being possibly weaker than it had been back in 1975. It was losing its direction while she still had her hand on the helm. Without her, however, it drifted along largely rudderless. With Thatcher and her abrasive, dominating personality, issues so often seemed first and foremost to be about her. A truly great leader would have seen to it that the party that was handed on to her successors was altogether stronger as the result of her efforts. She did make things extremely difficult for John Major. She simply would not fade away and whatever he said or did, he could feel her disapproval and her breath on the back of his neck. The Tory victory in the 1992 election was generally unexpected but the Party itself was floundering.

One aspect of Thatcher's legacy was that it led to the election of Blair's successive governments and talk at the time that the Tories had become unelectable because New Labour had stolen their thunder. Blair used the 1992 election defeat of Labour as an excuse for ruthless reforms of his party which would make it into a rigid command structure for obedience to the leadership and the removal of any vestigial commitment to socialism. Many years previously Sir Keith Joseph had said that one day there would be a Labour leader who would tell his Party and the country that capitalism and markets were the best way of improving the living standards of the people. When that happened, he had said, that would be the most important achievement of the Conservative Party. How right he was. Thatcher's mantle was assumed not so much by Major as by Tony Blair. When it came to egocentricity if not for abrasiveness, he was every bit a match for Thatcher. He was happy to be seen as her worthy successor and, when Prime Minister, to continue and enlarge upon many of the policies associated with Thatcherism. His proud creation, 'New Labour' was actually nothing new at all. It was superficial, glitzy. It initially looked and sounded plausible but it soon became evident that it had no substance, like the man. It was the old reformism of the Labour Party taken to its ultimate conclusion but it was Thatcher's legacy, a truly toxic one for socialism. In November 2010 Nigel Lawson commented, "By inflicting three successive election defeats on Labour…she forced Labour to go back to the centre and recognise the changed realities of Britain in the 1980s and 1990s." In being so under her thrall and seeking to continue with Thatcherism, Blair, to his eternal shame, rendered the Labour Party virtually pointless. Out went Clause 4, the famous 'socialist clause' in the Party's constitution. Thatcher, with her hatred of anything to do with the word 'socialism', had the last laugh and the laugh, although it wasn't funny, was on Blair although he, of course, was too full of himself to realise it. Britain, after all, has already got the Conservatives and the Liberal Democrats. It does not need a third quasi-Tory party.

Blair's 'New Labour' can be seen as the policies of Thatcherism continued but in glossier packaging and surrounded by much more in the way of vacuous hyperbole. Blair was an unashamed enthusiast of privatisation, of price mechanisms, of welfare reforms and the pursuit of the profit motive. He was constantly lacing what he said with words such as 'radical' and 'modernising'. With his faux sincerity, a slightly manic look in his eyes and a semi-permanent humourless grin, he used those words in a way that suggested that any policies and measures which could be described as 'radical' and 'modernising' were ipso facto virtuous. However the seemingly endless reform and reorganisation frequently led to chaos, tying what was left of the public sector up in inflexible red tape. League tables abounded everywhere but were the services provided, in education and the health service, for example, actually any better for being subjected to a continuous rolling programme of revision and reform? Blair and Brown found they were riding a carousel marked 'change for its own sake' which neither of them had the gumption to realise was out of control yet not actually going nowhere.

Blair made no bones about his admiration for Thatcher and, like her, his aversion to anything that smacked of socialism. His policies were those of neo-liberalism but contained a larger chunk of content borrowed from American enterprise culture. He was an advocate of supply-side economics, wishing to continue Thatcher's attempts to remove barriers to economic enterprise and he argued that doing so would enable consumers to enjoy more choice of goods and services at low prices. Blair continued deregulation and the privatisation of much of the already shrunken public sector, applying the criteria of the market to the provision of a wider range of services. He also enthusiastically embraced Thatcher's encouragement of inward investment from overseas and the neo-liberal concept of the globalisation of capitalism. The decline of 'traditional' manufacturing was allowed to continue and the idea was that this would be more than compensated for by the growth of information and communication technology and the so-called 'culture' industries such as fashion, film, pop music and advertising.

Blair took Thatcherism to its logical conclusion by the way it stigmatised the unemployed. They were now seen as unwilling to work, a misdemeanour for which they should be punished by being forced into employment, almost always low-paid and meaningless work. Thatcher's authoritarian policies were widened as 'failing' schools, hospitals and local authorities were brought under ever closer scrutiny. An army of inspectors, auditors and scrutineers hectored and bullied workers in the public sector. It was by no means unknown for inspections to lead to suicides among those being inspected, sometimes even before the inspection actually took place, such was the stress they created. It was also not uncommon for inspectors of educational establishments to be ex-teachers who had been hopeless practitioners in the classroom. Despite the assurances of the spin doctors, were the services provided by schools and hospitals, for example, actually any better for all this nastiness masquerading as 'reform'? Everywhere even those who still had jobs peered anxiously over their shoulders, desperate not to catch the eye of a supervisor as there was a boom in workplace bullying and harassment. It was the age of the sneak, the snitcher and the toady. And the age of the cowed, insecure and frightened worker.

Thatcher was not one to go gentle into that Good Night. After leaving formal politics she embarked on a lucrative second career as a writer and lecturer on the international celebrity circuit. She spent much time inveighing against the European Union which she was fond of saying was a project that was doomed to ultimate failure. She was insistent that Britain should leave the Union and join the North American Free Trade Area. Whatever the topic and whenever she had the opportunity, Thatcher could be guaranteed to hold forth on it and in doing so to continue to ruffle feathers.

She remained the subject of controversy. In 1998 she called for the release from custody of the aged former Chilean dictator Pinochet. He had been seized by the Spanish authorities who wanted him to stand trial for violations of human rights. Despite the fact that this man had cold-bloodedly ordered the slaughter or torture of huge numbers of those who had opposed him and had brought down the democratically-elected left government of Allende with American assistance, she went to visit him when he was staying in the UK under conditions of house arrest, saying that she owed it to him for his help during the Falklands War. The notoriety of his crimes against humanity made a mockery of Thatcher's claims of standing for democracy and freedom.

There was nothing repentant about Thatcher. As late as April 2009 when the capitalist world was becoming embroiled in what was looking as if it might be the most severe crisis since the 1930s, she made it clear that she thought that the economic measures she had applied had been successful. It was a contradictory event. Overall, public spending was reduced from about 50% of GDP to just below 40% in the years 1979-97 when the Tories were in office but spending on welfare had continued to increase inexorably to constitute about 66% of all public spending. Social security benefits fell in relations to the wages of the employed but the bill for paying for the unemployed continued to grow. The cash bill, that is. Lives were blighted and some cut short as a result of Thatcher's politics. Communities had their hearts torn out. Despair, drink, drugs and crime resulted. In 1980 there were 3,000 registered drug addicts in Britain. By 1996 that figure had risen to 43,000.

There was much that was dissolute and seedy about the 1980s. It witnessed a considerable deterioration of both the natural and built environments. Failure to invest sufficiently in infrastructure meant that roads, railways and public utilities fell into serious disrepair. Beaches and rivers were filthy and litter and graffiti were everywhere. There were major scares about health standards especially as regards eggs and beef. Between 1980 and 1988 the number of reported cases of food poisoning increased by 169 per cent. A number of railway accidents and other disasters were found to be directly attributable to cost-cutting and corner-cutting by the companies or authorities concerned in their race for profits. The business ethos of the decade was that of 'get rich quick' and this was totally endorsed by Thatcher and her governments who have to bear a large degree of responsibility. The Thatcher years were years of regress not progress.

The period of Thatcher's last government witnessed a substantial economic boom across the capitalist world. In Britain the trade unions and the miners in particular had been put in their place, the ordinary people were now mini-capitalists with their own homes and their portfolios of shares, the City of London was the envy of finance capitalists everywhere and the former Soviet bloc was in total disarray. The idea began to be put about that we had now reached the 'end of history'. Socialism in whatever guise had been shown to be totally unworkable and capitalism was triumphant, now meeting and satisfying the needs of folk across the globe, in economies which seemed to be increasingly interlinked and interdependent. A few more small cosmetic reforms here and there and utopia would soon be achieved. It was only a matter of time, or so they thought. The capitalist triumphalists of the 1990s are now being forced to eat their words..

The forces of the New Right managed to sow widespread confusion and dismay in the political left. Resulting from serious setbacks on both the political and industrial fronts in the late 1980s and early 1990s, triumphalist pro-capitalist ideologues were able to use rhetoric to convince many on the left that socialism was no more than a phantasm, as unrealistic as the possibility of finding the philosopher's stone. Others on the left beat their breasts and tore out their hair believing that so much that they thought was crucial to socialism had been rendered outdated and irrelevant by the new world of rampant individualism, free markets and the enterprise ethic. What price the practices of collectivism, class consciousness, trade unionism, economic planning and public ownership in a post-industrial world where manual occupations and employment in manufacturing were giving way to a new industrial order based on the provision of services?

The New Labour leadership bought into this nonsense despite the fact that a major financial crash had been narrowly avoided in 1987 and then only by the concerted efforts of several western governments working together. The democratic changes that had opened up the Labour Party in the late 1970s and early 1980s had been clawed back and the leadership now jettisoned the socialist baby with what was left of its socialist bathwater and went over to wholehearted and unashamed support for capitalism especially because, according to them, it was now demonstrably crisis-free. One of them, Gordon Brown, was to say memorably a few years later that he had found the cure for capitalist boom and bust – and that was just before the beginning of a crisis which may yet prove to be the most serious capitalism has ever faced! The Labour Party was now basically a pro-capitalist party and it was only continued funding from the trade unions and the presence of some senior union figures in the policy-making bodies of the Party that maintained any vestigial link with the organised working class. Brown, incidentally, is among those who have called for Thatcher to be accorded a state funeral.

The ideas of socialism received a severe setback by the triumphant and seemingly inexorable onward march of Thatcher's 'market forces' and their direct lineal descendent in the form of 'New Labour' under Messrs Blair and Brown. A decade and more of rampant capitalism took its toll of genuine socialists but provided succour for most of those Labour Party and trade union leaders who used it to 'prove' that socialism was out-of-date and irrelevant and went on to push their organisations' policies, procedures and practices even further to the right. This they called the politics of 'realism'.

Thatcher played an important role in attempting to popularise radical right-wing ideas about the nature and role of the state, the utility of markets and how society should be organised. It would be foolish to deny that from the 1980s through to at least the mid-2000s, the New Right, although by no means homogeneous, was able to dominate the ideological agenda in Britain and elsewhere across the world. Thatcher was both a product of New Right thinking and a major contributor to New Right ideas in practice and she passed so much of this on to her successors in New Labour. A huge ideological assault was launched on the political left in general which left them staggering and reeling, largely divided, defeatist and unable to develop a viable sustained socialist critique of the New Right. This was remarkable given, as we have noted above, the far from unanimous and often even lukewarm reception for much New Right theory and practice.

An argument could be put forward that there was nothing especially new or radical about Thatcher's view of the world or in the policies carried out by her governments. While Conservative ideology reflects and seeks to further the material interests of a fairly narrow, generally rich and powerful stratum of society who obtain their wealth from and owe their position to the primacy of private enterprise, the Party's undoubted historical success has been due to its flexibility and pragmatism. The Tories have a remarkable record in adapting what they say and do to changing circumstances. They have been the undisputed party of property, privilege and inequality yet they have managed to generate electoral support right across the social spectrum. To maintain the continuing social system they have had to employ different tactics at different times. Thatcher was fortunate to come to office when the post-war consensus was tired and largely discredited. Thatcher's brand of Conservatism drew on the New Right and a variety of other influences and was enabled to perhaps look more radical than it actually was when contrasted with the 'Butskellism' of the previous decades. Her main purpose was to restore the viability of British capitalism. She and the Prime Ministers who followed her managed to achieve a significant shift in the economy in favour of private enterprise. This, however, was not the same thing as excising the malignant underlying problems of capitalism and restoring the patient to perfect health.

Moreover, Thatcher, Blair and Company, like others before them, found that socialism and those with socialist ideas could not simply be wished away. As technology has become more ubiquitous and sophisticated and the national economies of the world have become increasingly interlinked, interdependent and dominated by global corporate capitalism, so new layers of activists have appeared on the scene. Many express concerns about environmental issues or the activities of international big business or the death, terror and destruction the USA has unleashed overseas in pursuit of its global imperial interests. An anti-capitalist movement has developed, not necessarily at present rooted in the traditional organisations of the working class and not always consciously socialist. However the ongoing travails of the capitalist system are reaching into every corner of this planet and affecting untold millions of people. They are angry and are likely to become far angrier. They will ask questions which capitalism will not be able to answer and the ideas of socialism will come under scrutiny once more as people look for a way out. In that situation it will be important that lessons are drawn from the experiences of the past. An understanding of major historical events of the past will be of importance in the struggles of the future. A leadership needs to be created which is rooted in an understanding of the processes of history and is able to connect the everyday struggles of ordinary people across the globe with the inability of capitalism to provide a decent existence for a large proportion of the world's population. The alternative to capitalism can only be a socialist one.

The author does not normally give too much credence to the utterings of clerical gentlemen but he felt it was worth ending on this note. Here are the words of one anonymous priest he could happily take to his heart.

Individualism and socialism correspond with opposite views of humanity. Individualism regards mankind as made of disconnected, or warring atoms; socialism regards it as an organic whole, a vital unity formed by the combination of contributory members mutually interdependent. He continues: *The method of socialism is co-operation, the method of individualism is competition. The one regards man as working with man for a common end; the other regards man working against man for private gain.*

Amen to this priest's words.

BIBLIOGRAPHY

Aaronovitch, Sam, *The Road from Thatcherism; An Alternative Economic Strategy,* (London, 1981).
Arnold, Bruce, *Margaret Thatcher,* (London, 1984).

Baker, Kenneth, *The Turbulent Years, My Life in Politics,* (London, 1993).
Beynon, Hugh (ed.), *Digging Deeper. Issues in the Miners' Strike,* (London, 1985).
Brown, Gordon, *Margaret Thatcher and the Betrayal of Britain's Future,* (Edinburgh, 1989).

Callinicos, Alex & Simons, Mike, *The Great Strike: The Miners' Strike of 1984-5 and its Lessons,* (London, 1985).
Campbell, John, *Margaret Thatcher,* 2 Volumes, (London, 1993 and 2004).
Cockerell, Michael, *Live from Number 10: The Inside Story of Prime Ministers and Television,* (London, 1988).
Coleman, Terry, *Thatcher's Britain: A Journey through the Promised Lands,* (London, 1987).
Cormack, Patrick, *Right Turn: Eight Men who changed their minds,* (London, 1978).
Crick, Michael, *Scargill and the Miners,* (London, 1985).

Evans, Eric, *Thatcher and Thatcherism,* 2nd edition, (London, 1997).

Gamble, Andrew, *The Free Economy and the Strong State: The Politics of Thatcherism,* 2nd edition, (London, 1994).
Gilmour, Ian, *Dancing with Dogma: Britain under Thatcherism,* (London, 1992).
Glasgow University Media Group, *Really Bad News,* (London, 1982).
Graham, Cosmo & Prosser, Tony, *Waiving the Rules: The Constitution under Thatcher,* (Milton Keynes, 1981).
Gould, Brian et al, *The Politics of Monetarism,* (London, 1979).

Hall, Peter, *Governing the Economy: The Politics of State Intervention in Britain and France,* (London, 1986).
Hall, Stuart & Jacques, Martin (eds.), *The Politics of Thatcherism,* (London, 1983).
Harris, Robert, *Gotcha! The Media, the Government and the Falklands Crisis,* (London, 1983).
Hayes, Mark, *The New Right in Britain: An Introduction to Theory and Practice,* (London, 1994).
Hennessey, Peter, *The Prime Minister,* (London, 2001).
Holden, Triona, *Queen Coal, Women and the Miners' Strike,* (Stroud, 1985).
Holmes, Martin, *The First Thatcher Government, 1979-83: Contemporary Conservatism and Economic Change,* (London, 1985).
----------- , *Thatcher and Thatcherism: Scope and Limitations, 1983-7,* (London, 1989).
Hoskyns, John, *Just in Time: Inside the Thatcher Revolution,* (London, 2000).
Hutton, Will, *The State we're in,* (London, 1996).

Jenkins, Peter, *Mrs Thatcher's Revolution, The Ending of the Socialist Era,* (London, 1987).

Jenkins, Simon, *Accountable to None: The Tory Privatisation of Britain,* (London, 1995).
----------------, *Thatcher and Sons. A Revolution in Three Acts,* (London, 2007).
Johnson, Christopher, *The Economy under Mrs Thatcher, 1979-1990,* London, 1991).
Jones, Nicholas, *Strikes and the Media: Communication and Conflict,* (Oxford, 1986).
Jones, Owen, *Chavs: The Demonisation of the Working Class,* (London, 2011).

Kavanagh, Dennis, *Thatcherism and British Politics: The End of Consensus,* (Oxford, 1990).
--------------- & Seldon, Anthony (eds), *The Thatcher Effect: A Decade of Change,* (Oxford, 1989).

Lawson, Nigel, *The View from No.11: Memoirs of a Tory Radical,* (London, 1992.)
Letwin, Shirley Robin, *The Anatomy of Thatcherism,* (London, 1992).

McInnes, John, *Thatcherism at Work: Industrial Relations and Social Change,* (Milton Keynes, 1987).
Marsh, David, *The New Politics of British Trade Unionism: Union Power and the Thatcher Legacy,* (Basingstoke, 1992).
Milne, Seamus, *The Enemy Within: The Secret War against the Miners,* 3rd edition, (London, 2004).
Minogue, Kenneth & Biddiss, William (eds.), *Thatcherism: Personality and Politics,* London, 1994.
Molyneux, John, *Will the Revolution be Televised: A Marxist Analysis of the Media,* (London, 2011).

Nevin, Michael, *The Age of Illusions: The Political Economy of Britain,* (London, 1983).

Ponting, Clive, *Whitehall: Tragedy and Farce,* (London, 1986.)

Raban, Jonathan, *God, Man and Thatcher,* (London, 1989).
Richards, Andrew, *Miners on Strike, Class Solidarity and Division in Britain,* (Oxford, 1996).
Riddell, Peter, *The Thatcher Era,* (Oxford, 1991).
Ridley, Nicholas, *My Style of Government: The Thatcher Years,* (London, 1991).
Roy, Subroto & Clarke, John, (eds.), *Margaret Thatcher's Revolution. How it Happened and What it Meant,* (London, 2005).

Samuel, Raphael et al. *The Enemy Within: Pit Villages and the Miners' Strike of 1984-5,* (London, 1986).
Skidelsky, Robert (ed.), *Thatcherism,* (London, 1988).

Taafe, Peter & Mulhearn, Tony, *Liverpool, A City that dared to fight,* (London, 1988).
Taylor, Robert, *The Trade Union Question in British Politics: Government and the Unions since 1945,* (Oxford, 1993).
Thatcher, Margaret, *The Downing Street Years,* (London, 1993).
----------------------, The Path to Power, (London, 1995).

Thornton, Peter, *Decade of Decline: Civil Liberties in the Thatcher Years,* (London, 1989).
Timmins, Nicholas, *The Five Giants: A Biography of the Welfare State,* (London, 1995).

Urban, George, *Diplomacy & Disillusion at the Court of Margaret Thatcher,* (London, 1986).

Vinen, Richard, *Thatcher's Britain: The Politics and Social Upheavals of the 1980s,* (London, 2010).

Walters, Alan, *Britain's Economic Renaissance: Mrs Thatcher's Reforms,* (Oxford, 1986).
Widgery, David, *Preserving Disorder,* (London, 1989).
Williams, Granville, *Shafted: The Media, the Miners' Strike and the Aftermath,* (London, 2005).
Williamson, Nigel, *The New Right: The Men behind Mrs Thatcher,* (Nottingham, 1984).
Wilson, Edgar, *A Very British Miracle: The Failure if Thatcherism,* (London, 1992).
Wright, G. (ed.), *ABC of Thatcherism 1979 to 1989,* (London, 1989).
Wrigley, Chris, *British Trade Unions, 1945-1995,* (Manchester, 1997).

Website

Margaret Thatcher Foundation: www.margaretthatcher.org